THE GREATEST AND THE GRANDEST ACT

CIVIL RIGHTS BILL PASSES · 1866

THE GREATEST AND THE GRANDEST ACT

THE CIVIL RIGHTS ACT OF 1866 FROM RECONSTRUCTION TO TODAY

EDITED BY CHRISTIAN G. SAMITO

Southern Illinois University Press
CARBONDALE

Southern Illinois University Press
www.siupress.com

Printed in the United States of America

Frontispiece: Allyn Cox, *Civil Rights Bill Passes, 1866*, mural (oil on canvas). ARCHITECT OF THE CAPITOL.
Cover image: detail from frontispiece, showing former slave Henry Garnet speaking with newspaper editor Horace Greeley, who supported African American suffrage.

21 20 19 18 4 3 2 1

Library of Congress Cataloging-in-Publication Data
Names: Samito, Christian G., editor.
Title: The greatest and the grandest act : the Civil Rights Act of 1866 from Reconstruction to today / edited by Christian G. Samito.
Description: Carbondale : Southern Illinois University Press, 2018. | Includes bibliographical references and index.
Identifiers: LCCN 2017033595 | ISBN 9780809336524 (paperback) | ISBN 9780809336531 (ebook)
Subjects: LCSH: United States. Civil Rights Act of 1866. | United States. Constitution. 14th Amendment | Civil rights—United States. | African Americans—Civil rights—History—19th century. | BISAC: history / United States / Civil War Period (1850–1877). | history / United States / 19th Century. | law / Civil Rights. | law / Legal History.
Classification: LCC KF4558 14th .G74 2018 | DDC 342.7308/5—dc23 LC record available at https://lccn.loc.gov/2017033595

Printed on recycled paper. ♲

CONTENTS

THE GREATEST AND THE GRANDEST ACT

INTRODUCTION

Christian G. Samito

In December 1865, Secretary of State William H. Seward declared the Thirteenth Amendment ratified by three-fourths of the states, and within weeks Congress had to take up the matter of how to give it more practical effect. Even before the amendment's adoption, southern state legislatures began enacting laws that offered one possible model of freedom for emancipated slaves: these Black Codes afforded African Americans some rights but heavily restricted them at the same time. Many Black Codes included provisions that regulated contracts and wages for African Americans, imposed on them licenses at exorbitant fees for certain trades or occupations (thus denying access to economic mobility), prohibited them from possessing weapons, and provided for their arrest if they quit their employment without "good cause." Legislation applicable to loosely defined vagrants (Alabama, for instance, included in its definition of vagrant a "stubborn or refractory servant" and a "laborer or servant who loiters away his time") in many former slave states subjected unemployed black people to heavy fines and sometimes authorized their being hired out or forced to labor as part of a chain gang. Some Black Codes also sought to inhibit the ability of white people to teach former slaves.[1]

On January 5, 1866, Senator Lyman Trumbull of Illinois introduced what would become the Civil Rights Act of 1866. During debate, Trumbull noted that this bill meant "to give effect to [the Thirteenth Amendment] and secure to all persons within the United States practical freedom." Referencing Black Codes that discriminated against African Americans to "deny them certain rights, subject them to severe penalties, and still impose upon them the very restrictions which were imposed upon them in consequence of the existence of slavery," Trumbull emphasized that "there is very little importance in the general declaration of abstract truths and principles"—the freedom of the slaves and the principles of the Declaration of Independence—"unless they can be carried into effect." At the same time, Trumbull assured his fellow senators that the bill concerned itself only with civil rights and not political ones.[2]

Some opponents challenged the measure on the grounds that it subverted federalism: it applied nationwide and broke with the traditional view that state law created most of the rights we today associate with national citizenship. "Can any man believe that the founders of this Republic . . . would have ever entered into the Union," asked Democratic senator Willard Saulsbury of Delaware, "if they had supposed that in the short term of eighty years their children would be subjected to the absolute control and the omnipotent will of the Federal Congress?" Saulsbury further queried, "What becomes of the powers of the States? What becomes of the rights of the States? Sir, they have not even the privilege of administering their criminal laws; they have not the privilege of saying who shall give evidence and who shall not in their own courts; they have not the privilege of saying who shall hold property and who shall not." Senator Garrett Davis of Kentucky bluntly summed up a racial objection to the bill: "This is a white man's Government," and "the negro is not a citizen here" unless made so by force.[3]

On the other hand, Republican senator Jacob Howard of Michigan asserted that the bill did not invade the "legitimate rights of the States" but "simply gives to persons who are of different races or colors the same civil rights." Moreover, Howard trusted that, having employed "nearly two hundred thousand" black men "in the prosecution of our just and righteous war," the nation could not "now be found so recreant to duty, so wanting in simple justice, as to turn our backs upon the race and say to them, 'We set you free, but beyond this we give you no protection; we allow you again to be reduced to slavery by your old masters, because it is the right of the State which has enslaved you for two hundred years thus to do.'" In response to Senator Davis's admonition that "the power to change the Constitution is a power simply to amend; it is not a power to revolutionize . . . it is not a power to change our form of Government," Republican senator Lot Morrill of Maine asked, "Are we not in the midst of a civil and political revolution which has changed the fundamental principles of our Government in some respects? Sir, is it no revolution that you have changed the entire system of servitude in this country?" According to Morrill, the changes created a "revolution grander and sublimer in its consequences than the world has witnessed hitherto." Trumbull reminded the Senate that the measure would apply to white and black people and asked what could be so repugnant about legislation providing that all of them should have equal rights.[4]

Toward the end of the debates, Republican senator Henry Wilson of Massachusetts provided an eloquent summation on February 2, 1866, reminding his colleagues that at least six of the former Confederate states "passed laws wholly incompatible with the freedom of these freedmen," laws "as iniquitous as the old slave codes." Wilson proclaimed to the Senate that pursuant to the Thirteenth Amendment and

> by the will of the nation freedom and free institutions for all, chains and fetters for none, are forever incorporated in the fundamental law of regenerated and united America. Slave codes and auction blocks, chains and fetters and bloodhounds are things of the past, and the chattel stands forth a man with the rights and the powers of the freemen. For the better security of these new-born civil rights we are now about to pass the greatest and the grandest act in this series of acts that have emancipated a race and disenthralled a nation.

Later that day, the Senate approved the bill by a vote of 33 to 12, with 5 members not voting. The House of Representatives followed suit on March 13, 1866, by a vote of 111 to 38, with 34 representatives not voting.[5]

President Andrew Johnson vetoed the measure on March 27, 1866, offering his opinion that the freed people were not fit for citizenship and stating that he believed the legislation inappropriately revised the relationship between the federal and state governments by now allowing the federal government to interfere with a state's ability to discriminate between the races as its government saw fit. On April 9, 1866, exactly a year after Confederate general Robert E. Lee's surrender at Appomattox, the House of Representatives joined the Senate's earlier vote to overturn Johnson's veto, and the bill became law.[6]

This book examines various aspects of the first federal civil rights statute in American history, one that specified in its first section that "all persons born in the United States and not subject to any foreign power, excluding Indians not taxed, are . . . citizens of the United States" and that

> such citizens, of every race and color, without regard to any previous condition of slavery or involuntary servitude, except as a punishment for crime whereof the party shall have been duly convicted, shall have the same right, in every State and Territory in the United States, to make and enforce contracts, to sue, be parties, and give evidence, to inherit, purchase, lease, sell, hold, and convey real and personal property, and to full and equal benefit of all laws and proceedings for the security of person and property, as is enjoyed by white citizens, and shall be subject to like punishment, pains, and penalties, and to none other. . . .[7]

Section 1 of the act provided a definition of national citizenship rights in the law for the first time, and, in harmony with the Republican Party's free labor ideology, it included economic rights of contract and property as well as a means of court enforcement so as to provide black people—and all Americans—with greater access to the growing capitalist economy as a right of citizenship. Yet, where the act altered the practice of federalism, it did not abandon it even as it recognized a greater role for the federal government in defining citizenship rights in contrast to the almost wholly state-based model that came before. According to legal historian Herman Belz, Republicans intended by the act "that within diverse states all persons, regardless of race, must enjoy equally the benefit of whatever laws existed for the protection of person and property," and their goal was "to guarantee intrastate equality before the law." Thus, according to Belz, the "nationalization of civil rights" followed "the peculiar pattern of American federalism." And, where the act was a race-conscious measure, it also intended to afford black Americans with rights equal to, but not greater than, those enjoyed by white Americans.[8]

Under Section 2 of the act, depriving someone of the rights outlined in Section 1 or subjecting someone to different punishment for having previously been a slave or because of that person's color or race became a misdemeanor for which one could be fined up to a thousand dollars and suffer imprisonment for up to one year. And several provisions of the act expanded the power of the federal government by enabling it to enforce the rights newly associated with national citizenship: Section 3 conferred on U.S. courts jurisdiction to enforce the rights granted in Section 1; Sections 4 and 5 required that U.S. attorneys, marshals, commissioners, Freedmen's Bureau agents, and any other officer appointed by the president arrest and prosecute at the expense of the federal government persons who violated the act; and Section 6 made it a criminal act to obstruct their efforts. Section 8 permitted the president to direct judges, marshals, and district attorneys to relocate to any location within their judicial district where the president believed offences had been or were likely to be committed against the provisions of the act "for the purpose of the more speedy arrest and trial of persons charged with a violation" of it; and Section 9 authorized the president "to employ such part of the land or naval forces of the United States or of the militia, as shall be necessary to prevent the violation and enforce the due execution of this act." Pursuant to Section 10, all questions of law arising in any cause of action under the act could be taken for final appeal to the Supreme Court.

Significant portions of the act remain in effect to this day, giving modern relevance to its history and operation. Fearing the act could be revised or repealed by a subsequent Congress, Republicans again turned to the amendment process and by June 1866 proposed to the states the Fourteenth Amendment, which provided a national definition of citizenship in the Constitution ("All persons born or naturalized in the United States, and subject to the jurisdiction thereof, are citizens of the United States and of the State wherein they reside") and ensured that these citizens were entitled to "equal protection of the laws" and "due process of law."[9] The Civil Rights Act of 1866 and the Fourteenth Amendment ratified in 1868 thus also served as nation-state building measures: they affirmed the power of the federal government to define who was a U.S. citizen (it did so by rejecting Supreme Court chief justice Roger Taney's race-based exclusion of black people in his ruling in *Scott v. Sandford*) and what that status meant.[10]

Thus, the Civil Rights Act of 1866 had great historical significance as the moment in Reconstruction when the federal government first sought to define national citizenship and protect civil rights. In a break with prior expectations that states would specify and protect the rights people enjoyed, the U.S. government now played a greater role in demarcating and defending the rights associated with a newly emphasized concept of national citizenship. Moreover, the act has helped shape civil rights jurisprudence since its enactment and operates as more than aspirational language: to this day, plaintiffs rely on the parts of it that are still in effect in filing claims in federal court.

Yet, despite its importance for historians, lawyers, litigants, and American citizens as a whole, the act largely has been overshadowed in public discussion by the Fourteenth Amendment. Part of this stems from the fact that the act can seem inaccessible, providing specificity in technical language in contrast with the more aspirational and general constitutional language provided by the amendment and the vibrant and ongoing discussion that has ensued about what it means and how it applies. And while historians and legal scholars have recognized the importance of the act when examining it, often in the context of writing about the Fourteenth Amendment or the broader Reconstruction, they usually do not consider each other's scholarship to the extent they should when looking at legal-based topics.

The essays in this book fall into three general sections intended to help historians, attorneys, and the broader public better understand an act that has helped to frame rights debates and affect people's lives for over a century and a half. The first group of essays examines the history and legal ramifications of various aspects of the act and highlights competing impulses within it. The act had radical elements—it was a wartime measure and a race-conscious one that defined national citizenship for the first time and included in it African Americans, including former slaves, in stark contrast to Chief Justice Taney's ruling in *Dred Scott* roughly a decade earlier. On the other hand, the act worked within the existing structure of federalism and did not go so far as to address certain rights and privileges such as suffrage. Michael Les Benedict opens the book by examining the tension that existed between the narrower view of citizenship in constitutional law and the broader, more republican definition that took root in constitutional politics and how the narrower view trumped the broader one as the courts became the primary enforcing institution of the Fourteenth Amendment. Moreover, the drafters of the act declined to include voting in the rights it granted with citizenship, despite the important role suffrage played in understandings of citizenship at the time. The next two essays examine more radical aspects of the act. Rebecca E. Zietlow investigates how the Thirteenth Amendment operated to overturn the *Dred Scott* case, as the civil rights act passed pursuant to its enforcement provision declared that all persons born in the United States are citizens, including black people. Michael Vorenberg then analyzes the oft-neglected Section 9 of the act, which allows the president to use the nation's military in its enforcement. According to Vorenberg, the act was a wartime measure, and alongside its provisions about equal citizenship are measures providing for military enforcement—in effect, announcing that the Civil War would not truly end until the equal rights measures had taken permanent root. Finally, Millington Bergeson-Lockwood investigates New England's role in the passage of the act and how prior antislavery activism and relations with the free black population in this region shaped visions of citizenship that later influenced the act.

In the next section, contributors provide a fine-grained analysis of the act as it operated on the ground in several regions during Reconstruction and show that, despite its grand ambitions, the act remained contested in practice and politics. Aaron Astor examines the border states of Kentucky and Missouri, not subject to Congressional Reconstruction policy because both states had remained in the Union and where many white people considered the act as an unconstitutional threat to the power of the states to manage civil, social, and legal relationships between the races. Jeff Strickland focuses on the Deep South state of South Carolina, which on December 21, 1865, passed its Black Code reminiscent of the slave code abolished by the ratification of the Thirteenth Amendment just days earlier. Strickland focuses on the arguments made by white South Carolinians assailing the Civil Rights Act and, in contrast, the activism of black South Carolinians in its support. R. Owen Williams considers the act and its interpretation by the federal judiciary in its first decades and shows how, at the same time it was contested on the ground in parts of the United States, the court also tempered some of its more radical elements through judicial rulings.

In the final part, three essays consider various aspects of how the act has been interpreted and used; in doing so they look back to history but also bring the act into the modern era and address its application and importance to contemporary issues. Richard L. Aynes investigates the act in terms of contract rights, one of the basic tenets behind free labor as a concept and a critically important right to this day. George Rutherglen examines the act in the context of the post–World War II civil rights era, particularly in regard to affirmative action and how the legislative history and reception of the Civil Rights Act of 1866 bears upon race-conscious remedies for racial discrimination. And, in conclusion, Darrell A. H. Miller analyzes the act insofar as it looks backward to slavery and the aftermath of the Civil War as well as forward to the Civil Rights Movement, and he shows this piece of legislation to be a gateway between the legal world that the Reconstruction Congress left behind and the more complicated one that followed.

Readers may be surprised not to see essays examining how Irish Americans, German Americans, or women engaged with the act during the decades following its passage. The omission is not by oversight. In my own research regarding Irish Americans and citizenship during the Civil War era, I did not find enough of a discussion of the act within that ethnic community to sustain an essay. Scholars asked to consider writing about German Americans and women found the same for their respective groups (although that should not preclude people from making further investigation). As for immigrants, this lack of discussion should not be surprising: while the act defines as citizens people *born* in the United States, excluding people subject to any foreign power (for example, a diplomat's child born here) and Native Americans not taxed (because their allegiance was to their tribal nation), the Fourteenth Amendment proposed to the states in June 1866, along with subsequent other legislation, addressed immigration and naturalization issues. Thus, for instance, Section 1 of the Fourteenth Amendment, in relevant part, states, "All persons born or naturalized in the United States, and subject to the jurisdiction thereof, are citizens of the United States and of the State wherein they reside."[11]

History and law professors contributed essays to this volume, and, while this introduction is not the place for a larger consideration as to how specialists in each discipline can learn from each other, we hope the participation of scholars from both fields helps foster greater interdisciplinary dialogue. Of note is that law professors wrote all three of the essays that move between the past and the present. The interpretations presented herein are those of individual authors, and I have deliberately taken a light hand in editing their scholarship particularly because there are tensions between various essays, just as there are tensions within an act that had radical and conservative elements, that was influenced by wartime developments but also undermined by local politics, and that was tempered by a judiciary before being revived again into a still-used piece of legislation. Where there are differences in thought, we hope to encourage other scholars to think about and build upon the essays in this book.

Notes

1. Christian Samito, ed., *Changes in Law and Society during the Civil War and Reconstruction: A Legal History Documentary Reader* (Carbondale: Southern Illinois University Press, 2009), 190.
2. *Cong. Globe*, 39th Cong., 1st Sess., 474, 476 (January 29, 1866).
3. Ibid., 477, 479 (January 29, 1866) (Saulsbury); 528 (January 31, 1866) (Davis).
4. Ibid., 504 (January 30, 1866) (Howard); 562 (January 31, 1866) (Davis); 570 (February 1, 1866) (Morrill); 599 (February 2, 1866) (Trumbull).
5. Ibid., 603 (Wilson), 606–7 (February 2, 1866); 1367 (March 13, 1866).
6. Ibid., 1857–1860 (veto message); 1861 (April 9, 1866).
7. Civil Rights Act of 1866, 14 Stat. 27, Sec. 1. The full text of the act is included in the appendix to this volume.
8. Herman Belz, *New Birth of Freedom: The Republican Party and Freedmen's Rights, 1861–1866* (1976; repr., New York: Fordham University Press, 2000), 164–65.
9. U.S. Const., Fourteenth Amend., Sec. 1.
10. Scott v. Sandford, 60 U.S. 393 (1857).
11. For more, see Christian G. Samito, *Becoming American under Fire: Irish Americans, African Americans, and the Politics of Citizenship during the Civil War Era* (Ithaca: Cornell University Press, 2009), chaps. 7 and 8.

1

"MEMBERSHIP OF A NATION, AND NOTHING MORE"

The Civil Rights Act of 1866 and the Narrowing of Citizenship in the Civil War Era

Michael Les Benedict

On January 5, 1866, Illinois senator Lyman Trumbull, the chairman of the Senate Judiciary Committee, introduced "A Bill to protect all Persons in the United States in their Civil Rights, and furnish the Means of their Vindication." Passed over President Andrew Johnson's veto in April 1866, the Civil Rights Act came to define the basic rights of citizenship. It was a progressive measure, a measure of racial justice. But it had the ironic effect of narrowing the rights of citizenship, divorcing it from its traditional ties to participation government. Even today the law conceives of citizenship more narrowly than do people in the broader society.

Citizenship is a hot topic now. In the last twenty years, a plethora of books and articles have discussed public culture in terms of citizenship, such as *State and Citizen*,[1] a compilation on the relationship between citizenship and state-building through the Civil War, and *Creating Citizenship in the Nineteenth-Century American South*, another compilation of essays on the subject.[2] Douglas Bradburn's *The Citizenship Revolution*[3] discusses how the American Revolution led to new understandings and definitions of citizenship. Nancy Isenberg's *Sex and Citizenship in Antebellum America* was one of the first books issued in this recent outpouring, as was Linda Kerber's *No Constitutional Right to Be Ladies: Women and the Obligations of Citizenship*.[4] Corinne Field's *The Struggle for Equal Adulthood: Gender, Race, Age, and the Fight for Citizenship in Antebellum America* broadens the scope.[5] A study of the contributions of women's history to the field of women's studies in general refers to the field as "Haunted by Citizenship."[6] Scholarly journals are filled with articles assessing some aspect of citizenship.[7]

Many of these books and articles discuss formal issues of citizenship, but most treat citizenship as a cultural construct involving civic participation rather than as a legal status.[8] Indeed, there is a whole field devoted to "cultural citizenship"—the panoply of behaviors and ideas that are related to civic belonging and participation.[9]

They demonstrate that citizenship has a number of meanings. The formal legal term that defines status and rights enforceable in courts is only one of them. It was not inevitable that American citizenship would be so narrowly conceived. But it was the paradoxical result of one the most progressive pieces of legislation in American history—the Civil Rights Act of 1866.

Before the Civil War, the legal term was ill defined. Delivering a formal opinion on African American citizenship in 1862, Attorney General Edward Bates marveled that "eighty years of practical enjoyment of citizenship . . . have not sufficed to teach us the exact meaning of the word, or the constituent elements of the thing we prize so highly."[10] Surprisingly few people had formally addressed the issue, and even fewer with any care. Treatise writer William Rawle wrote that the term was used as if everyone knew what it meant, and he did little to clarify it.[11] Supreme Court justice Joseph Story pithily explained, "Every citizen of a state is *ipso facto* a citizen of the United States."[12] But he was as silent as Rawle on what citizenship implied in the way of rights.

Legal commentators came closest to answering that question when discussing Article 4, Section 2, of the Constitution. It ordained, "The Citizens of each State shall be entitled to all Privileges and Immunities of Citizens in the several States." Story said that this clause "may be esteemed the basis of the union," but given that importance, he was surprisingly terse about interpreting it. It prevented states from treating the citizens of other states as aliens, he said. But he eschewed a discussion of what those privileges and immunities were, other than a reference to owning land.[13]

Courts did little better. Questions of citizenship sometimes arose in property disputes that turned on whether women or children were American citizens at the time of various transactions, and Congress passed a law governing the citizenship status of women married to foreigners. As a result the rules for determining the citizenship status of women were better developed than those involving men. Questions also arose when a dispute involved free African Americans. It was in these cases, more than in any others, that judges had discussed what it meant to be a citizen. And then there was the *Dred Scott* case, in which Chief Justice Roger B. Taney held that free African Americans were not citizens of the United States, no matter what their states said.[14] Taney provided a full exegesis on citizenship, but Americans proved unwilling to accept it. Beyond the *Dred Scott* decision, only the federal circuit court case *Corfield v. Coryell* had discussed the rights of citizenship at any length, and it was cited more often for its treatment of riparian law.[15] Attempting to define the privileges and immunities of U.S. citizens to be protected by the proposed Fourteenth Amendment "would be a somewhat barren discussion," the amendment's Senate manager shrugged in 1866, because the courts had said so little about it.[16]

But the term had been widely used in the public sphere, as it still is today. It has many meanings. And nearly all of them are broader than the narrow legal one that was embodied in the Civil Rights Act and then in the Fourteenth Amendment.

There were no "citizens of the United States" before the American Revolution, nor was the term "citizen" known to British law. Englishmen and Englishwomen were "subjects," not "citizens." The distinction reflected the difference between "those who justified authority via the inheritance of power . . . and those who justified it via the consent of the governed," historian Holly Brewer has explained.[17] All free American colonists—men and women, black and white, perhaps even members of the Native American tribes—had been subjects of the British monarch.[18] Being a subject was unrelated to active participation in governance. A subject owed loyalty and allegiance to the monarch and in return received protection. Subjects were represented by Parliament, but not because they voted for its members.

English subjects had rights. People regularly referred to the "rights of Englishmen," and Americans consistently claimed that they were entitled to them. The general understanding was that people had natural rights, but when they established societies, they gave up their "natural liberty" for "civil liberty"—liberty bound by law.[19] By the eighteenth century, the "rights of Englishmen" included the notion that they could be taxed only by the consent of their representatives in Parliament, but that did not imply a right to vote.[20] Being a "citizen" had nothing to do with it. Since the fourteenth century, the term "citizen" had referred to a subject who participated in the civic life of a town or city. In England there was a clear distinction between subjects of the Crown who were "gentlemen" and might play a role in the public life of the realm and a subject who was merely a "citizen" of a town. A "citizen" was a freeman, to be sure, but "a man of trade, not a gentleman," as Samuel Johnson put it in his celebrated dictionary.[21]

Americans had a different idea than metropolitan elites about what it meant to be represented in Parliament. In America, representation had to be "real," not "virtual." That implied popular participation in government, and this participation implied citizenship.[22] Therefore, the term "citizen" replaced "subject" when the American colonies repudiated their allegiance to Great Britain and the British Crown. By the 1800s every revised state constitution referred to "citizens" and none to "subjects." Citizenship conveyed a status more elevated than that of a mere subject. In America, the people are sovereign, but as Chief Justice John Jay put it in 1793, "They are sovereigns without subjects . . . , and have none to govern but themselves."[23] "The difference is immense," wrote David Ramsey. "Subjects look up to a master, but citizens are so far equal, that none have hereditary rights superior to others."[24]

In popular parlance there are a number of meanings ascribed to being a "citizen."[25] It may mean nothing more than being a denizen—that is, a permanent resident, or what a nineteenth-century legal analyst called a "domiciled inhabitant."[26] Americans speak of themselves as citizens of their hometowns and communities. What is a "senior citizen" other than an older inhabitant of any community? Surely one is not a "senior citizen" in contrast to being a "senior alien."

Americans used the term in the same loose way before the Civil War. After a "great conflagration" in 1802, the fire wardens posted an informational broadside "To the Citizens of the Town of Boston."[27] A broadside might inform "the Citizens of Worcester" that a "violin virtuoso" would give a "Grand Concert!" consisting of music "composed by the most celebrated European artists."[28] Courts too sometimes construed citizenship to mean mere residency. Georgia's courts determined that "all persons who are found within the limits of government, whether their residence be permanent or temporary, are to be deemed, so far, citizens . . . that the right of jurisdiction, civil and criminal, will attach" to them.[29] The Constitution gives federal courts jurisdiction over controversies between citizens of different states. Until the *Dred Scott* case changed the rule, federal judges said that citizenship for this purpose meant no more than residence.[30]

The word "citizen" may merely connote nationality—what passport one carries, what one writes on an international arrival card. It differentiates the citizen from the alien. In this sense citizenship is identical to "subject." This idea came out most clearly when lawyers considered the situation of women and children, citizens who did not have the right to participate in public life or the obligation to defend the community. As James Kent put it early in the nineteenth century, "Subject and citizen are, in a degree, convertible terms. . . . We are, equally with the inhabitants of all other countries, subjects, for we are equally bound by allegiance and subjection to the government of the land." In Kent's view, citizens were simply "free inhabitants, born within the United States, or naturalized under the law of Congress." That status did not imply much in the way of rights. According to Kent, free African Americans were citizens, but they were subject to whatever disabilities state legislators thought expedient.[31]

Sometimes courts too construed "citizen" and "subject" to mean the same thing. Perhaps the most remarkable instance was the North Carolina Supreme Court's holding that free black North Carolinians were citizens, a holding at odds with the law of every other slave state. "The term 'citizen' . . . is precisely analogous to the term subject in the common law," the court opined. The switch to "citizen" was due merely to the repudiation of the British government. Free black North Carolinians had been subjects before the Revolution, and they were citizens afterward.[32] It did not mean much in the way of rights.[33]

However, in a republic, citizenship can mean something more than mere nationality. We reflect this deeper notion when we speak of "good citizenship." That concept underlies President John F. Kennedy's oft-quoted admonition "Ask not what your country can do for you—ask what you can do for your country."[34] We regularly speak of voting as "the very essence of citizenship," as historian Vernon Burton recently did in a presidential address to the Southern Historical Association.[35] Recognizing that some citizens have been excluded from civic life by being denied the right to vote, we distinguish between formal citizenship and "full citizenship."[36]

These are the powerful echoes of what historians call republican citizenship. This was a concept that grew out of Roman and Renaissance Italian ideas of the citizen as an active member of the political community.[37] It also grew out of the special privileges granted to "citizens" of self-governing communities in medieval Europe. As late as 1768 Samuel Johnson defined "citizen" as "a freeman of a city."[38] Citizenship was by no means general in medieval and Renaissance cities; it was restricted to the small minority who participated in governance.[39]

In the revolutionary era, "the word 'citizen' was . . . detached from its municipal meaning and attached to the state."[40] The notion grew, in Europe as well as America, that a republic depended on the civic virtue of the people, that in a republic every man with a stake in the community partook of the citizen's right and obligation to participate in public life. A stake in the community did mean owning property, but property ownership was widespread in America—a fact that made republican notions of citizenship especially attractive there.[41]

Republican citizenship was active citizenship. The republican citizen served the community in official capacities and defended it when threatened. He put the welfare of the community ahead of his own personal interests. Citizenship required what Italian civic humanists had called *virtù*—"love of our country, resignation and obedience to the laws, public spirit, love of liberty, sacrifice of life and all to the public."[42] They were manly virtues. Republican citizenship was profoundly gendered. While all people who owed allegiance to a monarch were subjects, only men had been republican citizens. In most of the United States, it was profoundly racial as well. "Acts of citizenship: sitting on a jury, voting, and mustering in the militia" were, as historian Ariela Gross has put it, "the civic performance of white manhood."[43]

The notion of what constituted enough of a stake in the community to justify political as well as civil citizenship was radically transformed in the United States during the first decades of the nineteenth century, as liberal egalitarianism became a central American value. To contemporaries the democratic transformation meant primarily extending to all white men both the privileges and obligations of republican citizenship.[44] All white men were entitled to representation in government, effected through a public ritual of constant rounds of voting, widespread office holding, jury duty, and militia service, and the goal remained to secure the public welfare rather than special interests. Most obvious of all, the republican ideal of citizenship was reflected in the continued limitation of civic privileges and obligations to men.[45] By 1828 Webster's *American Dictionary* defined citizenship thus: "In *the U. States,* a person, native or naturalized, who has the privilege of exercising the elective franchise, or the qualifications which enable him to vote for rulers, and to purchase and hold real estate."[46]

State constitutions identified citizenship with civic life. They mentioned citizenship rather sparingly (and rarely defined it). As universal white male suffrage became the norm, voting was explicitly identified with citizenship.[47] Even states like Indiana and Michigan that permitted immigrants to vote required them to declare their intention of becoming citizens.[48] The constitutions likewise linked office holding explicitly to citizenship.[49] A number of them tied service in the militia to citizenship as well.[50]

State constitutions contained other indications that citizenship was bound together with civic life. Few of the provisions guaranteeing rights in a state referred to "citizens." Most of the Declarations of Rights embedded in state constitutions began with a provision stating that "all men" or sometimes "all freemen" had inherent and indefeasible rights to life, liberty, and property.[51] They provided that "no man" or "no freeman" could be deprived of life, liberty, or property except by due process or law, or according to the law of the land.[52] "No person" was to be imprisoned for debt.[53] Everyone had rights in criminal proceedings, so some provisions simply banned abuses, while others specified rights of which "no person" could be deprived.[54]

Only when the constitutions guaranteed freedoms associated with public life—freedom of assembly, freedom of speech and press, the right to hold office free of religious tests, and the right to bear arms—did they refer to the rights of "citizens" or "the people."[55] Anti-dueling provisions, which deprived offenders of the right to hold office, also often referred to citizens.[56] All political power was inherent in "the people."[57] It was "the people" who established constitutions, the highest of all political acts, including the U.S. Constitution.

Constitutional jurisprudents made similar linguistic choices. In his nineteenth-century book on government and liberty, Elisha H. Hurlbut referred to "individuals," "people," or "men" when discussing human rights. But in his chapter "Of the Elective Franchise," he spoke of "citizens," a term he did not use elsewhere.[58] Expositors of the Constitution addressed their work to "citizens." William Hickey prefaced his publication of the Constitution and other documents with the admonition that the Constitution "should be the fireside companion of the American citizen."[59]

As inhabitants of their states, citizens were entitled to all the civil rights their state constitutions guaranteed to everyone. But as *citizens* they had more rights than those. As David Ramsey wrote at the time the nation was founded, "The citizen of a free state is so united to it as to possess an individual portion of the common sovereignty," while a mere inhabitant "has no farther connection with the state . . . than such as give him security for his person and property. . . . Citizenship confers a right of voting at elections and many other privileges not enjoyed by those who are no more than inhabitants."[60] Nearly seventy-five years later, a congressman insisted that black Pennsylvanians were not citizens of their state. The people of Pennsylvania had settled that question "definitely" when they amended their constitution "so that to be a 'white' man is one of the necessary constitutional qualifications of the elector."[61] In other words, the right to vote defined citizenship.

The close association between national citizenship and civic rights was manifest in formal discussions from the beginning of the Republic. One reason that Federalists wanted to increase the waiting period for naturalization in the 1790s was because of the general understanding that citizenship conferred political rights.[62] Thus, when a Federalist representative proposed banning naturalized foreigners from holding office, he avowed that he was for giving immigrants every civil right, "but as to the rights of citizenship, he was not willing they should be enjoyed except by persons born in this country."[63] William Rawle explained, "In a republic the sovereignty resides essentially and entirely in the people. Those who compose the people, and partake in this sovereignty are citizens, they alone can elect and are capable of being elected to public offices, and they alone can exercise authority within the community."[64]

Northerners and southerners argued about whether free African Americans were citizens during the Missouri Crisis of 1820. If they were, they were entitled to the benefit of Article 4 of the Constitution, which secured to citizens of each state the privileges and immunities of citizens in other states. In that case Missouri could not ban black immigration, as it proposed doing. (Nor, by implication, could any other state.) Civic rights, especially the right to vote, were the prime indices of citizenship in that debate. A Virginia representative denied that free African Americans were citizens. "A citizen is he who is entitled to the freedom and privileges of the body politic, and has a share in its government," he insisted.[65] A Massachusetts representative described the privileges and immunities that black citizens of Massachusetts shared with white citizens: "all the broad and essential rights of citizens—the right . . . , to hold real and personal estate; the right of course to hold and convey land; the right to trial by jury; the right to the writ of habeas corpus; and, in this government, the all-important right of the elective franchise."[66]

In assessing whether Virginia's "free persons of color" were citizens of the United States, U.S. attorney general William Wirt opined that only those with full rights of citizenship in their states could be citizens of the United States. It was not enough simply to owe allegiance—that is, to be a subject of their state. That "is no evidence of citizenship," he wrote.[67] Even though Virginia statutes seemed to include free African Americans when referring to citizens[68] (a fact Wirt carefully avoided noting explicitly), they still were not citizens of the United States. "Such people have very few of the privileges of the citizen of Virginia," he observed. "They can vote at no election" and "are incapable of any office . . . , civil or military." They could not be witnesses against a white man in court, nor were they enrolled in the militia "and are forbidden even to have in their possession military weapons."[69]

Although they defined women as citizens, judges often made the same connection between voting and citizenship when gender was not at issue. In deciding whether a male litigant had become a citizen of a state to which he had moved, the Supreme Court held that voting there was "conclusive" evidence.[70] In his concurring opinion in the *Dred Scott* case, Justice Peter V. Daniel found it easy to deny that an African American was automatically a citizen of the state where he lived. Nowhere could one find "an exposition of the term *citizen* which has not been understood as conferring the actual possession and enjoyment . . . of an entire equality of privileges, civil and political," he wrote.[71]

Judges who denied the citizenship of African Americans regularly pointed to the laws barring them from civic privileges and responsibilities as conclusive. "Free people of color have never been considered or treated . . . as possessing the rights and privileges of citizens," Kentucky's highest court opined in a leading case. "On the contrary, they are incapable of holding the lowest office in the government; they do not enjoy the right of suffrage, and cannot even be a witness in a civil case." These were "the privileges which are peculiarly characteristic of a citizen."[72] When Georgia's highest court ruled that African Americans were not citizens of the state, it pointed out that "they are not entitled to bear arms, vote for members of the legislature, or to hold any civil office."[73]

As noted above, the sole federal case that attended extensively to the privileges and immunities of citizenship was *Corfield v. Coryell*. That case was brought by a New York oysterman challenging New Jersey's law restricting exploitation of its oyster beds to its own citizens. Did the law deny him the privileges and immunities of citizenship guaranteed by Article 4 of the Constitution? Supreme Court justice Bushrod Washington, sitting as a circuit court judge, cataloged the privileges and immunities of citizenship. They included, he said, those rights that were "in their nature, fundamental; which belong, of right, to the citizens of all free governments." Among them were the right to the protection of government; the right to life, liberty, and property; the right to travel for professional, trade, or other purposes; and the right to have access to the courts. To these "fundamental" rights he added "the elective franchise." A *visitor*, Washington concluded, was entitled only to those rights "deemed to be fundamental"—rights that even a noncitizen might enjoy. Fishing was not a fundamental right, and so the New York plaintiff had no right as a citizen of the United States to fish New Jersey's oyster beds. But Washington's formulation meant that New Jersey could not have denied the plaintiff's right to vote on the same basis as its own citizens if he had moved there permanently. That was a privilege of citizenship.[74]

Washington's opinion was consistent with the idea that citizens had both civil and political rights, with the latter being the particular mark of citizenship. But some analysts held the opposite—identifying basic rights with citizenship while political rights were special privileges given only to some citizens. This view seemed particularly compelling when considering the status of women. After all, they were citizens, and yet they did not vote.[75] A U.S. statute explicitly declared that foreign women became citizens if they married an American man.[76]

However, the concept of citizenship was so heavily gendered that people rarely noticed the inconsistency of treating civic rights as essential to citizenship while denying them to female citizens. Attorney General Caleb Cushing tried to deal with the conundrum in an 1851 opinion. It was true that white women and children could not vote, but they were nonetheless "constituent members of the political sovereignty." If *none* of the members of a class of inhabitants exercised political rights, as was true of African and Native Americans, the members of that class could not be considered citizens. If *some* of the members of the class voted, as with white people, all the members of that class were citizens.[77] The Kentucky Court of Appeals offered a similar explanation: women and children "partake of the quality of those adult males who belong to the same class and condition of society," the judges explained, "and of course they will or will not be citizens, as the adult males of the same class are or are not so."[78] Thus the fact that the law explicitly defined women as citizens did not negate the idea that voting was one of the privileges of male citizenship.

Paradoxically, those who sympathized with black citizenship were more likely than those who opposed it to associate citizenship with civil rather than political rights. Examples occurred during the Missouri Crisis debates. While many northern congressmen argued that the exercise of voting rights was proof of black citizenship in a number of northern states, that argument left African American residents of other states out in the cold. To avoid this, some sympathizers denied the essential link between citizenship and civic rights. One northern congressman specified the right simply to pass freely from place to place as one of "the peculiar and distinctive characteristics of a citizen of a State." "Indeed, vastly the greatest proportion of citizens of a State have no other external mark of their citizenship," he observed, referring to women and children. Yet women and children "enjoy the privilege of citizenship . . . as completely as the man who has, in addition, the qualification of a voter, or a juryman."[79] Likewise, in the *Dred Scott* case, dissenting Supreme Court justice Benjamin R. Curtis repudiated the notion that only voters were citizens. "Whether native-born women, or persons under age, or under guardianship because insane or spendthrifts, be excluded from voting or holding office, or allowed to do so, I apprehend no one will deny that they are citizens of the United States."[80]

In contrast, most of those who denied that African Americans were citizens saw political rights as the central element of citizenship. Pennsylvania's black residents were not citizens, Judge John Fox ruled in an important 1838 case. Not being a citizen, a black man could not vote, "yet his civil rights, as distinguished from political, are by the law, precisely the same as those of a white man."[81]

There is yet another definition of citizenship: the notion that a citizen is an accepted member of the community. Rogers Smith has pointed out that Americans have oscillated between a liberal, egalitarian, and ecumenical concept of citizenship and a concept that stresses exclusivity based on race and ethnic origin. For many Americans, citizenship is more than a status entitling one to individual rights; it has been a matter of "full membership in the American civic community."[82] Kenneth Karst observes that "real membership in the community is more than a legal status. . . . Citizenship means . . . belonging."[83]

One can discern this definition of citizenship in the Missouri Crisis debates. African Americans lived in the American states when they united to fight Britain, a northern congressman urged. "This was their native country, and as dear to them as to us. Thousands of them were free born, and they composed a part of the people in the several States. They were identified with the nation, and its wealth consisted, in part, of their labor. They had fought for their country, and were righteously included in the principles of the Declaration of Independence."[84] This argument defined citizenship not in terms of the right to vote but in terms of membership in a community. As a southerner put it in the same debate, "A person, to be a citizen under one Government, must be a member of the civil community. . . . His rights result from his association with it."[85] This means more than merely residing somewhere. Citizens in this sense are those who are accepted into full fellowship in the community. They appear to share its heritage and values. They are insiders rather than outsiders. Federal courts sometimes incorporated *belonging* into their assessments of citizenship. When a state resident claimed to have become a citizen of a new state, a federal judge explained, "the question of law . . . must always be, has the person so removing, become incorporated into the new society, so as to be a member of it, in like manner as he was of the political family from which he emigrated?"[86]

That sense of belonging is what the German revolutionary refugee Carl Schurz wanted of citizenship. The future American journalist and politician decided against settling permanently in England. "The stranger remains a stranger here," he wrote his brother. "Under such circumstances I cannot feel at home. If I cannot be the citizen of a free Germany, at least I can be a citizen of free America."[87]

A German liberal might reasonably hope to become part of the American people. But that seemed a forlorn hope for African Americans. British visitor Edward Dicey observed in 1862 that "a free Negro citizen does not enjoy the full rights of citizenship." Black people were not only discriminated against but also completely segregated, excluded from the society of the white population. They are, he wrote, "a pariah people."[88] For African Americans, Stephen Kantrowitz writes, "'citizenship' meant being legally and politically vested, but it also meant something more.... It meant knowing and being known; it meant a warm welcome to the full duties, rights, privileges, and pleasures of American life."[89] It was, he writes, "a vision of belonging."[90]

African Americans only dreamed of such acceptance. Still, they harnessed the connection between citizenship and belonging. Black Californians bolstered their claims to citizenship by contrasting themselves to Chinese immigrants. "We are Americans by birth, habits, custom, education and religion," an African American newspaper editor insisted. Unlike the Chinese, "we are part and parcel of the country, homogenous with the American people."[91] From this perspective, one cannot be a citizen unless one is accepted as a member of the community. Thus Mae M. Ngai writes of "alien citizens"—"American citizens by virtue of their birth in the United States but who are presumed to be foreign by the mainstream of American culture and, at times, by the state."[92]

Those who opposed black citizenship consistently denied that African Americans could be part of the people of the United States. During the Missouri Crisis debates, a Virginia congressman expressed the common feeling. "Indians, free negroes, mulattoes, slaves! Tell me not . . . that the Constitution, when it speaks of *We the people,* means these," he expostulated.[93] At Ohio's constitutional convention in 1851, Democratic activist William Sawyer insisted, "Every man in his own place." If African Americans colonized Liberia, "they should enjoy there everything which [an

American citizen] enjoyed here." Another delegate agreed: "Ohio was a state for the white man. The negroes were intruders amongst us."[94] As a leading southern case opinion put it, the free African American "resides among us, and yet is a stranger. A *native* even, and yet not a citizen."[95] African Americans were, in the words of the Mississippi Supreme Court, "alien strangers."[96]

Chief Justice Roger Taney's opinion in the *Dred Scott* case is the best-known judicial articulation of citizenship as belonging. "The words 'people of the United States' and 'citizens' are synonymous terms," he said. The question was whether free African Americans "compose a portion of this people." "We think they are not," he wrote. Taney carefully avoided making possession of political rights the test of citizenship at the time of the framing. Whether they had voted or not, Negroes "had for more than a century before been regarded as . . . altogether unfit to associate with the white race, either in social or political relations." They "were not regarded as a portion of the people or citizens of the Government then formed." If they were not part of the people of the United States, they could not be citizens of the United States.[97]

As the Civil War shifted attitudes toward African Americans, northerners more and more came to think of their black neighbors as citizens in some meaning of the word or another. But only a minority could conceive of them as voters. The logical result was a growing belief that citizenship did not necessarily imply political rights, and the old examples of women and children were available to bolster the notion. So when Abraham Lincoln's attorney general, Edward Bates, opined in 1863 that all free Americans were citizens, he refused to define citizenship according to "some right or privilege." "No error can be greater" than defining it according to the right to vote, he wrote. "There is no district in the nation, in which a majority of the known and recognized citizens are not excluded, by law, from the right of suffrage." Lunatics, criminals, other disqualified men, women, and children were all denied the vote. "And yet, I think, no one will venture to deny that women and children and lunatics . . . may be citizens of the United States."[98]

When Lyman Trumbull and his Judiciary Committee first reported the Civil Rights Bill to the Senate, it did not define citizenship. It simply forbade discrimination "in civil rights or immunities among the inhabitants of any State or Territory of the United States on account of race, color or previous condition of slavery."[99] The Civil Rights Bill counteracted the proposition embodied in newly passed southern Black Codes that public safety justified deprivation of basic rights. It did not, as first presented, counteract southern denial of black citizenship. The bill was designed, as its title declared, to protect "all persons" in their civil rights. Its provisions guaranteed equal civil rights to the "inhabitants" of the states and territories of the United States. Omitting references to "citizens" but instead referring to "all persons" and to "inhabitants," both the title and the language of the bill reflected the distinction between the personal rights guaranteed to everyone and the political privileges that belonged to citizens alone.

When Trumbull reported the bill back from the Judiciary Committee to the Senate three weeks later, it included a new first clause defining citizenship. Trumbull did not explain the reason for the alteration, but it reflected changing understandings of citizenship in the North. White southerners adhered to the traditional conception that citizenship related to civic rights and responsibilities. That is why the Black Codes continued to treat African Americans as "colored persons" or "negroes" rather than as citizens. Therefore a Mississippi legislator who opposed the Black Codes reassured his colleagues that extending equal civil rights to African Americans would not make them citizens. "A negro could never become a citizen of the United States unless he was first invested with the right of suffrage by a sovereign state," he said.[100] For southerners, the right to vote remained, in the words of another Mississippi legislator, "the great distinguishing right between citizens and denizens."[101]

In contrast, the vast majority of Republicans had come to believe that African Americans *were* citizens. But the aspect of citizenship that most enlisted Republican sympathy was not its connection with voting and holding office but its connection with belonging. Nearly three hundred thousand black men had taken up arms in the Union cause. The great black abolitionist leader Frederick Douglass had seen the potential. He had urged African American men to enlist and thereby adopt "the great national family of America."[102] He asked northerners pointedly, "Shall we be citizens in war, and aliens in peace?"[103] Black military service became a compelling argument for citizenship during the war.[104] It was, of course, an argument for republican citizenship—citizenship identified with governance and defense of the polity—but it also was powerful proof of African American commitment to America, evidence of belonging all the more compelling when contrasted with the effort of white southerners to separate themselves from the people of the United States.

Most northerners were committed to recognizing African Americans as citizens, but extending political rights remained politically explosive.

The president whom Republicans had elected was dead-set against black suffrage. Enough rank-and-file Republicans opposed it to jeopardize the party's prospects if its leaders made it an issue.[105] Reluctance to make black enfranchisement a national issue was not only a manifestation of continued racism; voting qualifications had always been a matter for states to decide. Transferring that authority to the federal government seemed to strike at the heart of states' rights.

If Republicans wanted to declare that African Americans were citizens, they would have to distinguish the rights of citizens from the right to exercise political power. A long tradition was in place that insisted African Americans were citizens even where they held no political rights. Trumbull and his Senate Judiciary Committee did the same.

When Trumbull explained the bill, he made his narrow conception of citizens' rights clear. He emphasized *Corfield v. Coryell* and quoted its catalog of citizens' rights. He acknowledged that Justice Washington had included the right to vote, but he dismissed the importance of the inconvenient language. *Corfield* meant the citizen was "entitled to the great fundamental rights of life, liberty, and the pursuit of happiness," Trumbull told his colleagues. The problem was that white southerners "have not regarded the colored race as citizens, and on that principle many of their laws making discriminations between the whites and the colored people are based." The Civil Rights Bill, making African Americans citizens, would knock the props from under that position.[106]

But Democrats knew that citizenship had meant much more. They were particularly concerned with the clause forbidding discrimination generally "in civil rights or immunities . . . on account of race, color or previous condition of slavery." A Democratic senator asked Trumbull to explain exactly what that meant. Trumbull responded that it referred to the specified list of rights that followed. "This bill has nothing to do with the political rights or *status* of parties," he insisted. "It is confined exclusively to their civil rights, such rights as should appertain to every free man."[107] Trumbull's response divorced political rights from citizenship and conflated the rights of citizenship and the fundamental rights that belonged "to every free man." The language of the bill reflected that conflation. It declared African Americans citizens, but it continued to guarantee to all "inhabitants" the rights that Trumbull now identified with citizenship.

Despite Trumbull's explanations, the identification of citizenship with political rights remained strong. A Unionist senator from West Virginia worried that "if you make these people citizens of the United States, I should feel that they were entitled to the right of suffrage."[108] A Johnson-supporting Republican feared the bill would throw open the doors of citizenship to the children of the Chinese immigrating to the Pacific coast. That would mean "an end to republican government there, because . . . those people have no appreciation of that form of government."[109] In response Trumbull reiterated, "The bill is applicable exclusively to civil rights. It does not propose to regulate the political rights of individuals; it has nothing to do with the right of suffrage, or any other political right."[110] Delaware's Democratic senator Willard Saulsbury sought to make that distinction explicit, moving to amend the clause forbidding discrimination in civil rights generally by adding the words "except the right to vote in the States." Trumbull denied the amendment was necessary. "That is a political privilege, not a civil right," Trumbull repeated.[111]

Radical Republicans like Massachusetts senator Charles Sumner conceived the privileges of citizens as consisting of both civil and political rights. In his view, the Civil Rights Bill protected the former, merely putting protection of the latter off for another day. Three days after the Senate sent the bill to the House, Sumner urged his colleagues to pass an enfranchisement statute modeled on it. Protection of political rights was as essential as protection of civil rights, "and the power is as ample in one case as in the other," Sumner insisted. The Civil Rights Bill "establishes the power of Congress, without further amendment of the National Constitution, to protect every citizen in all his rights, including of course the elective franchise."[112]

Sumner's proposal reinforced Democrats' apprehensions. Democrats denied that the Thirteenth Amendment's enforcement section justified passage of the Civil Rights Bill. The amendment ended slavery. It said nothing about the status of African Americans once free, and therefore the second section gave Congress no authority to define it. Congress could only counteract efforts to reimpose slavery itself. To hold that the amendment gave Congress general power to protect freedom gave it an unbounded power. As one Democrat put it, "If, to protect the negroes in their freedom you have the right to confer upon them all the civil rights and immunities contemplated by this bill, you have the right to carry your legislation to any extent that the whim or caprice of gentlemen may dictate."[113] Sumner's call for a black suffrage statute was a prime example. Once again, Trumbull insisted the rights of citizenship were limited to those the bill specified. The bill guaranteed "the rights of citizens," he said. "And what are they? The great fundamental rights set forth in this bill."[114]

The House Judiciary Committee reinforced the idea that the rights of citizenship were limited to civil rights as it amended the Senate bill so that it protected the rights of "citizens" rather than "inhabitants." The chairman of the committee, James F. Wilson, forcefully divorced citizenship from political rights. The privileges and immunities of citizenship did not include voting, "for suffrage is a political right." "Civil rights are the natural rights of man," he explained, "and these are the rights which this bill proposes to protect every citizen in the enjoyment of."[115]

Wilson's language implied that everyone was entitled to the rights specified in the Civil Rights Bill. (They were, he said, "the natural rights of man.") But citizens had a special claim for protection of those rights. They are "the things which belong to him as a constituent member of the great national family."[116] As amended, the bill protected only citizens. Wilson's explanation amounted to a repudiation of the republican definition of citizenship and the adoption of the old notion of protection in exchange for allegiance.

House Democrats doubted that one could read the privileges and immunities of citizenship so narrowly. Andrew J. Rogers asked, "What broader words than privileges and immunities are to be found in the dictionary? . . . The right of suffrage is not a natural right. It is a civil right." He pointed out that Justice Washington had included it among the privileges and immunities of citizenship in *Corfield v. Coryell*. Pass this bill, and "you will allow the negroes of this country to compete for the high office of President of the United States."[117] Republicans scorned the notion. "Nobody can successfully contend that a bill guarantying simply civil rights and immunities is a bill under which you could extend the right of suffrage, which is a political privilege, and not a civil right," one replied.[118]

Wilson could dismiss Rogers's criticism as Democratic carping. But he could not so easily dismiss the objection when it came from John A. Bingham, a respected lawyer and now a member of the Joint Committee on Reconstruction, where he was working hard to fashion what became the rights-protecting first section of the Fourteenth Amendment. Bingham had indicated he was going to speak on the bill, and Wilson no doubt knew what he was going to say.[119] He decided on a preemptive strike, moving to add a new section to the bill—"That nothing in this act shall be so construed as to affect the laws of any State concerning the right of suffrage"—and the House agreed.[120]

But Bingham was not deterred. "The term civil rights includes every right that pertains to the citizen under the Constitution, laws, and Government of this country," he insisted. That included political rights. "The term 'political rights' is only a limitation of the term 'civil rights,' and . . . signifies that class of civil rights which are more directly exercised by the citizen in connection with the government of his country."[121] Once again Wilson denied it. "This bill refers to those rights which belong to men as citizens of the United States and none other," he said.[122] Bingham's concerns went further than the meaning of civil rights, however. Like Democrats, he did not believe that the Thirteenth Amendment justified congressional civil rights legislation. That would take another constitutional amendment like the one he was composing.[123]

Enough Republicans shared Bingham's concerns to send the bill back to the Judiciary Committee. The committee then removed the clause banning discrimination in civil rights generally, leaving only the specific list. That is the way the bill passed.[124] The clear implication of the law was now that the civil rights that the bill specified constituted the rights of citizenship. That satisfied nearly all the worried Republicans. The change did not reconcile Bingham, however. He voted against the bill, the only Republican in the House to do so.

Later that year, Congress sent the Fourteenth Amendment to the states for ratification. Its first section, authored by Bingham, echoed the Civil Rights Act's citizenship clause and barred the states from abridging the privileges and immunities of citizens of the United States. In explaining the first section, Bingham had to acknowledge that it did not treat voting as one of the privileges of citizenship. The second section conceded the states' rights to deny the vote to citizens by reducing their congressional representation if they did so. That "excludes the conclusion that by the first section suffrage is subjected to congressional law," he observed.[125]

By the time Congress sent the Fourteenth Amendment to the states for ratification, it seemed clear that it and the Civil Rights Act implied a narrow legal definition of citizenship. Republicans had taken such a course because they thought a definition that established black suffrage would be politically suicidal. Ironically, southern intransigence led to a seismic shift in public opinion. By 1867 Republicans were emboldened to make impartial suffrage part of a new program of Reconstruction, and in 1869 they proposed a Fifteenth Amendment barring racial discrimination in voting rights anywhere in the United States. The fact that black enfranchisement required a new constitutional amendment, beyond the Civil Rights Act and the Fourteenth Amendment that declared African Americans citizens, reconfirmed the idea that voting was a privilege that could be granted or withheld from citizens as public policy dictated.

Nonetheless, the notion that citizenship implied political rights remained powerful in the popular mind. In 1875 an elite observer grumbled that "a citizen without suffrage is hardly conceived of."[126] Relying on this long tradition, woman suffragists hoped the courts might agree that voting was indeed among the privileges of American citizenship. But the restrictive legal meaning of citizenship had been set. The Supreme Court dashed their hopes. The term "citizen," the Court observed, "has been considered better suited to the description of one living under a republican government" than the term "subject." But that carried no particular implication. Citizenship "is understood as conveying the idea of membership of a nation, and nothing more."[127]

Notes

1. Peter Thompson and Peter S. Onuf, eds., *State and Citizen: British America and the Early United States* (Charlottesville: University of Virginia Press, 2013).
2. William A. Link et al., eds., *Creating Citizenship in the Nineteenth-Century American South* (Gainesville: University Press of Florida, 2013).
3. Douglas Bradburn, *The Citizenship Revolution: Politics and the Creation of the American Union, 1774–1804* (Charlottesville: University of Virginia Press, 2009).
4. Nancy Isenberg, *Sex and Citizenship in Antebellum America* (Chapel Hill: University of North Carolina Press, 1998); Linda Kerber, *No Constitutional Right to Be Ladies: Women and the Obligations of Citizenship* (New York: Hill and Wang, 1998).
5. Corinne T. Field, *The Struggle for Equal Adulthood: Gender, Race, Age, and the Fight for Citizenship in Antebellum America* (Chapel Hill: University of North Carolina Press, 2014).
6. Amy L. Brandzel, "Haunted by Citizenship: Whitenormative Citizen-Subjects and the Uses of History in Women's Studies," *Feminist Studies* 37 (Fall 2011): 503–33.
7. A title search in the *America: History and Life* database undertaken February 5, 2017, brought up 1,498 articles with "citizenship" in the title, although an indeterminate number related to Canadian rather than U.S. history.
8. See, for example, Christine N. Buzinde and Iyunolu F. Osagie, "Slavery Heritage Representations, Cultural Citizenship, and Judicial Politics in America," *Historical Geography* 39 (2011): 41–64; and Gabriel Milner, "The Tenor of Belonging: The Fisk Jubilee Singers and the Popular Cultures of Postbellum Citizenship," *Journal of the Gilded Age and Progressive Era* 15 (October 2016): 399–417.

9. See Nick Stevenson, "Culture and Citizenship: An Introduction," in *Culture and Citizenship*, ed. Nick Stevenson (London: Sage, 2001), 1–10; and Gershon Shafir, "Introduction: The Evolving Tradition of Citizenship," in *The Citizenship Debates: A Reader*, ed. Gershon Shafir (Minneapolis: University of Minnesota Press, 1998), 1–28.
10. Horace Binney to Francis Lieber, March 14, 1864, quoted in Michael Vorenberg, "Emancipating the Constitution: Lieber and the Theory of Amendment," in *Francis Lieber and the Culture of the American Mind*, ed. Charles R. Mack and Henry H. Lesesne (Columbia: University of South Carolina Press, 2005), 26; Bates in *Official Opinions of the Attorneys General of the United States*, 10:382, at 383 (November 29, 1862).
11. William Rawle, *A View of the Constitution of the United States of America*, 2d ed. (Philadelphia: Philip H. Nicklin, 1829), 85–86.
12. Joseph Story, *Commentaries on the Constitution of the United States*, 2d ed. (Boston: Little and Brown, 1851), 2:466, 544.
13. Ibid., 452, 544.
14. Scott v. Sandford, 60 U.S. 393 (1857).
15. Corfield v. Coryell, 6 F. Cas. 546 (C.C.E.D. Pa. 1823) (No. 3,230).
16. *Cong. Globe*, 39th Cong., 1st Sess., 2765 (May 23, 1866).
17. Holly Brewer, *By Birth or Consent: Children, Law and the Anglo-American Revolution in Authority* (Chapel Hill: University of North Carolina Press, 2005), 131.
18. For the status of American colonists, as well as the foundations of that status in English law, see James H. Kettner, *The Development of American Citizenship, 1608–1870* (Chapel Hill: University of North Carolina Press, 1978), 13–131.
19. William Blackstone, *Commentaries on the Laws of England*, 4 vols. (New York: Harper and Brothers, 1847), 1:125–29. See John Phillip Reid, *The Concept of Liberty in the Age of the American Revolution* (Chicago: University of Chicago Press, 1988).
20. Blackstone, *Commentaries*, 1:169–71.
21. Gordon Wood, *The Radicalism of the American Revolution* (New York: Alfred A. Knopf, 1992), 233; Samuel Johnson, *A Dictionary of the English Language*, 3d ed. (Dublin: W. G. Jones, 1768).
22. Bernard Bailyn, *The Ideological Origins of the American Revolution* (Cambridge, Mass.: Harvard University Press, 1967), 161–75.
23. Chisholm v. Georgia, 2 U.S. (2 Dall.) 419, 470 (1793).
24. David Ramsey, *Dissertation on the Manner of Acquiring the Character and Privileges of a Citizen of the United States* (Charleston, S.C.: n.p., 1789), 33.

For a vibrant, insightful analysis of the change, see Douglas Bradburn, *The Citizenship Revolution: Politics and the Creation of the American Union, 1774–1804* (Charlottesville: University of Virginia Press, 2009), 19–60.

25. For a good discussion, somewhat different from what follows, see Michael Vorenberg, "Abraham Lincoln's 'Fellow Citizens'—before and after Emancipation," in *Lincoln's Proclamation: Emancipation Reconsidered,* ed. William A. Blair and Karen Fisher Younger (Chapel Hill: University of North Carolina Press, 2009), 151–69.
26. John Codman Hurd, *The Law of Freedom and Bondage in the United States,* 2 vols. (Boston: Little, Brown, 1858–62), 2:274.
27. *To the Citizens of the Town of Boston* (Boston: n.p., 1802), broadside at the Massachusetts Historical Society, Boston (digital copy available in Early American Imprints, Series II: Shaw-Shoemaker, 1801–1819, No. 1930).
28. *Flagg Hall. Friday Evening, March 8th 1850. Grand Concert! To the Citizens of Worcester* (N.p., [1850]) (digital copy in Readex American Broadsides and Ephemera, First Series, No 7603).
29. Molyneaux v. Seymour, Fanning & Co., 30 Ga. 440, 441 (1860).
30. Cooper v. Galbraith, 6 F. Cas. 472, 475 (No. 3193) (1819).
31. James Kent, *Commentaries on American Law,* 3d ed., 4 vols. (New York: Clayton and Van Norden, 1836), 2:258n.
32. State v. Manuel, 4 N.C. 20, 26 (1838). There was more to the reasoning than this. The judges pointed out that black freemen had exercised the right to vote until the state constitution was revised in 1835.
33. See State v. Newsom, 27 N.C. 250 (1844). See also Richard C. Rohr, "The Free Black Experience in Antebellum Wilmington, North Carolina: Refining Generalizations about Race Relations," *Journal of Southern History* 78 (August 2012): 615–38.
34. John F. Kennedy, inaugural address, January 20, 1961, in *Inaugural Addresses of the Presidents of the United States from George Washington to George W. Bush,* Senate Document 101–10 (Washington, D.C.: Government Printing Office, 1989), 308.
35. Vernon Burton, "The South as Other, the South as Stranger," *Journal of Southern History* 79 (February 2013): 42.
36. For example, Joseph R. Washington, *Rulers of Reality and the Ruled Races: The Struggle of Black Ministers to Bring Afro-Americans to Full Citizenship in America* (Lewiston, N.Y.: E. Mellen Press, 1990).
37. Adrian Oldfield, *Citizenship and Community: Civic Republicanism and the Modern World* (New York: Routledge, 1990), 31–49; J. G. A. Pocock, *The Machiavellian Moment* (Princeton, N.J.: Princeton University Press, 1975).

38. Johnson, *Dictionary of the English Language*, s.v. "citizen."
39. Derek B. Heater, *A History of Education for Citizenship* (New York: Routledge Falmer, 2004), 80–98. For general histories of citizenship, consult also Oldfield, *Citizenship and Community*; and Andreas Fahrmeir, *Citizenship: The Rise and Fall of a Modern Concept* (New Haven: Yale University Press, 2007).
40. Heater, *History of Citizenship*, 150. For the change in revolutionary America, see Rogers M. Smith, *Civic Ideals: Conflicting Visions of Citizenship in U.S. History* (New Haven: Yale University Press, 1997), 70–114.
41. Heater, *History of Citizenship*, 111–48; Michael Schudson, *The Good Citizen: A History of American Civic Life* (New York: Free Press, 1998), 49–89; Gordon Wood, *The Creation of the American Republic, 1776–1787* (Chapel Hill: University of North Carolina Press, 1969), 53–70.
42. "Preceptor" (Boston, 1772), quoted in Smith, *Civic Ideals*, 84. See the discussions of Renaissance ideals of citizenship in Oldfield, *Citizenship and Community*, 31–49, and in Pocock, *Machiavellian Moment*.
43. Ariela Gross, *What Blood Won't Tell: A History of Race on Trial in America* (Cambridge, Mass.: Harvard University Press, 2008), 49. See Mark E. Kann, *A Republic of Men: The American Founders, Gendered Language, and Patriarchal Politics* (New York: New York University Press, 1998).
44. Wood, *Radicalism of the American Revolution*, 227–369; Lee Benson, *The Concept of Jacksonian Democracy: New York as a Test Case* (Princeton: Princeton University Press, 1961), 3–20.
45. Alexander Keyssar, *The Right to Vote: The Contested History of Democracy in the United States* (New York: Basic Books, 2000), 26–52; Schudson, *Good Citizen*, 90–132; Sean Wilentz, *Chants Democratic: New York City and the Rise of the American Working Class, 1788–1850* (New York: Oxford University Press, 1984), 91–97; Mary P. Ryan, *Women in Public: Between Banners and Ballots, 1825–1880* (Baltimore: Johns Hopkins University Press, 1990).
46. Noah Webster, *American Dictionary of the English Language*, 2 vols. (New York: S. Converse, 1828), 1:381.
47. For examples, Const. of Alabama (1819), Art. 3, Sec. 5; Const. of Arkansas (1836), Art. 4, Sec. 2; Const. of California (1849), Art. 2, Sec. 1; Const. of Connecticut (1818), Sec. 2; Const. of Florida (1838), Art. 6, Sec. 1; Const. of Illinois (1848), Art. 6, Sec. 1; Const. of Indiana (1851), Art. 2, Sec. 2; Const. of Iowa (1846), Art. 3, Sec. 1; Const. of Michigan (1850), Art. 7, Sec. 1; Const. of Mississippi (1832), Art. 3, Sec. 1; Const. of Ohio (1851), Art. 5, Sec. 1; Const. of New York (1846), Art. 2, Sec. 1; Const. of Pennsylvania

(1838, as amended 1857), Art. 1, Sec. 2, Art. 2, Sec. 2, Art. 3, Sec. 1, Art. 6, Sec. 1; Const. of Virginia (1851), Art. 3, Sec. 1.

48. Const. of Indiana (1851), Art. 1, Sec. 2; Const. of Iowa (1846), Art. 7, Sec. 1; Const. of Michigan (1850), Art. 7, Sec. 1.

49. For examples, Const. of Alabama (1819), Art. 3, Sec. 4, 12; Const. of Arkansas (1836), Art. 4, Sec. 4; Const. of California (1849), Art. 4, Sec. 5 (legislators must be qualified electors and thus U.S. citizens); Const. of Florida (1838), Art. 4, Sec. 4, 5; Const. of Georgia (1798), Art. 1, Sec. 6, 8, Art. 2, Sec. 3; Const. of Illinois (1848), Art. 3, Sec. 3, 4, Art. 4, Sec. 4; Const. of Indiana (1851), Art. 4, Sec. 7, Art. 5, Sec. 7; Const. of Iowa (1846), Art. 4, Sec. 4, 5, Art. 5, Sec. 3; Const. of Kentucky (1850), Art. 1, Sec. 4, 16, Art. 3, Sec. 4; Const. of Michigan (1850), Art. 4, Sec. 5, Art. 5 Sec. 3; Const. of Mississippi (1832), Art. 3, Sec. 7, 14; Art. 5, 14; Const. of Pennsylvania (1838, as amended 1857), Art. 1, Sec. 3, 5, 8, Art. 2, Sec. 4; Const. of Virginia (1851), Art. 5, Sec. 3.

50. For examples, Const. of Indiana (1851), Art. 12, Sec. 1; Const. of Iowa (1846), Art. 7, Sec. 1; Const. of Michigan (1850), Art. 17, Sec. 1; Const. of Ohio (1851), Art. 9, Sec. 1.

51. For examples, Const. of Florida (1838), Art. 1, Sec. 1; Const. of California (1849), Art. 1, Sec. 1; Const. of Illinois (1848), Art. 13, Sec. 1; Const. of Iowa (1846), Art. 1, Sec. 1; Const. of Ohio (1851), Art. 1, Sec. 1; Const. of Pennsylvania (1838), Art. 9, Sec. 1. ("All men" or "all persons" had the right to worship freely); Const. of Alabama (1819), Art. 1, Sec. 3, 5; Const. of California (1849), Art. 1, Sec. 1, 4; Const. of Conn. (1818), Art. 1, Sec. 3; Const. of Florida (1838), Art. 1, Sec. 3; Const. of Illinois (1848), Art. 13, Sec. 3; Const. of Iowa (1846), Art. 1, Sec. 3, 4; Const. of Ohio (1851), Art. 1, Sec. 7; Const. of Pennsylvania (1838), Art. 9, Sec. 3.

52. For examples, Const. of Florida (1838), Art. 1, Sec. 8; Const. of Illinois (1848), Art. 13, Sec. 8.

53. For examples, Const. of Alabama (1819), 18; Const. of California (1849), Art. 1, Sec. 15; Const. of Illinois (1848), Art. 13, Sec. 15; Const. of Iowa (1846), Art. 1, Sec. 19; Const. of Pennsylvania (1838), Art. 9, Sec. 16.

54. Const. of Alabama (1819), Art. 1, Sec. 10–13, 16–17, 20, 28; Const. of California (1849), Art. 1, Sec. 3–8; Const. of Connecticut (1818), Art. 1, Sec. 9, 10, 13, 14; Const. of Florida (1838), Art. 1, Sec. 10–13, 16; Const. of Illinois (1848), Art. 13, Sec. 9–14; Const. of Iowa (1846), Art. 1, Sec. 9–13, 17; Const. of Ohio (1851), Art. 1, Sec. 5, 8–10; Const. of Pennsylvania (1838), Art. 9, Sec. 6, 9, 10, 13, 14, 18.

55. For examples, Const. of Alabama (1819), Art. 1, Sec. 8, 22, 23; Const. of California (1849), Art. 1, Sec. 9, 10; Const. of Connecticut (1818), Art. 1, Sec.

5, 16, 17; Const. of Florida (1838), Art. 1, Sec. 5, 20; Const. of Illinois (1848), Art. 13, Sec. 21, 23; Const. of Iowa (1846), Art. 1, Sec. 20; Const. of Ohio (1851), Art. 1, Sec. 3, 11; Const. of Pennsylvania (1838), Art. 9, Sec. 7, 20, 21. The one anomaly in this regard is the use of the term "the people" when describing who had a right against unreasonable searches and seizures. See, for example, Const. of California (1849), Art. 1, Sec. 19; Const. of Iowa (1846), Art. 1, Sec. 8; Const. of Ohio (1851), Art. 1, Sec. 14. One element of the explanation is that this language carried over from the first state constitutions, when illicit searches, seizures, and general warrants were associated not only with high-handed British enforcement of the Navigation Acts but with the prosecution of the radical Whig newspaperman and hero John Wilkes. See George F. E. Rude, *Wilkes and Liberty: A Social Study of 1763 to 1774* (Oxford: Clarendon Press, 1962); Peter D. G. Thomas, *John Wilkes: A Friend to Liberty* (New York: Oxford University Press, 1996). For the Wilkes controversy in America, see Pauline Maier, "John Wilkes and American Disillusionment with Britain," *William and Mary Quarterly* 20 (July 1963): 373–95.

56. For examples, Const. of California (1849), Art. 1, Sec. 9; Const. of Iowa (1846), Art. 1, Sec. 5.
57. For examples, Const. of Alabama (1819), Art. 1, Sec. 2; Const. of Illinois (1848), Art. 13, Sec. 2; Const. of Iowa (1846), Art. 1, Sec. 2; Const. of Ohio (1851), Art. 1, Sec. 2, 4; Const. of Pennsylvania (1838), Art. 9, Sec. 2.
58. E. H. Hurlbut, *Essays on Human Rights and Their Political Guaranties* (New York: Greeley and McElrath, 1845).
59. William Hickey, *The Constitution of the United States of America . . .*, 3d ed. (Philadelphia: n.p., 1848), viii.
60. David Ramsey, *A Dissertation on the Manner of Acquiring the Character and Privileges of a Citizen of the United States* (Charleston, S.C.: n.p., 1789), 3–4.
61. Charles Biddle, *The Alliance with the Negro: Speech of Hon. Charles J. Biddle, of Pennsylvania; Delivered in the House of Representatives of the United States, March 6, 1862* ([Washington, D.C.]: L. Towers and Co., [1862]), 2.
62. Kettner, *Development of American Citizenship*, 235.
63. *Annals of Congress*, 3d Cong., 2d Sess., 1568 (May 2, 1795) (hereafter cited as *AC*).
64. Rawle, *View of the Constitution*, 85–86.
65. *AC*, 16th Cong., 2d Sess., 555–56 (December 9, 1820).
66. Ibid., 637 (December 12, 1820).

67. "Rights of Free Virginia Negroes," *Official Opinions of the Attorneys General*, 1:506–9, at 508 (November 7, 1821).
68. "An Act declaring who shall be deemed citizens of this Commonwealth . . . ," December 23, 1792, in *A Collection of All Such Acts of the General Assembly of Virginia of Permanent and Public Nature as Are Now in Force* (Richmond: Pleasants and Pace, 1803), 216. The law was not changed to limit citizenship to "free white persons" until the 1840s. Code of Virginia, title 2 (citizenship), ch. 3, sec. 1 (1849).
69. "Rights of Free Virginia Negroes," 508.
70. Shelton v. Tiffin, 47 U.S. (6 How.) 163 (1848).
71. *Dred Scott*, 60 U.S. at 476.
72. Amy v. Smith, 11 Ky. 326, 334–35 (1822).
73. Cooper v. City of Savannah, 4 Ga. 68, 72 (1848).
74. *Corfield* , 6 F. Cas. 546.
75. See, for example, Kent, *Commentaries on American Law*, 2:258n ("The privilege of voting, and the legal capacity for office, are not essential to the character of a citizen; for women are citizens without either").
76. Statutes at Large of the United States of America 10:604 (February 10, 1855).
77. "Relation of Indians to Citizenship," *Official Opinions of the Attorneys General*, 8:748–56 (July 5, 1856) (quoted at 749).
78. *Amy*, 11 Ky. at 333.
79. *AC*, 16th Cong., 2d Sess., 571 (December 9, 1820) (Representative James Strong).
80. *Dred Scott*, 60 U.S. at 583.
81. John Fox, *Opinion of the Hon. John Fox: President Judge of the Judicial District Composed of the Counties of Bucks and Montgomery, against the Exercise of Negro Suffrage in Pennsylvania: Also, the Vote of the Members of the Pennsylvania Convention on the Motion of Mr. Martin to Insert the Word "White" as One of the Proposed Amendments to the Constitution* (Harrisburg, Pa.: Packer, Barret and Parke, 1838), 13.
82. Smith, *Civic Ideals*, 15.
83. Kenneth L. Karst, *Belonging to America: Equal Citizenship and the Constitution* (New Haven: Yale University Press, 1989), 10–11. Likewise, Judith N. Shklar, *American Citizenship: The Quest for Inclusion* (Cambridge, Mass.: Harvard University Press, 1991); Barbara Y. Welke, *Law and the Borders of Belonging in the Long Nineteenth Century United States* (New York: Cambridge University Press, 2010); Rebecca Zietlow, *Enforcing Equality:*

Congress, the Constitution, and the Protection of Individual Rights (New York: New York University Press, 2006) (stressing "rights of belonging").

84. *AC*, 16th Cong., 2d Sess., 598 (December 11, 1820) (Representative Joseph Hemphill).
85. Ibid., 615 (December 12, 1820) (Representative Louis McLane).
86. Butler v. Farnsworth, 4 F. Cas. 902 (C.C.E.D. Pa. 1821) (No. 2,240).
87. Hans L. Trefousse, *Carl Schurz: A Biography* (New York: Fordham University Press, 1998), 41.
88. A. M. Dicey, "The Free Negro," in Edward Dicey, *Spectator of America*, ed. Herbert Mitgang (Chicago: Quadrangle Books, 1971), 48–49.
89. Stephen Kantrowitz, *More Than Freedom: Fighting for Black Citizenship in a White Republic, 1829–1889* (New York: Penguin Press, 2012), 6.
90. Ibid., 4.
91. *San Francisco Pacific Appeal*, June 7, 1862, quoted in D. Michael Bottoms, *An Aristocracy of Color: Race and Reconstruction in California and the West, 1850–1890* (Norman: University of Oklahoma Press, 2013), 42.
92. Mae M. Ngai, *Impossible Subjects: Illegal Aliens and the Making of Modern America* (Princeton: Princeton University Press, 2004), 2.
93. *AC*, 16th Cong., 2d Sess., 505 (December 8, 1820) (Representative Philip Barbour).
94. *Reports of the Debates and Proceedings of the Convention for the Revision of the Constitution of Ohio, 1850–1851*, 2 vols. (Columbus: S. Medary, 1851), 1:56 (May 13, 1850), 2:337 (January 16, 1851).
95. Bryan v. Walton, 14 Ga. 185, 202 (1853).
96. Heirn v. Bridault, 37 Miss. 209, 224 (1859).
97. *Dred Scott*, 60 U.S. at 404, 407, 411.
98. "Citizenship," *Official Opinions of the Attorneys General*, 10:384–85 (November 29, 1862).
99. *Cong. Globe*, 39th Cong., 1st Sess., 211 (January 12, 1866).
100. Speech of B. F. [Simrall] in the Mississippi state legislature, *Meridian Clarion*, November 14, 1865, 2.
101. S. A. D. Steele, "Substance of Remarks Made by Hon. S. A. D. Steele in the [Mississippi] House of Representatives . . . on the 'Bill to confer Civil Rights on Freemen and for other purposes,'" *Jackson Daily Clarion*, November 19, 1865, 2.
102. Quoted in Wang Xi, "Make 'Every Slave Free, and Every Freeman a Voter': The African American Construction of Suffrage Discourse in the Age of Emancipation," in *Contested Democracy: Freedom, Race, and*

Power in American History, ed. Manisha Sinha and Penny von Eschen (New York: Cornell University Press, 2007), 124.

103. Frederick Douglass, *What the Black Man Wants: Speech of Frederick Douglass at the Annual Meeting of the Massachusetts Anti-slavery Society at Boston* [January 26, 1865], University of Rochester Frederick Douglass Project, https://www.lib.rochester.edu/index.cfm?PAGE=2946 (last consulted June 2, 2014). The date is from the version available in print in *The Frederick Douglass Papers: Series One, Speeches, Debates, and Interviews*, ed. John W. Blassingame, 5 vols. (New Haven: Yale University Press, 1979–), 4:61–63.
104. Mary F. Berry, *Military Necessity and Civil Rights Policy: Black Citizenship and the Constitution* (Port Washington, N.Y.: Kennikat Press, 1977); Christian G. Samito, *Becoming Americans under Fire: Irish Americans, African Americans, and the Politics of Citizenship during the Civil War* (Ithaca, N.Y.: Cornell University Press, 2009).
105. Michael Les Benedict, *A Compromise of Principle: Congressional Republicans and Reconstruction, 1863–1869* (New York: W. W. Norton, 1964), 100–16.
106. *Cong. Globe*, 39th Cong., 1st Sess., 474–76 (January 29, 1866).
107. Ibid., 476 (January 29, 1866) (inquiry by Senator James W. McDougall).
108. Ibid., 497 (January 30, 1866) (Senator Peter G. Van Winkle).
109. Ibid., 499 (Senator Edgar Cowan).
110. Ibid., 599 (February 2, 1866).
111. Ibid., 606.
112. Charles Sumner, *The Equal Rights of All: The Great Guaranty and Present Necessity, for the Sake of Security, and to Maintain a Republican Government* (Speech in the Senate, February 5 and 6, 1866), in *The Works of Charles Sumner*, 15 vols. (Boston: Lee and Shepard, 1870–1883), 10:217–18.
113. *Cong. Globe*, 39th Cong., 1st Sess., 1156 (March 2, 1866) (Representative Andrew J. Thornton). See ibid., 576–77 (February 1, 1866) (Senator Garrett Davis), 1120 (March 1, 1866) (Representative Andrew J. Rogers); and 1268 (March 8, 1866) (Representative Michael C. Kerr).
114. Ibid., 475 (January 29, 1866).
115. Ibid., 1117 (March 1, 1866).
116. Ibid., 1118.
117. Ibid., 1121–22.
118. Ibid., 1151 (March 2, 1866) (Representative Martin R. Thayer).
119. Ibid., 1271 (March 8, 1866).

120. Ibid., 1162 (March 2, 1866). (Bingham mentioned having discussed the bill privately with Wilson at ibid., 1291 [March 9, 1866]).
121. Ibid., 1291 (March 9, 1866).
122. Ibid., 1294.
123. Ibid., 1292–93.
124. Ibid., 1296, 1367 (March 13, 1866).
125. Ibid., 2542 (May 10, 1866).
126. Theodore Woolsey, introduction to *On Civil Liberty and Self-Government,* by Francis Lieber, 3d ed. (Philadelphia: Lippincott, 1875), 10. Woolsey was the longtime president of Yale University (then called Yale College).
127. Minor v. Happersett, 88 U.S. 162, 166–67 (1875).

2

THE OTHER CITIZENSHIP CLAUSE

Rebecca E. Zietlow

The first sentence of the Fourteenth Amendment declares that "all persons born or naturalized within the United States . . . are citizens of the United States."[1] This clause defined the criteria for U.S. citizenship and established birthright citizenship as a principle of constitutional law. Yet two years before the Fourteenth Amendment became law, the Reconstruction Congress had already declared "all persons born in the United States and not subject to any foreign power, excluding Indians not taxed . . . to be citizens of the United States."[2] This other citizenship clause, the preamble to the 1866 Civil Rights Act, directly contravenes the U.S. Supreme Court's ruling in *Scott v. Sandford* that freed slaves could not be citizens.[3] Yet the 1866 act was based on Congress's power to enforce the Thirteenth Amendment and came before the Fourteenth Amendment's citizenship clause was ratified. How could the members of the Reconstruction Congress have believed that they had the power to enact the other citizenship clause? The answer to this question has implications for the original meaning of the Thirteenth Amendment and its enforcement clause. Clearly, the members of the Reconstruction Congress believed that they had the power to overturn the Court's ruling in *Dred Scott* with this statutory provision. Either the Thirteenth Amendment had conveyed citizenship rights on free slaves upon the abolition of slavery, or members of Congress felt empowered to establish constitutional meaning on their own, notwithstanding the Court's contrary ruling.

Scholars have generally linked citizenship rights to the Fourteenth Amendment, not to the Thirteenth.[4] Historian Michael Vorenberg has argued that the framers of the Thirteenth Amendment did not link freedom to citizenship rights.[5] Yet the citizenship clause of the 1866 Civil Rights Act reveals a great deal about the scope and meaning of the rights of a free person that were protected by the Thirteenth Amendment. Antislavery activists had long argued that free black people were citizens and that their citizenship entitled them to fundamental human rights. The fact that members of the Reconstruction Congress based this citizenship clause in their power to enforce the Thirteenth Amendment is evidence that they believed that freed slaves had become citizens as soon as they were freed by that amendment. Either the Thirteenth Amendment had established freed slaves as U.S. citizens prior to the Fourteenth Amendment's citizenship clause, or the Thirteenth Amendment's enforcement clause empowered Congress to redefine the law of citizenship and overturn the Supreme Court's interpretation of the Constitution in *Dred Scott* before the Fourteenth Amendment constitutionalized that law.

As soon as Congress abolished slavery with the Thirteenth Amendment, members of Congress sought to enforce the fundamental human rights of the newly freed slaves. The first step in this process was to ensure that freed slaves were citizens of the United States, enforcing the long-standing arguments of antislavery activists and overruling the Supreme Court's decision in *Dred Scott*. Senator Lyman Trumbull introduced the bill that became the 1866 Civil Rights Act immediately after the Thirteenth Amendment became law.[6] Trumbull intended his bill to enforce the abolition of slavery, and his colleagues agreed.[7] With the citizenship clause, the act effected monumental change, transforming former slaves into equal citizens with the same rights as white citizens. As Trumbull declared, "The rights of citizenship *mean* something, and freed slaves were entitled to whatever citizenship meant."[8] Senator Jacob Howard explained that with "respect to all civil rights . . . there is to be hereafter no distinction between the white race and the black race."[9] Senator Henry Lane said that the act would ensure "that these freedmen shall be secured in the possession of all rights, privileges, and immunities of freedom; in other words, that we shall give effect to the proclamation of emancipation and to the constitutional amendment."[10] Thus, the 1866 Civil Rights Act provides a glimpse of those fundamental rights that those men believed to be inherent in freedom and furthers our understanding of the original meaning of the Thirteenth Amendment and its enforcement clause.

The act was based in Congress's new power to enforce the Thirteenth Amendment pursuant to its enforcement clause, Section 2.[11] Senator Trumbull explained that he believed that Section 2 enabled Congress to protect the fundamental rights of newly freed slaves and all other persons within their jurisdiction.[12] He explained that the act would "give effect to [the] declaration of freedom [in the Thirteenth Amendment] and secure to all persons within the United States practical freedom."[13] Senator Henry Lane agreed that the bill would "give effect to the proclamation of emancipation and to the constitutional amendment."[14] Thus, these members of the Reconstruction Congress, both of whom had supported the Thirteenth Amendment, made it clear that they believed the amendment empowered Congress to enact legislation that went well beyond ending the institution of slavery. The enforcement clause gave Congress the power to define and protect the fundamental rights to which free persons were entitled, including the right to be a U.S. citizen.[15]

Many members of the Reconstruction Congress believed that freed people were U.S. citizens with fundamental rights. In their view, the Thirteenth Amendment not only ended slavery but also recognized the citizenship rights of freed slaves. Prior to the Civil War, some antislavery activists had claimed that slavery violated the privileges and immunities of citizenship protected by Article 4 of the Constitution. During that era, most people linked citizenship rights to state citizenship, and they varied from state to state. Some states recognized free black people as citizens, while others refused to acknowledge them even as persons. Some antislavery constitutionalists sought to end this dynamic, advocating national rights of citizenship that were enforceable against all states. The Civil War transformed the balance of federalism, shifting the primary locus of citizenship rights to the federal government. After the war, supporters of the 1866 Civil Rights Act articulated the broad view of the fundamental rights of U.S. citizens held by the antebellum activists. Many argued that the Thirteenth Amendment transformed former slaves into U.S. citizens.

For those members of Congress who did not equate freedom with citizenship, the other citizenship clause reflects the scope of their power to enforce the Thirteenth Amendment with "appropriate" legislation. Did they believe that the amendment empowered them to overturn *Dred Scott* with a statute? If so, they thought that their enforcement power was broad indeed, broad enough to alter the Court's interpretation of constitutional law with a statute. In *City of Boerne v. Flores*, the twentieth-century Supreme Court ruled that Congress's power to enact "appropriate" legislation to enforce the Fourteenth Amendment is limited to remedying violations of the Constitution. However, the other citizenship clause provides evidence that members of the Thirty-Ninth Congress had a broader view of their power than that envisioned by the Court in *Boerne*. During the Reconstruction era, it was considerably more common for political officials to assert their own authority to interpret the Constitution than they do today, and many of the leaders of the Reconstruction Congress had been elected in part because of their outspoken opposition to the Court's *Dred Scott* decision. Thus, it is not surprising that they asserted their own authority to overturn the decision. The other citizenship clause thus casts light on the relationship between the Court and Congress in interpreting the Reconstruction amendments. It provides evidence that the members of the Reconstruction Congress believed that they, and not the Court, would play the primary role in determining the meaning of the Reconstruction amendments.

CITIZENSHIP AND THE RIGHTS OF A FREE PERSON

When the members of the Reconstruction Congress linked fundamental rights to citizenship, they were following in the footsteps of antislavery activists during the years leading up to the Civil War. At that time, the issue of whether free black people were citizens—and if so, what rights inhered therein—often surfaced in constitutional debates over slavery and the rights of free black individuals.[16] Antislavery activists invoked citizenship to challenge the institution of slavery and advocate for the rights of free black people. They claimed that such free persons were citizens with fundamental human rights. Some asserted their states' authority to recognize black people as citizens and demanded that other states respect those rights. Others linked fundamental rights to national citizenship and claimed that those rights were enforceable throughout the country. With the other citizenship clause, the members of the Thirty-Ninth Congress invoked this tradition and established the rights that had long been advocated by antislavery activists.

In Congress, disputes over citizenship rights date back as far as the debates over the Missouri Compromise. During that debate, Rhode Island senator James Burrill argued that a provision of Missouri's proposed constitution that would have prohibited free black people from entering the state violated the rights of citizenship established by the privileges and immunities clause of Article 4.[17] South Carolina senator William Smith rebuffed Burrill, objecting that black people were not citizens anywhere, so they were not subject to the clause's protections.[18] South Carolina representative Charles Pinckney agreed with Senator Smith. Pinckney insisted that the Article 4 clause had never been intended to apply to black people.[19] Kentucky representative Henry Clay brokered a compromise on this issue. Missouri was admitted on the condition that the state legislature could not enact any law that would violate the privileges and immunities clause.[20] This compromise allowed the members of Congress to avoid deciding whether free black individuals could be citizens.

In 1849, the issue of citizenship resurfaced in Congress during debates over the "Seaman's Acts," laws enacted by the states of South Carolina and Louisiana that authorized state police officers to arrest and imprison free black individuals who entered their states.[21] The Seaman's Acts responded to the arrest of Denmark Vesey, a free northern black man who allegedly traveled to Charleston to foment a rebellion. The southern legislators intended the acts to ward off the potential threat to slavery posed by free black people in the state.[22] Members of Congress from Massachusetts protested the Seaman's Acts because their state had a large shipping industry that employed many black sailors.[23] Said Massachusetts representative Charles Hudson, "In the state of Massachusetts the Black man was as much a citizen as a white man."[24] His colleague George Ashmun agreed that South Carolina was enforcing its law against "our citizens."[25] Both men linked rights to state, not federal, citizenship. Nonetheless, they articulated a national view of citizenship that would protect the rights of state citizens in all states. This view was particularly significant because by 1849, southern courts had become extremely reluctant to recognize the manumission of slaves under the laws of northern states. Thus, northern black people who traveled to southern states were in grave danger of being enslaved.[26] By claiming those free black individuals as citizens, northern states asserted a responsibility to protect their fundamental rights.

Outside of Congress, antislavery activists also linked fundamental human rights to citizenship. They cited the 1823 case of *Corfield v. Coryell*, in which Justice Bushrod Washington, riding circuit, described the rights of "citizens of all free governments," protected by the Article 4 privileges and immunities clause. According to Justice Washington, those rights included "protection by the government, the enjoyment of life and liberty, with the right to acquire and possess property of every kind, and to pursue and obtain happiness and safety . . . the right of a citizen of one state to pass through, or reside in, another state . . . to claim the benefit of writ of habeas corpus [and] to institute and maintain actions of any kind in the courts of the state."[27] Antislavery constitutionalists seized on this language to argue for a broad view of citizenship rights that were enforceable against state governments because they were based on Article 4.

In 1838, antislavery activist Theodore Dwight Weld wrote a treatise insisting that the federal government had an obligation to protect free black men and women who were loyal to the federal government.[28] He argued that Congress had the power to protect those rights by abolishing slavery in the federal territories. Liberty Party leaders James Birney and William

Goodell agreed with Weld that Congress could abolish slavery in exchange for slaves' allegiance and willingness to obey the law.[29] Birney agreed that a slave's duty to obey the law entitled him (or her) to protection and maintained that "without this protection—this security—we have no right to try him for violation of the laws of the country which deprives him of both."[30] These activists claimed that free persons of color were citizens, entitled to fundamental rights and the protection of the federal government.

Journalists Lysander Spooner and Joel Tiffany most fully developed this citizenship-based theory of rights. A lifelong resident of Boston, Spooner published a treatise titled *The Unconstitutionality of Slavery* in 1845.[31] In it, Spooner argued that slaves would immediately become U.S. citizens upon the abolition of slavery.[32] He continued, "If they would become citizens then, they are equally citizens now—else it would follow that the State governments had had an arbitrary power of making citizens of the United States."[33] Spooner argued further that all citizens were entitled to the equal protection of the law.[34] In his 1849 *Treatise on the Unconstitutionality of Slavery*, Joel Tiffany went even further than Spooner and claimed that even a slave was a citizen of the United States, entitled to the rights of citizenship.[35] According to Tiffany, all persons born within the United States, including slaves, were U.S. citizens, entitled to the protection of the U.S. government.[36] Tiffany relied on *Corfield* to support his broad view of citizenship rights that, he argued, were violated by the institution of slavery.[37] He wrote, "What is it, then, to be a citizen of the United States? It is to be invested with a title to life, liberty, and the pursuit of happiness, and to be protected in the enjoyment thereof, by the guaranty of twenty millions of people."[38] The Reconstruction Congress eventually adopted Tiffany's theory as the preamble to the 1866 Civil Rights Act.

In 1850, a majority of the members of Congress refuted the antislavery constitutionalists by adopting the Fugitive Slave Act of 1850.[39] That act assisted southern slave owners in capturing slaves who had escaped to northern states and contained scant procedural protections for free black people who were accused of being escaped slaves.[40] The act protected the rights of southern slave owners to their "property," implicitly rejecting any claim of individual rights that the fleeing slaves, or free black persons accused of being such, themselves might have enjoyed. By enacting this law, Congress adopted the southern position that free black people were not entitled to the rights of citizenship. Seven years later, the U.S. Supreme Court emphatically adopted the same position in the infamous case of *Scott v. Sandford*.[41]

Even after *Dred Scott,* Republican members of Congress continued to advocate a broad theory of citizenship rights. This was evident in the 1858 congressional debate over whether or not to admit the territory of Oregon into the Union as a state. In order to gain admission, Oregon submitted a proposed constitution to Congress for approval. One provision of the proposed constitution would have allowed Oregon to exclude free people of color and prohibit them from owning property, entering into contracts, and filing suit in Oregon state court.[42] Representative John Bingham of Ohio argued that these provisions violated the privileges and immunities clause of Article 4 because they denied the rights of citizenship to free black people. He explained, "It has always been understood that the citizens of each state of the Union are *ipso facto* citizens, of the United States."[43] This interpretation conflicted directly with the Court's decision in the *Dred Scott* case. However, Bingham refused to recognize the Court's decision as authoritative, asserting his own authority to recite principles of constitutional law.[44]

In his speech, Bingham articulated a vision of citizenship rights that was similar to that advocated by antislavery constitutionalists before him. His senatorial colleague from Maine William Fessenden agreed, "By the laws of Maine, and under the constitution of the state of Maine, free Negroes are citizens . . . just as much citizens of the state of Maine as white men," and insisted that he could not vote to admit a state that denied the privileges of citizenship to those men.[45] Senator Henry Wilson of Massachusetts concurred that the provision that would have denied to free black individuals access to state courts violated the privileges and immunities of free black citizens.[46] Representatives Henry Dawes and Clark Cochrane also claimed that the provisions preventing black people from entering into contracts, owning property, and suing in courts violated the Article 4 clause.[47]

Bingham went a step further than his colleagues, maintaining that the privileges and immunities clause protected the rights of national, rather than state, citizenship. He insisted that the clause "is senseless and a mockery, if it does not limit state sovereignty and restrain each and every State from closing its territory and the courts of justice against citizens of the United States."[48] Echoing Tiffany, Bingham explained that the privileges and immunities protected by the clause belonged to citizens "in," not "of," the several states.[49] This interpretation of Article 4 "implies the existence of substantive national rights which states may not deny."[50] By 1866, the majority of the Reconstruction Congress agreed with Bingham's theory of national citizenship rights.

Of course, not everyone agreed with Bingham and Fessenden. Some opponents simply cited *Dred Scott* to refute them.[51] Others argued that states could exclude whomever they chose, notwithstanding the privileges and immunities clause.[52] For example, Democratic Illinois senator Stephen Douglas, who later ran for president against Abraham Lincoln, pointed out that Illinois had a similar provision to Oregon's in excluding free black people. Douglas insisted that Oregon, like Illinois, had a sovereign right to do so.[53] This debate illustrates that the issue of citizenship rights continued to be contested. Democrats persisted in articulating a cramped view of the Article 4 privileges and immunities clause throughout the Civil War and into Reconstruction. Nonetheless, the views of Bingham, Fessenden, and Wilson are particularly significant because they were leaders in the Reconstruction Congress. Moreover, by 1866 most Republicans shared Bingham's and Fessenden's view that free black people were citizens, and they sought to enshrine that view into law with the other citizenship clause.[54]

In the mid-1850s, our country's political landscape underwent a seismic shift. In 1854, Congress enacted the Kansas-Nebraska Act, which nullified the Missouri Compromise and authorized new states to choose whether they wanted to allow slavery within their borders. Many Democrats left their party due to their outrage over Democratic support for the Kansas-Nebraska Act.[55] The Whig Party dissolved due to disputes over the act.[56] Antislavery politicians from both parties joined members of the Liberty and Free Soil Parties to form the new Republican Party, a party that advocated the end of slavery and the expansion of citizenship rights.[57] Indeed, the 1860 Republican Party platform declared the party to be "in favor of giving a full and efficient protection to the rights of all classes of citizens."[58] During Reconstruction, members of the Republican Party led the effort to fulfill this promise by enacting the 1866 Civil Rights Act.

THE *DRED SCOTT* DECISION AND OPPOSITION TO THE COURT

As support for the citizenship rights of free black people grew, so did opposition to the U.S. Supreme Court. The two trends were linked because anti-Court was largely due to the Court's rejection of the citizenship rights of black persons in *Scott v. Sandford*.[59] Dred Scott was a slave from the state of Missouri. He filed a petition for his freedom in the U.S. District Court, alleging that he became free when he traveled with his master to the free state of Illinois and the portion of the Louisiana Territory that is now known as the state of Minnesota.[60] Scott lost in a jury verdict and appealed to the U.S. Supreme Court, which rejected his petition. The Court held that Scott was not a citizen who could invoke the diversity jurisdiction of the U.S. courts. The *Dred Scott* opinion inspired a firestorm of opposition that undermined the Court's institutional authority. With the citizenship clause of the 1866 Civil Rights Act, Congress sought to overrule *Dred Scott*'s exclusionary holding that a person of African descent could not be a U.S. citizen, regardless of where that person was born. This citizenship clause stated the exact opposite—that freed slaves were U.S. citizens simply because they were born in the United States.

In his opinion in *Dred Scott*, Chief Justice Roger Taney described the question presented as whether "a Negro, whose ancestors were imported into this country, and sold as slaves, [could] become a member of the political community formed and brought into existence by the Constitution of the United States and as such become entitled to all the rights, and privileges, and immunities, guaranteed by the instrument toward the citizen," including the privilege of suing in the U.S. courts.[61] Justice Taney agreed with the antislavery constitutionalists that the rights of citizenship were broad. He described those rights as "the right to enter every other state whenever they pleased, singly or in companies, without pass or passport . . . the full liberty of speech in public and in private upon all subjects upon which its own citizens might speak; to hold public meetings upon political affairs, and to keep and carry arms wherever they went."[62] However, Taney used the breadth of those rights of citizenship to explain why free black people could not be entitled to those rights.[63] It was clear, said Justice Taney, that slaves were not "constitutional members of this sovereignty," so they were not intended to be included in the word "citizen."[64] This was the case because neither slaves nor their descendants were part of the "people" protected by the Constitution and Declaration of Independence. Instead, they were "considered as a subordinate and inferior class of beings who had been subjugated by the dominant race."[65] Under the *Dred Scott* decision, no person of African descent could be a citizen of any state or of the United States. Thus, the Court rejected a central tenet of antislavery constitutionalism.

Even though the *Dred Scott* Court found that the circuit court lacked jurisdiction, it also ruled on the merits of the case. The Court held that Congress violated the due process clause and unconstitutionally deprived slave owners of their property rights when it outlawed slavery in the free territories. Thus, the Court not only rejected the rights claims of slaves and free black persons but also constitutionalized the property rights of slave owners to their slaves. The *Dred Scott* decision denied the basic humanity of persons of African descent. It also posed a threat to the northern states because "it made slavery national, in the sense that slavery would be legal in any part of the United States where a state government had not abolished it."[66] Perhaps most important, it appeared that the *Dred Scott* case eviscerated Congress's power to decide the slavery issue on its own, through the political process.

Members of the Supreme Court had hoped in vain that their *Dred Scott* decision would resolve the issue of slavery once and for all. Instead, the decision ignited a firestorm of criticism that escalated into the Civil War. The decision inflamed northern fears about the expansion of slavery and emboldened southern leaders to demand nationalization of the institution.[67] Southerners argued that the opinion gave them a stamp of approval to expand slavery in the territories.[68] Northerners were outraged at *Dred Scott* and widely attacked the Court. The *Dred Scott* decision was a central political issue in the 1858 congressional election and the 1860 presidential election, an issue that contributed to the victory of candidates from the new Republican Party in both elections. The decision raised political consciousness in the North, leading "a considerable segment of the public to adopt views that were openly anti-Court and anti-judicial supremacy as well as anti-slave power."[69]

Some antislavery Republicans refused to accept the authority of the Court's ruling. Labeling *Dred Scott* a political decision, they challenged the Court's authority to interpret the Constitution. Chief Justice Taney had read his opinion aloud from the bench two days after the inauguration of pro-slavery president James Buchanan, promoting speculation that the decision was a political one.[70] Antislavery Republicans derided what they referred to as "Buchanan's" decision. For example, in 1858, Senator Fessenden proclaimed that he did not believe that *Dred Scott* "accurately states the law."[71] In April 1860, Representative Bingham defiantly exclaimed, "With Jefferson, I deny that the Supreme Court is the final arbiter on all questions of political power, and assert that the final arbiter on all such questions is the people. . . . While I could condemn armed resistance to any decision of the Supreme Court . . . I would claim for myself, in common with my fellow citizens the right to question their propriety, to denounce their injustice, and to insist that whatever is wrong therein shall be corrected."[72] After the Civil War, both of these men served on the influential Joint Committee on Reconstruction. They were leaders in the Congress that adopted the 1866 Civil Rights Act, with its citizenship clause purporting to overrule *Dred Scott*.

Abraham Lincoln also denounced the *Dred Scott* decision and made his opposition to it a principal campaign issue. Between March 1859 and April 1860, Lincoln made at least sixteen speeches in which he raised the specter of "a nationalization of slavery" and warned that a new "*Dred Scott* decision" would eventually "bring slavery up into the very heart of the North."[73] Conceding that the ruling bound the parties before it, Lincoln challenged the decision's authority as rule of law. For example, in a speech during the Lincoln-Douglas senatorial debate in October 1858, Lincoln stated that "we oppose [the *Dred Scott* decision] as a political rule which shall be binding on the members of Congress or the President to favor no measure that does not actually concur with the principles of the decision. [We] propose resisting it as to have it reversed if we can."[74] In his first inaugural address, Lincoln insisted, "If the policy of the Government upon vital questions affecting the whole people is to be irrevocably fixed by decisions of the Supreme Court . . . the people will have ceased to be their own rulers."[75]

Even after *Dred Scott*, antislavery activists continued to insist that freed black people were entitled to the rights of citizenship. In 1857, noted abolitionist Frederick Douglass gave a widely reproduced speech condemning the decision and responding to the Court's ruling.[76] In his speech, Douglass argued that the Preamble, the due process clause, the Fourth Amendment, and the prohibition on bills of attainder all "strike at the root of slavery" and, if "faithfully carried out, would put an end to slavery in every State in the American Union."[77] He concluded, "The Constitution, as well as the Declaration of Independence, and the sentiments of the founders of the Republic, give us a platform broad enough, and strong enough, to support the most comprehensive plans for the freedom and elevation of all the people of this country, without regard to color, class, or clime."[78] Douglass's speech reflects the unrepentant nature of the antislavery activists. "Freedom national" was their response to *Dred Scott*, a call that became the motto for the Republican Party.[79]

Thus, Abraham Lincoln and his antislavery allies did not treat the *Dred Scott* decision as the final word on whether free black people could be citizens. Their actions spoke even louder than words. During the Civil War, the Lincoln administration disregarded the *Dred Scott* decision and recognized black citizenship in a variety of contexts, including regulating coastal shipping and issuing passports and patents to black applicants.[80] Members of the Civil War Congress also disregarded *Dred Scott* when they abolished slavery in the territories and the District of Columbia.[81]

During Reconstruction, they directly challenged the Court's authority by enacting the citizenship clause of the 1866 Civil Rights Act. They could have only two justifications for doing so: either they were enforcing the Thirteenth Amendment–based citizenship rights, or they were using their enforcement power to establish those rights as a matter of statutory law, overruling *Dred Scott* by statute.

THE THIRTEENTH AMENDMENT AND THE RIGHTS OF CITIZENS

Shortly after the end of the Civil War, the Thirteenth Amendment became law. The rights of citizenship were central to debates over the first congressional measure to enforce the amendment, the 1866 Civil Rights Act. The Union victory confirmed that federal citizenship was paramount over state citizenship and enabled Congress to define the contours of those rights. In support of congressional power to enact the amendment, Senator Trumbull also invoked Congress's power over naturalization, insisting that "the authority to declare who shall be citizens of the United States is, as I understand, vested in Congress and nowhere else,"[82] and Congress's power to enforce the Article 4 privileges and immunities clause, which, Trumbull explained, secured to citizens "such fundamental rights as belong to every free person."[83] However, Trumbull relied mostly on Congress's power to enforce the brand-new Thirteenth Amendment, and his colleagues did the same.

In speeches justifying the use of their new power to enforce the Thirteenth Amendment, Trumbull and his colleagues invoked the citizenship-based arguments of the antislavery constitutionalists. For example, in his speech in support of the 1866 Civil Rights Act, Representative Martin Thayer indicated that he believed that freed slaves were entitled to the rights of citizenship by virtue of being free people. He argued that "the sole purpose of the bill is to secure to that class of persons the fundamental rights of citizenship . . . those rights which are common to the citizens of all civilized States."[84] Thayer explained that he believed that the Thirteenth Amendment was intended to abolish and destroy "all features of slavery which are oppressive in their character, which extinguish the rights of free citizens."[85] The congressmen claimed that freed slaves became U.S. citizens when the Thirteenth Amendment ended slavery.

In debates over the act, its supporters articulated a civic republican notion of citizenship, invoking the themes of antislavery constitutionalism. They argued that the freed slaves' allegiance to the federal government entitled them to federal citizenship rights. These members of Congress pointed out that many freed slaves had proven their allegiance by serving in the Union army, contributing significantly to the Union victory. Thus, they were entitled to the membership and protection of the federal government. For example, Senator Daniel Clark explained that the free black man became a citizen "when he helped to achieve the independence with the country equally with white men."[86] Representative William Windom opined that the "the colored soldier, who has worn the uniform of the Republic and periled his life for its defense," was entitled to "an equal right, nothing more, with the white rebel yet reeking with the blood of our murdered defenders."[87] Agreeing, Representative John Hubbard said that freed slaves were "loyal and faithful, every one . . . who had prayed to God for the success of the nation's banner." He insisted, "We owe them protection for their faithful allegiance."[88]

Thus, the act was based to a large degree on the Lockean notion of "allegiance and protection" as reciprocal rights, a central theme of the antislavery constitutionalists.[89] As Representative Hubbard explained, the measure was "intended to cast a shield of protection over four million American citizens."[90] The citizenship clause of the Civil Rights Act clearly was of central importance to it. It overrode the restrictive *Dred Scott* decision and justified the act's protections for freed slaves and others within Congress's jurisdiction. Many of the act's supporters believed that it merely restated the existing law after the Thirteenth Amendment came into effect.

OVERRULING *DRED SCOTT*

The citizenship clause found in the Civil Rights Act also casts light on the scope of Congress's power to enforce the Thirteenth Amendment. Supporters of the act maintained that Section 2 of the Thirteenth Amendment empowered them to overturn the Supreme Court's interpretation of the Constitution in the *Dred Scott* decision.

The 1866 act proclaimed freed slaves to be U.S. citizens, entitled to the fundamental rights of citizenship. This statutory position conflicted directly with the Court's ruling in *Dred Scott* that freed slaves could never be citizens. Indeed, opponents of the act cited *Dred Scott* and insisted that Congress lacked the power to define freed slaves as citizens or bestow citizenship-based rights upon them. Democratic senator Willard Saulsbury of Delaware explained, "If you intended to bestow upon the freed slaves all the rights of a free citizen, you ought to have gone further in your constitutional amendment."[91] Opponents of the act said that Section 2 was insufficient to support the 1866 act because the Thirteenth Amendment did nothing more than eradicate slavery. For example, Senator Edgar Cowan argued that "[the] amendment, everybody knows and nobody dare deny, was simply made to liberate the negro slave from his master. That is all there is of it."[92] Similarly, Senator Saulsbury insisted that "it does not of itself declare, and human ingenuity cannot torture it into meaning that the Congress of the United States shall invade the States and attempt to regulate property and personal rights within the States any further than refers simply and solely to the condition and *status* of slavery."[93] Senator Peter Van Winkle, a member of the Unconditional Unionist Party from West Virginia, asked whether Congress had the power to make people of African descent citizens of the United States.[94] Democratic senator Reverdy Johnson of Maryland invoked the southern argument against citizenship rights for black people, arguing that Congress lacked the authority to create birthright citizenship because slave states did not consider slaves to be citizens.[95] Other opponents of Reconstruction insisted that "enfranchisement of those unfit for republican citizenship" was inconsistent with republican ideals.[96] However, since most of those who advocated these restrictive views had opposed the Thirteenth Amendment to begin with, the Republican majority largely disregarded such critiques. With the other citizenship clause, they nationalized the rights of citizenship and bestowed them upon all people born in the United States, including the newly freed slaves. They emphatically rejected the opponents' arguments that they lacked the power to do so.

When reminded by their opponents of the *Dred Scott* decision, the Republicans' response was hostile to the Court. Representative James Wilson called the Court's opinion "a mere partisan subterfuge" that had been intended to support President James Buchanan's position on the issue of slavery in the territories.[97] Wilson pointed out that the decision had not been released until after the 1856 presidential election, opining that the late release was because "it was not safe to cast the monstrosities of that decision into the presidential campaign."[98] Pennsylvania representative John Bromall agreed and described the *Dred Scott* decision as "the political speeches of the judges of the Supreme Court of the United States . . . to celebrate the election of James Buchanan."[99] Thus, the Republicans in Congress rejected any limitations on their power imposed by the Court's precedent in *Dred Scott*.

Supporters of the act repeatedly asserted their authority to interpret and enforce the Constitution, notwithstanding the Court's contrary *Dred Scott* precedent. Senator Trumbull explained, "In my judgment, persons of African descent, born in the United States, are as much citizens as white persons who are born in the country. . . . If there were any question about it, it would be settled by the passage of a law declaring all persons born in the United States to be citizens thereof. That this bill proposes to do."[100] Virtually every member of Congress who spoke in support of the bill agreed with Trumbull that, notwithstanding *Dred Scott*, they had the power to recognize freed black people as citizens. As Representative Wilson explained, they believed that the provision of the bill defining citizenship was "but declaratory of existing law."[101] They asserted their authority to declare for themselves what "existing law" was.

On the question of whether they had the power to enact the 1866 act, the Reconstruction Republicans gave far more credence to their Republican colleague John Bingham than they had to their Democratic adversaries.[102] However, Bingham's critique was not directed at the citizenship clause, which was consistent with his theory of federal citizenship.[103] Bingham agreed that the citizenship clause was but "declarative of what is written in the Constitution."[104] Instead, Bingham was concerned that the Thirteenth Amendment had not authorized Congress to impose the limitations and remedies upon the states that made up the heart of the bill.[105] The conservative editor of the *New York Times*, Henry Raymond, shared Bingham's concern that Congress lacked the power to regulate state action by penalizing those who violated civil rights "under color of state law."[106] Representative Bingham was well respected, and the members of the Reconstruction Congress heeded his and Raymond's concern. The Reconstruction Congress acted quickly to pass the Fourteenth Amendment, which expressly makes rights enforceable against the states. However, Bingham's concerns did not dissuade the vast majority of the members of the House and Senate, who passed the act by an overwhelming majority over the veto of President Andrew Johnson, prior to the Fourteenth Amendment becoming law. It is clear that these members of Congress believed that they had the power to enact the citizenship clause. If the Thirteenth Amendment itself did not transform slaves into citizens, these members of Congress asserted the power to do so themselves, regardless of any contrary ruling by the Supreme Court.

THE FOURTEENTH AMENDMENT CITIZENSHIP CLAUSE

In the Fourteenth Amendment, Congress included a citizenship clause that was virtually identical to that of the 1866 act. The citizenship clause of the Fourteenth Amendment was intended to constitutionalize the act's citizenship clause. This thus raises the important question of whether the members of the Thirty-Ninth Congress feared that they lacked the power to enact the clause under the Thirteenth Amendment.[107] However, there is no evidence that the supporters in the Thirty-Ninth Congress had second thoughts about their power to enact the citizenship clause of the 1866 act. Rather, the evidence indicates that those members feared that future Congresses might reverse their legislation if it was not enshrined in the Constitution.

Congressional debates over the Fourteenth Amendment and the 1866 Civil Rights Act reveal several consistent themes. First, both measures responded to reports of widespread violations in the former Confederacy of fundamental rights enjoyed by the newly freed slaves and Union sympathizers. Members of Congress frequently cited testimony about these violations before the Joint Committee on Reconstruction. This testimony included letters from freed slaves and employees of Freedmen's Bureaus complaining about laws like the Black Codes and widespread violence against freed slaves.[108] Second, virtually all members of Congress who spoke in support of both measures stated that they believed that freed slaves were citizens of the United States and thus entitled to the fundamental rights of citizenship.[109] Both citizenship clauses clarify that the measures were intended both to establish and to protect those citizenship rights.

John Bingham proposed the original version of the Fourteenth Amendment, which did not include a citizenship clause. Neither did the version of the Fourteenth Amendment that was eventually approved by the House of Representatives. The second citizenship clause was added to the amendment only during the Senate debate. As Senator Howard introduced the amendment, Senator Benjamin F. Wade proposed the addition of the citizenship clause to clarify whose privileges and immunities would be protected by the amendment.[110] As we have seen, for many members of the Reconstruction Congress, the Fourteenth Amendment citizenship clause was "simply declaratory of existing constitutional law, properly understood."[111] Indeed, Richard Aynes has argued that the citizenship clause was "added in the Senate at the last moment to write into the Constitution the antislavery view that the Thirteenth Amendment granted citizenship along with freedom."[112]

As we have seen, most of the architects of the Civil Rights Act believed that native-born black people were already citizens, regardless of whether they had previously been slaves.[113] The Fourteenth Amendment's citizenship clause reflected the widely held understanding that freed slaves were entitled to the rights of citizenship. Thus, the Fourteenth Amendment did not cast doubt on the constitutionality of the other citizenship clause. However, they also knew that once the freed slaves were counted for purposes of apportioning membership in Congress, southern states would hold more seats in that body. The Thirteenth Amendment thus made it likely that southern Democrats would gain the majority in Congress, posing the risk that all Reconstruction legislation would be overturned, including the act and its citizenship clause.[114] Constitutionalizing the citizenship clause would simply prevent future courts or Congresses from denying black individuals those rights.

CONCLUSION

The Civil War marked a turning point in our constitutional history. The Reconstruction Amendments included the first provisions authorizing Congress to protect civil rights, and the 1866 Civil Rights Act was legislators' first attempt to do so. The 1866 act sought to bring freed slaves into the polity and recognize them as rights-bearing persons. The citizenship clause of that act reflected their legislators' inclusive spirit. The clause reveals that the members of the Reconstruction Congress viewed citizenship as a fundamental attribute of freedom. Members of the Reconstruction Congress also believed that their power to enact appropriate legislation to enforce the Thirteenth Amendment was broad enough to effectuate those rights, notwithstanding the contrary precedent of the U.S. Supreme Court.

Notes

1. U.S. Const., Fourteenth amend., Sec. 1.
2. Civil Rights Act of 1866, 14 Stat. 27. The full text of the act is included in the appendix.
3. Scott v. Sandford, 60 U.S. 393 (1857).
4. See, e.g., Richard Aynes, "On Misreading John Bingham and the Fourteenth Amendment," 103 *Yale L. J.* 57 (1993); Michael Kent Curtis, *No State Shall Abridge: The Fourteenth Amendment and the Bill of Rights* (Durham: Duke University Press 1986), 57–92.
5. See Michael Vorenberg, "Citizenship and the Thirteenth Amendment: Understanding the Deafening Silence," in *The Promises of Liberty: The History and Contemporary Relevance of the Thirteenth Amendment*, ed. Alexander Tsesis (New York: Columbia University Press, 2010), 58.

6. See S. 61, 39th Cong. (1866).
7. See *Cong. Globe*, 39th Cong., 1st Sess., 504 (statement of Senator Jacob Howard) ("Such was not the intention of the advocates of this amendment. Its intention was to make him the opposite of a slave, to make him a free man") (1866); ibid., 1124 (statement of Representative Burton Cook) ("It is idle to say these men will be protected by the States. . . . Those states have already passed laws which would virtually re-enslave them"); and ibid., 1151 (statement of Representative Martin Thayer) (if states are allowed to enact the Black Codes, "of what practical value is the amendment abolishing slavery in the United States?").
8. Ibid., 1757.
9. Ibid., 474, 504 (statement of Senator Howard).
10. Ibid., 592, 602 (statement of Senator Lane).
11. See ibid., 594, 594–607 (discussing the scope of the Section 2 power).
12. Ibid., 39, 43 (1865) (statement of Secretary Trumbull).
13. Ibid., 474 (1866).
14. Ibid., 594, 602 (statement of Senator Lane).
15. This is not to say that the Thirteenth Amendment protected only citizenship rights. As I have argued elsewhere, the rights protected by the Thirteenth Amendment included liberty and equality rights for all people. See, e.g., Rebecca E. Zietlow, "James Ashley's Thirteenth Amendment," 112 *Colum. L. Rev.* 1697 (2012); and "Free At Last! Anti-subordination and the Thirteenth Amendment," 90 *B.U. L. Rev.* 255 (2010).
16. For a detailed description of these debates, see Rebecca E. Zietlow, *Enforcing Equality: Congress, the Constitution and the Protection of Individual Rights* (New York: NYU Press, 2006), 26–29.
17. See David P. Currie, *The Constitution in Congress: The Jeffersonians, 1801–1829* (Chicago: University of Chicago Press, 2001), 246.
18. Annals of Congress, 16th Cong., 2d Sess., 56–72 (1821).
19. Ibid., 1134. Pinckney had indeed been a strong proponent of the rights of slaveholders during the convention. See Paul Finkelman, *Imperfect Union: Slavery, Federalism, and Comity* (Chapel Hill: University of North Carolina Press, 1981), 35.
20. Currie, *Jeffersonians*, 248.
21. *Cong. Globe*, 30th Cong., 2d Sess., 418 (1849).
22. See Finkelman, *Imperfect Union*, 236.
23. See *Cong. Globe*, 31st Cong., 1st Sess. (1850) (statement of Senator John Davis of Massachusetts).

24. Ibid., 30th Cong., 2d Sess., 418.
25. Ibid., 419.
26. See Finkelman, *Imperfect Union*, 223, 234.
27. Corfield v. Coryell, 6 F. Cas. 546, 551–52 (C.C.E.D. Pa. 1823) (No. 3,230).
28. Theodore Dwight Weld, *The Power of Congress over the District of Columbia* (New York: John F. Trow, 1838), 45.
29. James G. Birney, "Can Congress, under the Constitution, Abolish Slavery in the States?," *Albany Patriot*, May 12, 19, 20, 22, 1847; William Goodell, *Views of American Constitutional Law, in Its Bearing upon American Slavery* (Utica, N.Y., 1844).
30. Birney, "Can Congress . . . Abolish Slavery?," 19, 20, 22.
31. See William M. Wiecek, *The Sources of Antislavery Constitutionalism in America, 1760–1848* (Ithaca: Cornell University Press, 1977), 256–57.
32. See Randy E. Barnett, "Whence Comes Section One? The Abolitionist Origins of the Fourteenth Amendment," 3 *Journal of Legal Analysis* 165, 203 (2011).
33. Spooner, *The Unconstitutionality of Slavery* (Boston: B. Marsh, 1845), 94.
34. Ibid.
35. See Wiecek, *Sources of Antislavery Constitutionalism*, 269.
36. Ibid., 57.
37. Joel Tiffany, *A Treatise on the Unconstitutionality of Slavery, Together with the Powers and Duties of the Federal Government in Relation to That Subject* (Cleveland: J. Calyer, 1849; Miami, Fla.: Mnemosyne, 1969), 99 (citations refer to the later edition). See Alexander Tsesis, "A Civil Rights Approach: Achieving Revolutionary Abolitionism through the Thirteenth Amendment," 39 *U.C. Davis L. Rev.* 1773, 1805 (2006) (emphasizing this line of reasoning of antislavery constitutionalists).
38. Tiffany, *Treatise*, 56.
39. Fugitive Slave Act of 1850, 9 Stat. 462 (repealed 1864).
40. See Paul Finkelman, "Sorting Out *Prigg v. Pennsylvania*," 24 *Rutgers L. J.* 605, 622–23 (1993).
41. *Dred Scott*, 60 U.S. at 393.
42. See *Cong. Globe*, 35th Cong., 1st Sess., 402 (1858) (Bingham). Several other northern states already admitted to the Union, including Illinois and Missouri, also had constitutional provisions prohibiting the entry of free black people into the state. See Eric Foner, *Reconstruction: America's Unfinished Revolution, 1863–1877* (New York: HarperCollins, 1988).
43. *Cong. Globe*, 35th Cong., 1st Sess. (1858).

44. See ibid., 36th Cong., 1st Sess., 1839 (1860).
45. Ibid., 35th Cong., 1st Sess., 1964 (1858).
46. Ibid., 1966–67 (1858).
47. See, e.g., ibid., 2d Sess., 974–75 (1859) (Representative Dawes); 980 (Representative Cochrane).
48. Ibid., 1st Sess., 984 (1858).
49. Ibid., 2d Sess., 984 (1859).
50. Aynes, "On Misreading John Bingham and the Fourteenth Amendment," 57, 70.
51. See *Cong. Globe*, 35th Cong., 1st Sess. (1858) (Representative Clark of Missouri citing *Dred Scott* as authority for his position that black people are not, and cannot be, citizens of the United States).
52. See ibid., 1965 (1858) (Senators Trumbull and Douglas); 974 (Representative Comins).
53. Ibid., 1965 (1858).
54. See Curtis, *No State Shall Abridge*, 46.
55. Eric Foner, *Free Soil, Free Labor, Free Men: The Ideology of the Republican Party Before the Civil War* (New York: Oxford University Press, 1995), 128.
56. Ibid.
57. Ibid., 150.
58. See "Republican Party Platform of 1860," May 17, 1860, American Presidency Project, http://www.presidency.ucsb/edu/ws/index.php?pid=29620.
59. *Dred Scott*, 60 U.S. at 393.
60. Ibid., at 399.
61. Ibid., at 403.
62. Ibid., at 417.
63. Ibid., at 404. See James W. Fox Jr., "Citizenship, Party, and Federalism, 1787–1882," 60 *U. Pitt. L. Rev.* 421, 484 (1999).
64. *Dred Scott*, 60 U.S. at 404.
65. Ibid., at 407.
66. Finkelman, *Imperfect Union*, 315.
67. Robert Burt, *The Constitution in Conflict* (Cambridge: Harvard University Press, 1992), 193.
68. Curtis, *No State Shall Abridge*, 27.
69. Larry D. Kramer, *The People Themselves: Popular Constitutionalism and Judicial Review* (New York: Oxford University Press, 2004), 212.
70. Finkelman, *Imperfect Union*, 276.

71. *Cong. Globe*, 35th Cong., 1st Sess., 402 (1858).
72. Ibid., 36th Cong, 1st Sess., 1839 (1860).
73. *The Collected Works of Abraham Lincoln*, ed. Roy P. Basler, 9 vols. (New Brunswick: Rutgers University Press, 1953–55), 3:421. See Finkelman, *Imperfect Union*, 318.
74. *Collected Works of Abraham Lincoln*, 3:255.
75. *A Compilation of the Messages and Papers of the Presidents*, ed. James P. Richardson (New York: New York Bureau of National Literature, 1897), 6:5, 9–10. See Keith Whittington, *Constitutional Construction* (Cambridge: Harvard University Press, 2001), 13 (discussing Lincoln's position on *Dred Scott* as a means of constitutional construction).
76. See Frederick Douglass, "Speech on the Dred Scott Decision, delivered in New York, on the occasion of the Anniversary of the American Abolition Society, May, 1857," in Frederick Douglass, *Two Speeches* (Rochester: C. P. Dewey, printer, 1857), 27.
77. Ibid., 40, 41.
78. Ibid., 45.
79. See Foner, *Free Soil*, 97.
80. See Kramer, *People Themselves*, 209.
81. See ibid.
82. *Cong. Globe*, 39th Cong., 1st Sess., 475 (1866).
83. Ibid., 474. Article 4 lacks a congressional enforcement clause. However, Trumbull cited the Supreme Court's ruling in *Prigg v. Pennsylvania*, upholding Congress's power to enforce the Article 4 fugitive slave clause, as precedent for congressional enforcement of the privileges and immunities clause. (Ibid.) This theory helped to justify what opponents saw as the most troubling aspect of the law—the remedies that it created against state officials. For a detailed comparison of the enforcement provisions of the 1866 Civil Rights Act and the Fugitive Slave Acts, see Robert J. Kaczorowski, "Congress' Power to Enforce Fourteenth Amendment Rights: Lessons from Federal Remedies the Framers Enacted," 42 *Harv. J. Leg.* 187, 260–63 (2005).
84. *Cong. Globe*, 39th Cong., 1st Sess., 1151, 1152 (1866) (statement of Representative Thayer).
85. Ibid., n. 200.
86. Ibid., 528 (1866).
87. Ibid., 1159.
88. Ibid., 630.

89. See Douglas Smith, "Citizenship and the Fourteenth Amendment," 34 *San Diego L. Rev.* 681, 695 (1997); and Earl Maltz, *The Fourteenth Amendment and the Law of the Constitution* (Durham: Carolina Academic Press, 2003), 9.
90. *Cong. Globe,* 39th Cong., 1st Sess., 630 (1866).
91. Ibid., 477. See also ibid., 497 (statement of Senator Van Winkle); ibid., 528 (statement of Representative Rogers); and ibid., 504 (statement of Senator Johnson).
92. See ibid., 497, 499 (1866) (statement of Senator Cowan).
93. Ibid., 474, 476 (statement of Senator Saulsbury).
94. Ibid., 475 (1866).
95. Ibid., 1777 ("What doubt can there be but that if a State possessed the power to declare who should be her citizens before the Constitution was adopted that power remains now as absolute and conclusive as it was when the Constitution was adopted?").
96. See Rogers Smith, *Civic Ideals: Conflicting Visions of Citizenship in U.S. History* (New Haven: Yale University Press, 1997), 296.
97. *Cong. Globe,* 39th Cong., 1st Sess., 1115 (1866).
98. Ibid.
99. Ibid., 1263. See Curtis, *No State Shall Abridge,* 86.
100. *Cong. Globe,* 39th Cong., 1st Sess., 475 (1866).
101. Ibid., 1115. See also ibid., 1152 (statement of Representative Thayer); ibid., 528 (statement of Senator Clark); ibid., 570 (statement of Senator Morrill); ibid., 602 (statement of Senator Lane). See also Curtis, *No State Shall Abridge,* 91.
102. See *Cong. Globe,* 39th Cong., 1st Sess., 1033, 1033–34 (1866) (statement of Representative Bingham).
103. See generally, Curtis, *No State Shall Abridge,* 91.
104. *Cong. Globe,* 39th Cong., 1st Sess., 1291 (1866).
105. Ibid. See also Curtis, *No State Shall Abridge,* 81.
106. *Cong. Globe,* 39th Cong., 1st Sess., 1267 (1866).
107. Indeed, Congress reenacted the 1866 act in 1870, relying on its power to enforce the 14th Amendment. Enforcement Act of 1870, 16 Stat. 140, Section 18.
108. See Schurz Report on Condition of the South, *Cong. Globe,* 39th Cong., S. Exec. Doc. 2 (1865).
109. See, e.g., ibid., 1st Sess., 474 (1866) (statement of Senator Trumbull); ibid., 603 (statement of Senator Wilson); ibid., 1123 (statement of Representative

Cook); ibid., 1153 (statement of Representative Thayer); and ibid., 1832 (1866) (statement of Representative Lawrence).

110. Ibid., 2768 (1866). See also ibid., 2890 (1866).

111. Curtis, *No State Shall Abridge*, 91.

112. Richard L. Aynes, "Constricting the Law of Freedom: Justice Miller, the Fourteenth Amendment, and the Slaughter House Cases," 70 *Chi-Kent. L. Rev.* 627, 649 (1994).

113. See D. Smith, "Citizenship and the Fourteenth Amendment," 306.

114. See Mark Graber, "Constructing Constitutional Politics: Thaddeus Stevens, John Bingham, and the Forgotten Fourteenth Amendment," SSRN.com/abstract=2483355.

3

THE 1866 CIVIL RIGHTS ACT AND THE BEGINNING OF MILITARY RECONSTRUCTION

Michael Vorenberg

As the essays in this volume suggest, the Civil Rights Act of 1866 was a turning point in the history of U.S. civil rights. But what is less well known about the act is this: it was a turning point in the history of U.S. warfare.

This is an odd-looking assertion, to be sure. We think of the Civil Rights Act as a peacetime measure proposed, debated, and adopted after the Civil War was over. Congress did not begin to consider it until the session that began in December 1865, eight months after General Robert E. Lee's surrender at Appomattox. The authority behind it lay not in the war powers of the Constitution but in the enforcement clause of the Thirteenth Amendment, which was ratified at the end of 1865 and thus is generally regarded as a *postwar* measure.[1] By contrast, the act for renewing the Freedmen's Bureau, passed at the same time as the Civil Rights Act, was justified by "war powers" invoked as if the Civil War was not yet over.[2] Historians have followed this pattern, treating the Civil Rights Act as a measure designed for peacetime and thus of a different genre from legislation such as the Military Reconstruction Acts, justified by Republicans on the basis that the nation was still in wartime. Recent scholarly work, most notably Gregory P. Downs's *After Appomattox*, has redirected our attention to the centrality of military force in the theory and practice of Reconstruction, but even this work tends to treat the Civil Rights Act as outside the scope of armed intervention. The scholarly tendency is understandable. The act relied on courts and civil officials, not on armies and soldiers, in most of its enforcement provisions.[3]

But not in *all* of its enforcement provisions. Embodied in the Civil Rights Act of 1866 is a set of clauses that reveals a wartime sensibility and explicit war powers. The act provided an unprecedented power to the federal government to take military action against those who threatened or even were *suspected* of threatening the nation's security. The government could invoke this power without a declaration of war and without visible provocation. The mere suspicion of an attack on the United States or its citizens, including (indeed, especially) newly freed African Americans declared citizens by the act, was grounds enough for federal military intervention. To use modern parlance, the Civil Rights Act provided a legal basis for preemptive war. Today's military theorists who write about the history of the preemptive war doctrine, which the administration of President George W. Bush made famous in justifying the U.S. war on Iraq beginning in 2003, have neglected the use of that doctrine in the Civil Rights Act. Historians of the Civil War and Reconstruction also have overlooked the clauses of the act that embody modern notions of preemptive war. Putting these clauses of the Civil Rights Act into the history of the preemptive war doctrine helps us make some interesting connections between our own time and the Reconstruction era. It also helps us to see the Civil Rights Act of 1866 in a new light—as an innovative measure for the practice of war as well as a crucial tool for securing civil rights.

This essay lays out the argument for the significance of the act's military provisions through a set of steps that requires a bit of jumping back and forth across the timeline of U.S. history. First, it discusses what the military provisions of the act said. Then, it draws out the origins of those provisions in a complicated history beginning in the 1830s and stretching into the Civil War. Bringing us next back to 1866, the essay explains why events of that moment made the military provisions of the Civil Rights Act not mere vestiges of irrelevant older events but in fact significant potential weapons in the hands of Republicans seeking to use military force in unprecedented ways to achieve their objectives for Reconstruction. In particular, the essay focuses on Secretary of War Edwin M. Stanton, who in 1866–67 came to realize the distinctive power of the military provisions of the act in granting him broad discretionary power over the army as the president and the Supreme Court whittled away at the other tools justifying broad military action that he had used to that point. Then the essay asks whether Stanton's understanding of such broad powers within the act's military provisions were entirely his invention or were in line with how the framers of the act considered the measures. To answer the question, the essay returns to the congressional debates of 1866 over the act to examine what the lawmakers of that moment understood to be the meaning of the military provisions. The essay argues that congressmen had an understanding of the provisions very much in line with Stanton's and therefore that Stanton's contemplated use of the act for preemptive war purposes adhered to the original purpose of the act. Finally, the essay reflects on the significance of this underappreciated dimension of the act for today's civil rights law, the law of war, and the use of military power.

Like much scholarship on Reconstruction, this essay is engaged with whether this era represented a radical transformation in American law. For decades, scholars working on the question have focused primarily on African Americans' legal status, a subject at the heart of Reconstruction in general and of the Civil Rights Act in particular. More recently, the issue of Reconstruction's radicalism has been informed just as much by scholarship on the theory and practice of war, including pathbreaking studies on such topics as treason, the law of war, and military occupation. Inspired in large part by this newer strain of scholarship, this essay argues that the radical potential of the Civil Rights Act of 1866 lay at least as much in its enhancement of war powers as in its expansion of civil rights.[4]

THE MILITARY PROVISIONS OF THE CIVIL RIGHTS ACT

It is easy to overlook the features of the Civil Right Act that resonate with today's preemptive war doctrine. They are buried within the long, detailed, legalistic explanation of how the civil rights provisions described in the crucial first section are to be enforced. Most of the scholarship on the act focuses only on Section 1, much of which made its way into the first section of the Fourteenth Amendment. Because Section 1 of the Civil Rights Act and Section 1 of the Fourteenth Amendment have become the foundation of much modern civil rights law, they are the sections that tend to get the most attention. As for the enforcement provisions of the Civil Rights Act that follow Section 1, they get some scrutiny by legal scholars but usually only to point out how the authors of the act cleverly copied the clauses from the Fugitive Slave Act of 1850. The act of 1866 was meant to turn the act of 1850 on its head. The act of 1850 put the power of the federal government—specifically, the power vested in civilian legal authorities such as marshals, attorneys, judges—in the hands of the Slave Power. The act of 1866 put the same power in the hands of those who sought to destroy all vestiges of the Slave Power.

Yet, the act of 1866 went further. Unlike the act of 1850, it explicitly gave a role to the president. Section 4 expanded the group who would enforce the act to include not only civilian legal authorities but also members of the armed services, specifically "officers and agents of the Freedmen's Bureau [which by this point was part of the War Department], and every other officer who may be specially empowered by the President of the United States." Section 8 gave the president power to wheel all legal machinery into action in areas where violations of the act "have been or are likely to be committed." Section 9 authorized the president, "or such person as he may empower," to use any part of the U.S. Army, U.S. Navy, or a local militia "to prevent the violation" of the act. Taken together, these clauses, which might be called the "military provisions" of the Civil Rights Act, gave the president unprecedented power.[5]

The Fugitive Slave Act contained nothing similar; it did not mention the president or the armed services. Under the posse comitatus principle, local and national legal officers might call out the local militia to enforce the law.[6] But nothing in the law specified that the president would order armed men, either local or national, to intervene. It might be argued that those who supported the 1850 act believed that it implied that presidents could or even must use military power to enforce it. Presidents in the 1850s seem to have accepted this implication; President Franklin Pierce, for example, dispatched a dozen or so U.S. Army and Marine units to Boston in 1854 to make sure that the law was enforced in the infamous Anthony Burns episode. Pierce's secretary of war, Jefferson Davis, surely believed that the president had such power, even if only implicitly, under the Fugitive Slave Law.

In the Civil Rights Act of 1866, however, the presidential power was *explicit*. More important, the law clearly authorized the president to act preemptively. Under the Civil Rights Act, the president could deploy armed units not only to places where violations of the act were known to have occurred but also to places where they were "*likely* to be committed" (emphasis added). The military provisions of the Civil Rights Act thus gave broad discretionary powers to the president in his role as commander in chief. In theory, the mere suspicion of a conspiracy to abridge the civil rights of African Americans in some locale, southern or northern, was all the president needed as justification to send in the troops. The act thus took war powers under the Constitution to a new and potentially permanent new level, one with far-reaching implications for the Reconstruction era and for American society today.

PREEMPTIVE WAR FROM THE *CAROLINE* AFFAIR TO THE CIVIL RIGHTS ACT

Where did the military provisions of the Civil Rights Act come from? In part, they were simply a carryover from the bill to renew the Freedmen's Bureau, which was a more obvious effort to use the U.S. military on behalf of African American civil rights. But the part of the Civil Rights Act that spoke of the president using the military *preemptively* had roots in an episode of U.S. history that long predated the Civil War and Reconstruction. It was lifted directly from a law resulting from the "*Caroline* Affair," which took place almost thirty years before the Civil Rights Act was adopted.

The *Caroline* Affair and its aftermath are less familiar to U.S. historians than to international relations experts. Like many events neglected by historians, it began in Canada. In 1837, a group of Canadian rebels near Ontario looking to create a republic independent from Great Britain had found a number of sympathizers across the Niagara River in the United States. Near the end of that year, Canadian forces loyal to Britain received intelligence that the steamship *Caroline*, which flew a U.S. flag, was in fact owned by a Canadian rebel leader and that it was being used to transport arms and provisions to the rebels. Learning that the *Caroline* was moored on the U.S. side of the Niagara River, just upriver from the Falls, the loyalist commanders with a local militia crossed the river and fired rifles at the ship to drive those on board away. The scheme worked, though in the melee they killed a man aboard the vessel, Amos Durfee, an African American sailor. (American sympathizers with the rebels later propped up Durfee's dead body in front of a Buffalo tavern to whip up anger against the British; Alexander McLeod, a leader of the loyalist attack who boasted of killing Durfee, was eventually tried and acquitted in an American court for the murder.) Once the *Caroline* was unmanned, the British towed it to the middle of the river, set it afire, cut it loose, and let it drift to its destruction over Niagara Falls. The action led to further attacks on the British from the American side of the Niagara and to a minor diplomatic crisis between the United States and the United Kingdom. The diplomatic dispute dragged on for four years and was ultimately resolved as part of the Webster-Ashburton Treaty of 1842. Both sides agreed in that treaty that "self-defense" in certain situations justified the use of force by one nation against another. Yet Daniel Webster, the secretary of state whose name was on the treaty, always doubted whether the *Caroline* had been a serious enough threat to merit what the British had done. Webster's doubts presaged future skepticism about the doctrine of "anticipatory self-defense," later labeled "preemptive war," which was born with the *Caroline* Affair. What might be seen as self-defense by one party could be deemed outright aggression by another.[7]

Back in 1838, in the immediate aftermath of the attack on the *Caroline* and four years before the Webster-Ashburton Treaty, the U.S. Congress passed a bill authorizing legal and military action against any U.S. citizens who plotted or took action against an ally or neighbor of the United States. President Martin Van Buren, a Democrat who, like his predecessor Andrew Jackson, believed in strong presidential power, signed the bill into law. The language of the law was very much in line with the "anticipatory self-defense" principle enshrined in the treaty adopted four years later. Sections 7 and 8 of the act explicitly authorized the president to enforce the law using federal legal and military power against those who violated it or were "likely" to violate it.[8] These two sections were lifted verbatim by the authors of the Civil Rights Bill of 1866 and ultimately appeared in the final act as Sections 8 and 9. As for the act of 1838, it had expired long beforehand; Congress had put a two-year limit on it, and it chose not to renew the act in 1840.

The *Caroline* Affair was not forgotten, though. For example, during the famous "*Trent* Affair" of 1861, Secretary of State William Henry Seward invoked the *Caroline* precedent and the Webster-Ashburton Treaty to justify the United States seizing from a British ship, the *Trent*, two agents of the rebellion, James Mason and John Slidell. British diplomats rejected the relevance of the *Caroline* Affair, and ultimately Seward released the Confederates.[9] The episode revealed among other things that U.S. authorities remembered the principle of justified preemptive action established in the *Caroline* Affair. But the principle could be invoked only in relations with Great Britain and only by referring to the Webster-Ashburton Treaty. Because the 1838 act had expired, there was nothing left in American law allowing for preemptive action against U.S. citizens contemplating activities that threatened national security.

The Civil Rights Act of 1866 remedied this deficit by bringing back into domestic law the key provisions of the 1838 act. This time, though, the primary danger was not American citizens plotting to help Canadian rebels against the British Crown. Such a danger still existed, to be sure: anti-British Fenians were more active than ever in the immediate aftermath of the Civil War on both sides of the U.S.-Canadian border.[10] But the greater threat lay to the south: unreconstructed Confederates keeping up their rebellious ways by refusing to accept the new status of African Americans as free people with rights. This was the threat targeted by the military provisions of the Civil Rights Bill. If adopted, the resulting act would be the only statute in U.S. law providing the president with the extraordinary power to use the armed forces in preemptive ways on American soil. Yet the lure of this power was not enough to sway Andrew Johnson to sign the bill. He vetoed it. However, Congress overrode the veto to make the bill into law. Against his own protests, Johnson had become arguably the most powerful commander in chief in American history. But the new power he had, the power to make preemptive war authorized by the Civil Rights Act, was not a power he was interested in using.

If Johnson was not an advocate of the military provisions of the act, how did they enter the final version? Most likely, Senator Lyman Trumbull, the primary architect of the Civil Rights Act, had included the provisions as part of a larger political strategy to win Johnson's favor. Well aware of accusations against congressional Radical Republicans that they meant to seize all power from the president, Trumbull, a former Democrat and now a moderate Republican, saw in the military provisions copied from an 1838 act a way to reassure doubters that the presidency would have at least as much power during Reconstruction as it had had during the Civil War. Trumbull took to heart the advice he had received from trusted allies such as his fellow Illinoisan Charles Ray, the editor of the *Chicago Tribune*, who had stressed that congressional Republicans must not engage in "a war with the President," as such a war would lose the party much-needed grassroots support.[11] When opponents of the Civil Rights Bill protested that the military provisions would allow the federal government to replace local and state law with martial law, Trumbull and his fellow moderate Senator William Fessenden pointed out that no such result had followed from the adoption of similar provisions in 1838. And how radical could such clauses be, Trumbull asked, if they had been signed into law by a Democrat, President Van Buren? Yes, chimed in Fessenden. The 1838 act made for a "good precedent." It "was passed under a good Democratic Administration."[12]

Here was a familiar ploy. Trumbull had used a similar political strategy two years before to try to make Democrats less hostile to the Thirteenth Amendment, the antislavery measure that the Civil Rights Act was meant to enforce. When opponents of the amendment warned of the radical disruption it would cause—the demise of the white race, the destruction of the household order, and the obliteration of constitutional government—Trumbull had calmly reminded them that the language of the amendment was drawn from the Northwest Ordinance, a law drafted by Thomas Jefferson, the sainted father of the Democratic Party. How radical, then, could the amendment be? When the Republican senator Charles Sumner offered substitute language that had a more radical tinge, Trumbull had marshaled forces against his colleague from Massachusetts, claiming that the traditional words of Jefferson the Democrat were preferable to any new ones crafted by a Republican.[13] Now he was doing the same thing, though this time he was seeking the favor not of congressional Democrats but of the Jacksonian Democrat in the White House, Andrew Johnson.[14]

Was Trumbull simply doing some rhetorical posturing in 1866 when he invoked a Democratic administration as the source of the military provisions of the Civil Rights Act? Only in part. He genuinely wanted support for the measure from moderate Republicans and particularly from Andrew Johnson. He thought he had been successful in wooing Johnson. He met with the president about the bill before the congressional debate began and received Johnson's assurance of support. Or at least that is what Trumbull remembered.[15] Johnson later denied ever having such a discussion. Most likely, Trumbull did discuss the bill with Johnson but Johnson never read it. Instead, he probably relied on the summary of it offered by Trumbull, who would have given it a conservative gloss: the measure merely enforced the Thirteenth Amendment, which Johnson had endorsed; it would not upend the political or racial order of the country; and it reaffirmed the power of the president. On this last point, Trumbull would have described the military provisions, which kept the armed forces entirely under the president and outside of any congressional control. Once debate on the bill began, Johnson heard a distorted version of the bill described by those he trusted most, northern Democrats and southern Unionists. This version, unlike Trumbull's, mandated black suffrage, the end of states' rights, and the congressional usurpation of all presidential powers. No wonder that Johnson denied ever talking about the bill with Trumbull. The bill he was hearing about was nothing like the one Trumbull had discussed with him, though they were of course exactly the same.

WHY THE MILITARY PROVISIONS OF THE CIVIL RIGHTS ACT MATTER

If Johnson was not interested in using the power that the military provisions of the Civil Rights Act gave him, were the provisions irrelevant? Johnson's successor, Ulysses S. Grant, might have been willing to invoke them, but we will never know, as he did not have to. By the time Grant became president, Congress had adopted the Military Reconstruction Acts, which gave Grant all the military authority he needed to use the military on behalf of the freed people. So why, if at all, should historians care about the military provisions of the Civil Rights Act? President Johnson did not use them, and President Grant did not need them.

First, it is important to remember that when the Civil Rights Act was being debated, Republicans in Congress assumed that Johnson would sign it—doubters heard Trumbull promise that he would—and they did not, indeed could not, foresee the need for the Military Reconstruction Acts that came in 1867. From the perspective of congressional Republicans, the military provisions of the Civil Rights Act, along with the Freedmen's Bureau Act, represented all the enhanced war power that the new nation needed. Only an obstructionist president determined to avoid the use of force in the South impelled Congress to consider legislation beyond these 1866 measures.

Second, of all the military-oriented measures passed by Congress in the early years of Reconstruction, the relevant provisions of the Civil Rights Act were the most revolutionary. All the other acts, including the Freedmen's Bureau Act, were assumed to be limited in space and time. They applied only to the states that had rebelled, and they stopped operating in each state as soon as it returned to the Union. The Civil Rights Act, in contrast, applied to all states and had no time limit. All the other legislation required an overt act to trigger a federal response. The Civil Rights Act, though, allowed for military intervention in instances where a threat was merely "likely." This principle of preemptive action to protect American citizens from discrimination, harassment, and attack informed federal military intervention in the states from the Enforcement Acts of the early 1870s (also known as the Ku Klux Klan Acts) to the National Guard mobilizations of the post–World War II period.[16]

Finally, even though President Johnson was not interested in using the military provisions of the Civil Rights Act, his secretary of war, Edwin Stanton, was. And because the act gave the new military power not only to the president but also to "such person as he may empower" to command armed forces, the military element of the Civil Rights Act was very much a live weapon so long as Stanton remained in office. Did Stanton understand the potential power of the military provisions of the act? Absolutely. Indeed, at a crucial moment in the winter of 1866–67, after it became clear that the War Department would be stripped of the powers it had assumed during the Civil War but before Republicans had settled on the remedy, the passage of the Military Reconstruction Acts and the impeachment of Johnson, Stanton looked to the military provisions of the 1866 act as the legal tool that would allow him to continue to use the armed forces to carry out the Republicans' reconstruction program.

STANTON AND THE MILITARY PROVISIONS OF THE CIVIL RIGHTS ACT

A flurry of unpredictable events led Stanton to realize the potential military power of the 1866 act. In February 1866, Johnson vetoed the bill renewing the Freedmen's Bureau. Congress was unable to override the veto and so set to work to craft a new bill that would keep the bureau alive. The bureau thus technically expired in March 1866. That meant that a major instrument for allowing military intervention in the South had disappeared. Congress would enact a renewal in July, though in March 1866, Stanton could not have predicted this development. He certainly could not have known what power this renewed bureau would give to the army. At about the same time the bureau expired, Congress passed the Civil Rights Bill. Johnson vetoed the measure on March 27. Among his many criticisms of the bill was that it seemed "to imply a permanent military force that is to be always at hand, and whose only business is to be the enforcement of this measure over the vast region where it intended to operate."[17] Less than a week later, on April 2, Johnson issued his proclamation declaring that a "cessation of hostilities" existed in all states but Texas. In Johnson's view, the Civil War was now over everywhere but Texas, and he was ready to renounce all the war powers that the federal government had assumed during the war.

The day after Johnson issued his proclamation, the U.S. Supreme Court made a move that some read as another signal that the war had ended. Two years earlier, in Indiana, the army had arrested Lambdin P. Milligan and four other men who planned to set free Confederates imprisoned in the North. Milligan and his associates sued to have their case heard by a civilian court. The petition for a writ of habeas corpus finally came before the U.S. Supreme Court in early 1866. On April 3, Chief Justice Salmon P. Chase announced the unanimous decision of the Court to issue the writ. Milligan was released. However, Chase did not say how the Court had come to its decision, and the Court issued no written opinion on the case for another nine months.[18] Without a published opinion, federal and state authorities did not know what relevance the case had, if any, to the issue of whether the Confederate states were under military control. The Court could have issued the writ on the narrow grounds that the Habeas Corpus Act of 1863 did not allow for suspension of the writ in areas where Union courts were operative and thus had no effect in Indiana. That line of reasoning would leave open the possibility that martial law was still constitutional in the South. Or did the Court mean to invalidate martial law *everywhere?* That was certainly how President Johnson and his supporters read the Court's announcement—as a validation of Johnson's proclamation the day before declaring civil law restored everywhere in the South but Texas. As it turned out, this did indeed turn out to be the Court's position when it issued its decision nine months later. Like Johnson's proclamation, the majority opinion, authored by Justice David Davis, was effectively a declaration that the Civil War was over and that military trials of civilians were now unconstitutional. (Chase and three other justices issued a less sweeping, concurring opinion that allowed military trials and martial law in the South.) But the Court's position was not clear until it published *Ex Parte Milligan* in January 1867. In April 1866, nine months before, no one could say for sure what the Supreme Court's position was on the use of the army in the South. Johnson's conservative allies were quick to say that the Court had put the final stake in the war, but in reality, the Court at this moment had been anything but definitive.[19]

Beginning in April 1866, then, Stanton saw the army operating in a kind of limbo.[20] Already the size of the army had suffered major reductions because of demobilization. The occupying force in the South had been reduced from about two hundred thousand in the summer of 1865 to forty thousand in April 1866. Now, between the actions of the president and the Supreme Court, what few troops remained faced the prospect of being rendered irrelevant or even unconstitutional.

Stanton knew, though, that he still had much latitude with the army. His relations with Andrew Johnson remained amicable, and Johnson still deferred to him when it came to managing the military. During the summer of 1866, Stanton continued to oversee his department with little interference from Johnson, even while Johnson and the Radicals engaged in an increasingly fierce war of words. In July, with the passage of a new Freedmen's Bureau Act—this time Congress was able to override Johnson's veto—Stanton still had all the tools he needed to keep the army at the bidding of the Radicals.

Over the next six months, though, the fragile relationship between Johnson and his secretary of war became strained to the point of breaking, making it increasingly difficult for Stanton to use the army to enforce the Reconstruction policies of congressional Republicans. The two men were careful to be civil to one another in their public statements and even in their private correspondence (hence little evidence of animosity exists in the historical record). Stanton did not want to give the president any clear reason to fire him. Nor did he want to resign. If he left his post, the Radicals would lose what little purchase they still had on the executive. Johnson, too, had to step carefully. If he fired Stanton or even voiced displeasure with him, he might lose the support of General-in-Chief Ulysses S. Grant, and that was sure to lose him the potential support of the many northerners who revered the general. So Johnson simply kept Stanton in place and used his power as commander in chief to undermine his secretary. Stanton would get no help from the Supreme Court, either, even though Chief Justice Chase was a fellow radical. The Court remained firm in its position that, with the war over, wartime legislation enabling the army to oversee civil affairs was no longer in effect. By the beginning of 1867, Stanton's tool chest of laws enabling military reconstruction stood nearly empty. The only implements left would be the military provisions of the Civil Rights Act.

The final stage of the inevitable split between Stanton and Johnson began on August 20, 1866, when the president issued his final proclamation declaring the Civil War at an end. A similar proclamation by Johnson on April 2 had declared the war over in all the states but Texas, but this one included Texas, and it went even further than the April proclamation in declawing the military. The "insurrection is at an end," the final proclamation announced, and "peace, order, tranquillity, and civil authority now exist in and throughout the whole of the United States of America."[21]

Did civil law now trump military law everywhere? That was certainly the interpretation given to the proclamation by local and state officials throughout the South. A U.S. Army officer who arrested a white man for beating an African American might now find himself arrested by a sheriff for assault or even kidnapping. U.S. troops stationed in a town might be rounded up by deputized white southerners for disturbing the peace. Such actions seemed justified under Johnson's proclamations, which declared the insurrection over, "civil authority" restored, and military law "in time of peace dangerous to public liberty."[22] Soon Stanton was receiving reports of southern police arresting and imprisoning scores of U.S. soldiers. When army commanders demanded their release, state authorities refused to comply, and local courts denied requests for writs of habeas corpus. Soldiers were just as vulnerable to arrest in states that had not seceded as in those that had. In Maryland, for example, the legislature passed laws granting compensation to state authorities for expenses incurred in resisting U.S. army interference with freed people. It also prohibited the state comptroller from using state monies to pay bounties of Marylanders serving in the U.S. Army.[23] White southerners opposed to Reconstruction read Johnson's proclamation as a signal that the president meant to stand aside as the states chased out the army.

Johnson may indeed have had such a purpose when he issued his August 20 proclamation, but he was not ready to move against Stanton and Grant, both of whom remained determined to sustain the army's power in the South. Even as he proclaimed that civilian authority superseded military rule, the president let stand the general orders given by Grant and authorized by Stanton that protected U.S. forces from civilian arrest and interference.

Such general orders had been the legal foundation of military occupation since the beginning of the Civil War. They were the Civil War–era equivalent of a modern "status of forces" agreement, which protects U.S. troops from civilian arrest in an occupied region in, say, Afghanistan. Before President Johnson began issuing his end-of-war proclamations, the most important general order protecting troops in occupied areas was General Order No. 3, issued by Grant in January 1866. By this order, which Grant issued "to protect loyal persons against improper civil suits and penalties in the late rebellious States," the soldiers, federal officials, and African Americans in an occupied area could transfer any charges brought against them by local or state authorities to a federal or military court.[24] After Johnson issued his April 2, 1866, proclamation declaring the war over everywhere but Texas, Grant issued a new general order, General Order No. 44, which was meant to have the same effect as General Order No. 3 and to carry the message that, despite Johnson's proclamation, the army in the South was still protected from civilian prosecution. Stanton approved Grant's move and perhaps helped engineer it.[25]

Johnson's final end-of-war proclamation of August 20, 1866, did not explicitly overturn the general orders protecting soldiers from civilian prosecution, but it did understandably create confusion as to whether those orders were still in effect. In Asheville, North Carolina, for example, Major W. W. Rollins was shocked when local police arrested his men for obstructing civilian law. When he protested, he "was at once indicted and arrested and bound in heavy bonds" and dragged to court. He managed to secure his release and on September 4 wrote to the adjutant general, the head legal officer of the army, asking "at what date . . . the rebellion cease[d] to exist" and whether the general orders protecting U.S. soldiers were still in effect.[26] Obviously the end-of-war proclamation that President Johnson had issued two weeks before, on August 20, had not struck Rollins as the final word on military authority in the South. In New Orleans, General Phil Sheridan, who commanded the Department of the Gulf, also regarded the general orders as still in effect despite Johnson's proclamation. But he conceded that the proclamation had caused "increased indolence on the part of the functionaries of the civil law in Florida and Texas."[27] Sheridan wrote to the adjutant general asking for confirmation that the general orders were still in effect. An officer in the adjutant general's office replied that the president's proclamation did indeed annul the general orders.[28] A surprised Sheridan asked for Grant's opinion. Grant replied that the Civil Rights Act could not be enforced without the general orders. And since he had received no word from above—meaning from Stanton or Johnson—that the general orders were revoked, they must still be in effect. Grant asked Stanton in late November to affirm his judgment, but Stanton offered no response.[29] To counter Grant's interpretation was to end military reconstruction. To confirm it was to make public his opposition to Johnson. So Stanton stayed silent, believing that his best strategy was to hold onto his office and thus to keep military reconstruction in place—at least until congressional Republicans could find some way to counter Johnson's moves.

Stanton's strategy became impossible to sustain when the U.S. Supreme Court finally published the *Ex Parte Milligan* decision on January 1, 1867. As Mark E. Neely has pointed out, the *Milligan* case did very little if anything in the long run to change the course of Reconstruction in the South.[30] But at the moment that the decision was issued, no one knew what that long run looked like, and the decision struck many as the death knell of military reconstruction. *Milligan* said that the army had no jurisdiction in areas where civilian courts were operative. Johnson's August 20, 1866, proclamation declared that civilian courts were operative everywhere. Taken together, the Court's ruling and the president's proclamation meant that the army had no legal authority in the South. General Orders No. 3 and No. 44 protecting U.S. soldiers were now inoperative. Southern state officials might now deputize masses of white men and authorize them to arrest and imprison anyone in Union uniform.

What could Stanton and like-minded Republicans do to avert what amounted to a rebirth of the Civil War that President Johnson had declared over? Congress was in the process of creating a Military Reconstruction Act that would effectively put the entire South under martial law. But in January 1867, that bill seemed a long way from becoming law. Congress had to craft the final language and vote on it, then submit it to Johnson, and then vote again on it after the president issued the inevitable veto. Another option to sustain the army—also too time-consuming—was to secure a new Supreme Court opinion that qualified *Milligan*. Stanton and leading legal officials of the War Department searched for a test case that might get the Supreme Court to allow military courts to trump civilian authority in at least some occupied areas.[31] But even if they could find the perfect case, getting the Court to hear it and rule on it could take months, even years. In the meantime, what legal basis could be found to allow the army to operate in the South?

The answer was the Civil Rights Act, specifically its military provisions. Because the legal authority for the act came not from open-ended wartime exigency but from the second clause of the Thirteenth Amendment, a measure surely meant for times of peace as well as war, the act could withstand the nullifying power of *Milligan*, which dealt only with legislation enacted specifically to prosecute the war, such as the Habeas Corpus Act of 1863.

In the face of an obstructive president and Supreme Court, Stanton and his Republican allies were ready to use the act's military provisions to sustain the army in the occupied South. Immediately after the *Milligan* decision was published, Senate Republicans pressed the president for something that Congress had been requesting for months: an investigation by the army into possible violations of the Civil Rights Act. The purpose was to force Johnson to concede that there had been overt violations, not to mention planned violations (the act covered both types). Johnson would then have to abide by the terms of the act and use the army on behalf of the freed people. From the perspective of congressional Republicans, this was not much to ask. Johnson merely had to keep doing with the army what he had done with it so far: leave it to Stanton to manage. The only difference would be that the legal basis for military action would now rest entirely on the Civil Rights Act. Stanton was in on this plan—he probably helped craft it—and he held out a narrow hope that Johnson would go along with it. On February 9, he drafted a new proclamation for Johnson to issue. He took a piece of War Department stationery, crossed out "War Department" and wrote in "Executive Mansion," and then began writing with his own hand but in the voice of Andrew Johnson. The proclamation began with a reprint of Section 9 of the Civil Rights Act, which Stanton had cut out and pasted to his draft. The proclamation then pointed out that this section had effectively become part of military law by General Order No. 50. That order, issued back in 1866, did nothing more than inform commanders of the text of the Civil Rights Act. Until this moment, the order had been trivial compared to General Orders Nos. 3 and 44. But now that the *Milligan* decision effectively nullified those two orders, General Order No. 50 was all that was left in military law to authorize the army to operate unmolested in civilian areas. The presidential proclamation drafted by Stanton ended with an order to all military departments that they "employ the power of the United States . . . to prevent the violation and enforce the due execution" of the Civil Rights Act.[32]

At about the time that Stanton drafted the proclamation for Johnson—not at Johnson's bidding but on his own initiative—he began assembling a list of violations of the Civil Rights Act that had been reported to the War Department. Congress had demanded such a report from the president a month before. Stanton expected Johnson to forward the list to Congress and probably hoped as well that Johnson would include the proclamation invoking the Civil Right Act to authorize a military response.

Stanton's scheme for using the Civil Rights Act to sustain military power in the South was short-lived, which helps explain why historians have neglected it. At a cabinet meeting on February 15, 1867, less than a week after Stanton drafted the new proclamation for Johnson, the president and the war secretary finally had a public falling-out. Johnson was furious at the report of abuses that Stanton had prepared for the president to send to Congress. It was based on hearsay and rumor, Johnson snarled, though he sent it anyway to comply with Congress's request.[33] He rejected the proclamation enforcing the Civil Rights Act that Stanton had drafted. He would never again defer blindly to Stanton, and he began taking steps to remove him from office. Those steps led eventually to Johnson's impeachment in the House of Representatives and his near-conviction in the Senate. While that drama played out, Congress passed the Military Reconstruction Acts over Johnson's vetoes, enabling Stanton and Grant to continue to use the army to implement Reconstruction. In the avalanche of events rushing forward in the war between Johnson and the Radicals, the military provisions of the Civil Rights Act, which Stanton had briefly contemplated as the cornerstone of a military reconstruction program, would be forgotten.

THE ORIGINAL INTENT OF THE MILITARY PROVISIONS

When Stanton in early 1867 came to regard the military provisions of the Civil Rights Act as a possible foundation of congressionally directed military reconstruction, was he inflating the power of those provisions? Put another way: Would the framers of the Civil Rights Act in 1866 have agreed with the way that Stanton in 1867 interpreted its military provisions? A careful reading of the congressional debate does not yield a simple answer to this question, but the preponderance of evidence suggests that Stanton's understanding of the military provisions was generally in line with that of the Republicans who argued for the act months before.

The military provisions did not receive as much attention as other sections of the bill, especially Section 1, but they did lead to some of the most interesting discussions during the debate. Perhaps the most striking question raised by the provisions was this: Was the country still in a state of war, and if not, how could such proactive military measures be legitimate? On one side were those who declared that the nation was in a state of peace and therefore the military provisions were inappropriate if not dangerous. Unsurprisingly, this was the position of those who opposed the bill, such as Senator Garrett Davis of Kentucky. To believe Davis was to think that all violence had magically disappeared from the land. Just as incredible as the "magnitude of the conflict, and the fierce and determined energy with which it was fought on both sides," Davis said, was "the suddenness of its termination, the completeness of the submission of so many million insurgents, and their universal desire to return to the Government against which they had risen."[34]

Republicans were more skeptical about whether harmony reigned, but for the most part they acknowledged that the war was over. When Representative Schuyler Colfax of Indiana, the Speaker of the House of Representatives, opened the first session of the Thirty-Ninth Congress on December 4, 1865, he sounded almost as celebratory as Davis: "The Thirty-Eighth Congress closed its constitutional existence with the storm-cloud of war still lowering over us; and, after a nine months' absence, Congress resumes its legislative authority in these council halls, rejoicing that from shore to shore in our land there is peace."[35]

While all Republicans agreed with Colfax that armed combat had ended, most were more equivocal as to whether the state of the country might fairly be described as at "peace." Representative James Wilson of Iowa offered a typical view of the Republicans. Yes, he said, widespread "armed resistance" had ended, but the country was still in a state of war—hence the presence of the Freedmen's Bureau, an arm of the War Department, throughout the South. This position resembled the well-known "grasp of war" approach made famous by the U.S. attorney and international law expert Richard Henry Dana. In a speech at Boston in July 1865, Dana defended the U.S. government's power to impose black suffrage on the former states of the

Confederacy because the South was still in the "grasp of war." Dana came earlier than some white Republicans to the cause of black suffrage, but his "grasp of war" approach was in the Republican mainstream. He believed that the U.S. military should maintain power in rebellious areas and slowly yield that power to civilian authorities when their willingness to enforce federal policy could be trusted. The federal government would determine the exact mix of military and civilian control in the South, just as it had done during Lincoln's time. When Dana gave the speech, he regarded the country as in the same state of active war as before the Confederate surrenders of April 1865.[36] A year later, when Congress debated the Civil Rights Act, Republicans like James Wilson were more likely to regard the Civil War as genuinely over. But that only meant that the federal government had loosened its grip on the South, not that it had let go entirely. The U.S. military was not to behave as if still at war, ferreting out armed rebels everywhere. Rather, it was to act in a targeted way, seeking to identify and halt only those who sought to interfere with the principle of equality before the law described in Section 1 of the Civil Rights Bill. If such a surgical use of the armed forces was not possible, Wilson argued, then and only then would "a perpetual state of constructive war . . . be a great blessing to very many American citizens."[37]

The Republican contention that the nation was somewhere between a condition of war and peace left open a wide range of interpretation of what the U.S. military was actually allowed to do. Those of a more radical persuasion envisioned a long-term military presence in the South that would vigilantly protect African Americans and genuine white Unionists from the violence of white southerners who only pretended to be loyal. Senator Jacob M. Howard reported of a white man in Texas who had hoisted a U.S. flag over his house only to be confronted by neighbors demanding that he take it down. "They could submit to be conquered," they told him, "but that for him to stick up the old flag over his house was a little too much for them to bear." When the Unionist refused, the mob killed him. This was why the army was needed throughout the South: to stand between dangerous false Unionists on one side and true Unionists, black and white, on the other.[38]

Such statements gave fuel to the arguments of the bill's critics that it would lead to a vast military occupation of the South. That fear had been voiced by opponents of the Republicans from the start of Reconstruction. Now the scale of the imagined military tyranny of the future took on new dimensions. The army would occupy not only formerly seceded states but loyal states like Kentucky, Senator Garrett Davis predicted. Davis could always be relied upon for hyperbole when it came to imagining Republicans' sinister intentions. "These military gentlemen think they have a right to command and control everywhere," Davis warned during the debate on the Civil Rights Bill. "The military power is now rampant and triumphant, and all we have to do is to bow our heads."[39] Even calmer congressmen could see doom ahead. If the army were empowered to act in any way it wished to protect needy black people in the South, speculated the Democratic congressman Charles A. Eldredge, the intervention would never stop. Troops might well be sent to Massachusetts to watch over the poor and insane.[40]

Dire predictions such as these spiced up the debate, but they bore little connection to the reality on the ground. It is true that some Republicans wanted to maintain a large army in the South. Francis Lieber, who had grown up in militaristic Germany and later crafted the first U.S. code of war, said that the United States should retain 150,000 troops for southern occupation.[41] But such arguments had gained little traction in a war-weary nation. After the Grand Review in Washington, D.C., in late May 1865, the demobilization of nearly one million Union soldiers moved at an astonishing pace. Numbering roughly 40,000 by the time of the Civil Rights Bill debate, the postwar army was twice as large as the prewar army, but it was small compared to what was needed simply to maintain the Freedmen's Bureau, and it was still shrinking. Hugh McCulloch, the Treasury secretary, confided to Charles Sumner that the nation could hardly afford to pay for an army that would occupy the South with any effectiveness.[42] Nations in Europe with populations comparable to the United States maintained armies at least three times the size of the Reconstruction era force. Historians continue to argue about many facets of Reconstruction, but they agree on at least one issue: the U.S. occupying army was much too small to accomplish even the most modest goals of the Republicans. The historian Mark Wahlgren Summers rightly contends that the paranoid fantasy of a "republic under siege" grew only more distorted during the debate over the Civil Rights Bill.[43] But the inflated rhetoric made for ineffectual propaganda. The reality of rapid demobilization made dubious the prospect of military despotism. "Although images of countless overbearing occupiers routinely graced popular literature (and eventually also film) in the years after the war," the historian Douglas R. Egerton writes, "the government demobilized rapidly after 1865, leaving but a skeleton force in place by the first months of 1866."[44] Anyone who knew the realities of the military situation in early 1866 could not imagine a return to a militarized nation—unless there was another war.

And that was precisely what the Republicans were trying to prevent when they supported the military measures of the Civil Rights Bill. They did not seek to perpetuate the war; they sought to prevent its return. Specifically, they aimed to cut short any rebirth of slavery or the Slave Power. Regardless of their differences over the best course of Reconstruction, Republicans shared a common understanding of history. The institution of slavery and the conspiracy that supported it, the Slave Power, were together the cause of the Civil War. Let these evil buds bloom again, and a war as fierce as the one just passed would return. As Henry Wilson explained, "the gigantic system of human slavery that darkened the land, controlled the policy and swayed the destinies of the Republic, has forever perished," yet remnants still plagued the country in the form of discriminatory action and legislation such as the "Black Codes" adopted by southern states beginning in the summer of 1865. All prior antislavery legislation leading to the Thirteenth Amendment had crippled the wicked institution, but without the Civil Rights Bill to enforce the amendment, the institution would rise again. The military provisions were needed "for the better security of these new-born civil rights," and they would help make the law "the greatest and the grandest act in this series of acts that have emancipated a race and disenthralled a nation."[45]

Notions of the reenslavement of African Americans and the resurgence of the Slave Power were more than idle concerns. They were legitimate fears. They had driven the Republican agenda during the war—James Oakes's recent work makes this point powerfully—and they were only slightly diminished by Lee's surrender at Appomattox. Ten days after the surrender, a Republican politician captured the spirit of his party in a private letter: "Slavery made the rebellion and murdered the President and starved our prisoners and has brutalized the community that has tolerated and sustained it, and it must be wiped away, every vestige of it and that without conditions and without delay."[46] Four months later, the journalist Whitelaw Reid traveled through the South and reported that "the aristocracy of slaveholders, their power unbroken," still controlled the region. "Every traveler in the South tells the same story," Reid wrote. If the United States failed to act proactively against these men, then "under some other name, State control, contract system, or something of the sort, slavery is certain to be re-established."[47]

Short of a long-term, full-scale military occupation of the South, which most Republicans conceded was not a viable option, what type of military intervention did Republicans envision would assure the death of slavery and the Slave Power? There was, of course, no single answer to this question that satisfied all Republicans. But most had in mind a vaguely understood two-pronged approach. First, a short-term, large-scale military intervention would take the form of the Freedmen's Bureau, already in place. The party disagreed with one another and with President Johnson over how long the bureau might be needed, but all understood that it was not to be a permanent institution. The second prong, as represented in the military provisions of the Civil Rights Act, was to be permanent but small-scale—sometimes inoperative entirely. The federal military would take on the traditional role of a local police force, a posse comitatus, in those areas so under the spell of the Slave Power that they could not be trusted to police themselves in accordance with the act. Once an area was shed of slavery and the influence of the Slave Power, the federal military would withdraw. But it might return upon a relapse of the disease of slavery, or even the threat of infection.

But how would federal authorities determine if their intervention under the Civil Rights Act was warranted? This question was at the crux of the conflict over the act's military provisions. Members of the opposition battered Senator Trumbull for an answer. They could understand the idea that state officials might call for federal military assistance if the local police force could not enforce national laws. That had happened in the North under the Fugitive Slave Law. But what was this new power concerning the federal military acting proactively, before any overt violation of law and without any call for assistance from the states? "What is meant in the bill by the preventive power of the military?" asked Democratic senator Thomas A. Hendricks of Indiana. "Before a crime is committed, before a wrong is done under this bill, the President, or any person whom he may appoint, may call in the military power of the Government to prevent a crime. How is that in aid of the courts of the country?"[48]

It was an excellent question. Trumbull's answer revealed just how revolutionary the military provisions were. First, he invoked the well-known power of the national government to call up the militias to put down treason. That power had been used in the weeks and months after the firing on Fort Sumter, and no loyal Unionists had questioned it then. From there, Trumbull made a great leap in logic. Wouldn't it be better, he asked, if federal authorities could intervene *before* a war-starting act like the one in Charleston in April 1861? Back then, if the government had slashed at the Slave Power when it was still conspiring to rebel, rather than waiting for the snake to strike first, then the Civil War could have been averted. In Trumbull's view, the government had already possessed this power before secession, it had failed to use it, and a preventable war had broken out. During the secession crisis, Trumbull argued, "if the men who were threatening rebellion . . . had been arrested for treason, of which, in my judgment, by setting on foot armed expeditions against the country, they were guilty; and if they had been tried and punished and executed for the crime, I doubt whether this great rebellion would ever have taken place." By the same logic, Trumbull reasoned, under the Civil Rights Act, the military could act preemptively to avoid another war. He offered a hypothetical situation: "Suppose that the county authorities in Muscogee county, Georgia, combine together to deny civil rights to every colored man in that county. For the purpose of preventing it, before they have done any act, I say the militia may be called out to prevent them from committing an act. We are not required to wait until the act is committed before anything can be done." Trumbull's scenario suggested a vision of military power that went well beyond the power to aid federal courts, such as had been used under the Fugitive Slave Law, and also beyond the power to react to overt acts of rebellion, such as had been used by Lincoln and Congress after the firing on Fort Sumter in 1861. The Fugitive Slave Law and the post-Sumter wartime acts of the Union government offered no precedents for the anticipatory military action that Trumbull described. He therefore had to reach back to the 1838 statute passed by Congress after the *Caroline* Affair. This was the only basis that he could find for the preventive war doctrine embodied in the Civil Rights Bill that he sponsored. Finally backed into a corner by Hendricks and the opposition, Trumbull read the 1838 statute to Congress and said it was a sound precedent for the military provisions of the Civil Rights Bill.[49]

Trumbull's invocation of the *Caroline* Affair was a remarkable move, not only from the perspective of his own time but from ours. On one level, it was a clever political trick. He reminded his Democratic opponents that it was a Democrat, Martin Van Buren, who had signed the 1838 act. That measure had not destroyed democracy then; its 1866 counterpart would not lead to military despotism now. On the level of legal doctrine, Trumbull's use of the 1838 act was even more innovative. In recent memory, the doctrine of preemptive war had been invoked by the Confederacy as justification for attacking the Union. The Confederate government in 1861 had reasoned that war was the only way to prevent the new Lincoln administration from destroying the Union and the Constitution by dissolving all state governments, freeing all slaves, and imprisoning all dissenters.[50] For Trumbull to use this same doctrine, albeit for the nobler cause of the protection of the freed people, was arguably a legitimization of the Confederacy's military moves of 1861. Trumbull did not mention Confederate notions of preventive war. He invoked only the *Caroline* Affair, something Confederate authorities had not done in 1861, but he certainly knew that the Confederates had used a preventive war argument. He had turned the Fugitive Slave Law on its head to construct crucial sections of the Civil Rights Bill. Maybe it was not such a stretch for him to turn the Confederate justification for war on its head to support the creation of a new power of preventive war.

RETHINKING THE MODERN SIGNIFICANCE OF THE CIVIL RIGHTS ACT

From the perspective of today, Trumbull's move is at least as remarkable as it was in 1866. His use of the *Caroline* Affair as the basis of broad preventive war powers anticipated the war powers doctrine of the twenty-first century. Only in the last decade or so, mostly in reaction to the U.S. invasion of Iraq in 2003, have legal theorists invoked the *Caroline* Affair to justify broad preventive war powers. Before then, most legal scholars and international lawyers used the *Caroline* Affair to argue for *narrow* preventive war powers. Their argument rested not on the 1838 statute but on the 1842 letter of Secretary of State Daniel Webster to Lord Ashburton clarifying the U.S. position. A sovereign power may act to stop a war, Webster wrote, but only if it could "show a necessity of self-defence, instant, overwhelming, leaving no choice of means, and no moment for deliberation."[51] In the build-up to the U.S. invasion of Iraq and then after that invasion, lawyers for the George W. Bush administration argued for a broader justification of preventive war. They coined the phrase "preemptive war." A preemptive war could be waged, so the argument ran, in reaction not only to immediate, overt threats, the sorts Webster had in mind in 1842, but also to *potential* threats, particularly those that jeopardized life on vast scale. Such threats included possible "weapons of mass destruction," which Iraq might possess or be close to acquiring. Today, those threats additionally include radical Islamic leaders planning or merely inciting attacks on the United States and its allies. When the Barack Obama administration used drone strikes against these people, some of them operating in countries allied with the United States, it invoked the preemptive war doctrine used by the prior administration. The preemptive war doctrine thus is not linked to any one political party, and by all accounts it is here to stay. It is also not new. It is a modern echo of the military provisions of the Civil Rights Act of 1866.

The 1866 military provisions, like the modern preemptive war doctrine, were based on a broad reading of the precedent of the *Caroline* Affair. Secretary of State Seward had taken a step in this direction in 1861 when he invoked the *Caroline* Affair as a precedent for stopping the *Trent*. But in that instance, the U.S. government was reacting against a known threat already underway: two Confederate agents heading to Europe to obtain foreign assistance. In 1866 Republicans were ready to act even in the absence of a known, overt threat. The potential for human abuse and treachery was all that was needed to justify strategic military intervention, Trumbull argued in 1866 during the Civil Rights Bill debate. A year later, Secretary of War Edwin Stanton was prepared to use a military provision of that law, Section 9, to keep the U.S. forces in the South in order to combat not only current, overt treachery but also plans for resistance that were merely embryonic. And as Stanton saw things, the power of Section 9 to justify preemptive strikes was untouched by either the presidential proclamation declaring the war over or the U.S. Supreme Court decision ruling military law in civilian areas unconstitutional. Preemptive strikes were as legitimate in times of peace as in times of war.

The position of Trumbull in 1866 and Stanton in 1867 was the same as that of the Bush administration in 2003: a small war was sometimes needed to slay a monster that could start a massive war. In Bush's time, the menace was weapons of mass destruction. In the post-Appomattox period, it was the Slave Power. Slavery might be outlawed, but the Slave Power remained. If the U.S. military did not attack it, or at least stand ready to do so, the Slave Power would deny African Americans their new rights and set the country once more on the road to war. As a group of French writers put it in a widely distributed pamphlet of 1866, slavery had been the "first negro question" inciting the country to Civil War; legal inequality was the "second negro question, destined to convulse the country like the first."[52]

That the Civil Rights Act of 1866 represented a new law of war, not merely a new law of rights, might at first seem surprising, but on reflection, the dual nature of the measure makes perfect sense. After all, the Emancipation Proclamation of 1863 had the same duality. As John Witt has argued in his important book on the U.S. laws of war, the same logic behind wartime emancipation lay behind the code of war that the U.S. government issued at nearly the same time and later used to justify some of its most aggressive military actions of the nineteenth and twentieth centuries.[53]

The Civil Rights Act of 1866, like the Emancipation Proclamation, was as much an innovation in the international law of war as in the domestic law of freedom. Yet, Americans today remember the act only in the context of civil rights—if they remember it all. The context of war was surely as important. Indeed, understanding the act as a military measure leads to an even greater appreciation of its significance. This was no mere parchment promise of equal rights. It was a declaration of war: a vow to use every weapon in the U.S. arsenal to protect the country's most vulnerable citizens.

Notes

1. On the Civil Rights Act as justified by the Thirteenth Amendment's enforcement clause, a position taken by Republicans of the time and opposed by Democrats and some border state Unionists, see Rebecca E. Zietlow, "The Other Citizenship Clause," in this volume.
2. Michael Les Benedict, *A Compromise of Principle: Congressional Republicans and Reconstruction, 1863–1869* (New York: W. W. Norton, 1974), 148.
3. Gregory P. Downs, *After Appomattox: Military Occupation and the Ends of War* (Cambridge, Mass.: Harvard University Press, 2015), 123–24. Downs acknowledges that the act "authorized the president to use the army or militia to enforce its provisions" (124), though he sees the act generally as part of the effort by congressional Republicans "to construct defensible rights in peacetime" (123).
4. On treason law during the Civil War and Reconstruction, see William A. Blair, *With Malice toward Some: Treason and Loyalty in the Civil War Era* (Chapel Hill: University of North Carolina Press, 2014); on the law of war, see John Fabian Witt, *Lincoln's Code: The Laws of War in American History* (New York: Free Press, 2012); on military occupation, see Downs, *After Appomattox*. For an excellent overview of legal developments in the period, see Laura F. Edwards, *A Legal History of the Civil War and Reconstruction: A Nation of Rights* (Cambridge: Cambridge University Press, 2015). For an argument about the Civil Rights Act of 1866 as a radical, transformative measure in civil rights law, see Robert J. Kaczorowski, "To Begin the Nation Anew: Congress, Citizenship, and Civil Rights after the Civil War," *American Historical Review* 92 (February 1987): 45–68, but this view must be moderated by the scholarship of Michael Les Benedict, including his essay in the current volume as well as his many other works cited in the volume's other essays.

5. Civil Rights Act of 1866, 14 Stat. 27. The full text of the act is included in the appendix.
6. Gautham Rao, "The Federal *Posse Comitatus* Doctrine: Slavery, Compulsion, and Statecraft in Mid-Nineteenth-Century America," *Law and History Review* 26 (Spring 2008): 1–56.
7. Howard Jones, *To the Webster-Ashburton Treaty: A Study in Anglo-American Relations, 1783–1843* (Chapel Hill: University of North Carolina Press, 1977), esp. 20–32, 118–60.
8. Statutes at Large of the United States of America 5:212–13 (March 10, 1838).
9. See Lord Lyons to Earl Russell, January 6, 1862, *Official Records of the Union and Confederate Navies in the War of the Rebellion*, ser. 1, vol. 1 (Washington, D.C.: Government Printing Office, 1894), 195–202, esp. 197, 199, 200.
10. Mitchell Snay, *Fenians, Freedmen, and Southern Whites: Race and Nationality in the Era of Reconstruction* (Baton Rouge: Louisiana State University Press, 2010).
11. Charles H. Ray to Lyman Trumbull, February 7, 1866, Trumbull Papers, Manuscript Division, Library of Congress, Washington, D.C.
12. *Cong. Globe*, 39th Cong., 1st Sess., 605–6 (February 2, 1866). See also Trumbull's statement on the relevant sections of the act in his response to Johnson's veto message: ibid., 1760 (April 4, 1866).
13. Michael Vorenberg, *Final Freedom: The Civil War, the Abolition of Slavery, and the Thirteenth Amendment* (Cambridge: Cambridge University Press, 2001), 55–59.
14. Johnson had been nominated to the presidential ticket in 1864 not as a Republican but as a candidate of an ostensibly nonpartisan "National Union" Party, though all recognized the party as the Republican Party in a new guise. Still, the appellation kept Johnson from having to renounce his longtime allegiance to the party of Andrew Jackson. On the depth of that allegiance, see Kenneth M. Stampp, *The Era of Reconstruction, 1865–1877* (New York: Random House, 1965), 50–82 ("Andrew Johnson: The Last Jacksonian").
15. *Cong. Globe*, 39th Cong., 1st Sess., 1755 (April 4, 1866).
16. The exact wording of Section 9 of the act was repealed in 1957 and replaced with wording much to the same effect in 10 U.S.C., Sec. 332 (Supp. 2009). See George Rutherglen, *Civil Rights in the Shadow of Slavery: The Constitution, Common Law, and the Civil Rights Act of 1866* (New York: Oxford University Press, 2013), 192n77.

17. Lillian Foster, ed., *Andrew Johnson, President of the United States: His Life and Speeches* (New York: Richardson, 1866), 277.
18. Because the Court issued the writ to Milligan in April 1866 but did not deliver its opinion justifying its action until January 1867—Chief Justice Chase explained when Milligan was freed that the Court would offer its full opinion at the next term—historians sometimes mistakenly date the opinion to 1866 instead of 1867. See Downs, *After Appomattox*, 148.
19. Witt, *Lincoln's Code*, 312–13; Samuel Klaus, ed., *The Milligan Case* (New York: Da Capo, 1970), 40–47, 82–83.
20. For fuller details of Stanton's approach to administering the army during this period, see Benjamin P. Thomas and Harold M. Hyman, *Stanton: The Life and Times of Lincoln's Secretary of War* (New York: Knopf, 1962), 476–500, which, unless otherwise noted, is the source of the narrative here provided of the widening split between Stanton and Johnson.
21. Andrew Johnson, "Proclamation 157—Declaring that Peace, Order, Tranquillity, and Civil Authority Now Exists in and Throughout the Whole of the United States of America," August 20, 1866, The American Presidency Project, http://www.presidency.ucsb.edu/ws/index.php?pid=71992.
22. See Andrew Johnson, "Proclamation 153—Declaring the Insurrection in Certain Southern States to be at an End," April 2, 1866, The American Presidency Project, http://www.presidency.ucsb.edu/ws/index.php?pid=71987; and Johnson, "Proclamation 157."
23. *Pennsylvania Freedmen's Bulletin*, May 1867, 216.
24. Thomas and Hyman, *Stanton*, 476.
25. See Downs, *After Appomattox*, 147, though Downs mistakenly implies that Grant invoked the Civil Rights Act to authorize General Order No. 44. In fact, the correspondence between Grant and Stanton makes clear that Grant believed that the authority preexisted the act—that it came from the United States still being in a state of war, even in the view of President Johnson—and that this preexisting authority could be used to enforce both the act and the Freedmen's Bureau Act; see Thomas and Hyman, *Stanton*, 499.
26. W. W. Rollins to Adjutant General, U.S. Army, September 4, 1866, Attorney General Papers, Letters Received, War Department, box 7, RG 60, National Archives, College Park, Md.
27. P. H. Sheridan to U. S. Grant, October 6, 1866, in Edward McPherson, ed., *A Political Manual for 1868* (Washington: Philp and Solomons, 1868), 309.

28. George K. Leet to P. H. Sheridan, October 17, 1866, in ibid., 309.
29. U. S. Grant to Edwin Stanton, November 22, 1866, in ibid., 308.
30. Mark E. Neely, *The Fate of Liberty: Abraham Lincoln and Civil Liberties* (New York: Oxford University Press, 1991), 160–84.
31. H. S. Fitch to Orville H. Browning, February 6, 1867, Andrew Johnson Papers, vol. 109, #14454–55, Library of Congress.
32. Draft proclamation in Stanton's hand, February 9, 1866, #14468, ibid.
33. For Stanton's report, see 39th Cong., 2nd Sess., serial set 1277, S. Exec. Doc. 29 (February 18, 1867), 12–43. For the cabinet meeting of February 15, 1867, see Theodore Calvin Pease and James G. Randall, eds., *The Diary of Orville Hickman Browning* (Springfield: Illinois State Historical Library, 1933), 2:130; and *Diary of Gideon Welles* (Boston: Houghton Mifflin, 1911), 3:42–45.
34. *Cong. Globe*, 39th Cong., 1st Sess., appendix, 185 (April 6, 1866).
35. Ibid., 5 (December 4, 1865).
36. Richard Henry Dana, "'Grasp of War' Speech," June 21, 1865, delivered in Faneuil Hall, Boston, Mass., reprinted in Richard Henry Dana Jr., *Speeches in Stirring Times and Letters to a Son*, ed. Richard H. Dana III (Boston: Houghton Mifflin, 1910), 234–72. See Harold M. Hyman, *A More Perfect Union: The Impact of the Civil War and Reconstruction on the Constitution* (New York: Alfred A. Knopf, 1973), 289.
37. *Cong. Globe*, 39th Cong., 1st Sess., 1119 (March 1, 1866).
38. Ibid., 503 (January 30, 1866).
39. Ibid., 599 (February 2, 1866).
40. Ibid., 1156 (March 2, 1866).
41. Francis Lieber to Charles Sumner, November 17, 1865, Francis Lieber Papers, Henry E. Huntington Library, San Marino, Calif.
42. Hugh McCulloch to Charles Sumner, August 22, 1865, Charles Sumner Papers, Houghton Library, Harvard University, Cambridge, Mass.
43. Mark Wahlgren Summers, *A Dangerous Stir: Fear, Paranoia, and the Making of Reconstruction* (Chapel Hill: University of North Carolina Press, 2009), 111.
44. Douglas R. Egerton, *The Wars of Reconstruction: The Brief, Violent History of America's Most Progressive Era* (New York: Bloomsbury Press, 2014), 119.
45. *Cong. Globe*, 39th Cong., 1st Sess., 603 (February 2, 1866).
46. Stanley Matthews to Salmon P. Chase, April 19, 1865, in *The Salmon P. Chase Papers*, vol. 5, *Correspondence, 1865–1873*, ed. John Niven (Kent, Ohio: Kent State University Press, 1998), 29.

47. "AGATE," August 8, 1865, Whitelaw Reid Papers, Manuscripts Divisions, Library of Congress.
48. *Cong. Globe,* 39th Cong., 1st Sess., 602 (February 2, 1866).
49. Ibid., 605–6.
50. For Confederate aggression in 1861 as "preventive war," see James M. McPherson, "The Fruits of Preventive War," *Perspectives on History* 41 (May 2003): 5–6.
51. Webster to Ashburton, July 27, 1842, *Treaties and Other International Acts of the United States of America* (Washington, D.C.: Government Printing Office, 1934), 4:449.
52. *Letter from MM. de Gasparine, Martin, Cochin, and Laboulaye, to the Loyal Publication Society of New York,* trans. Mary L. Booth (New York: C. S. Westcott, 1866), 9.
53. Witt, *Lincoln's Code.*

4

"IN ACCORDANCE WITH THE SPIRIT OF THE TIMES"

African American Citizenship and the Civil Rights Act of 1866 in New England Law and Politics

Millington W. Bergeson-Lockwood

In February 1867, Benjamin F. Roberts and twenty-three other black Bostonians petitioned the city's common council for the immediate deletion of the descriptor "colored" from the city tax bills and voting lists.[1] They stated that the city's use of the label "is an unnecessary appendage and calculated to uphold an old spirit of caste, which is detrimental to the best interests of our community."[2] Based on this petition, the council agreed to remove any racial designation from Boston's tax and voting documents. The special committee of the council declared in its official report that "the prayer of the petitioners is in accordance with the spirit of the times; as well as in harmony with that republicanism which recognizes all citizens as standing upon the same equality before the law."[3]

The council lauded the previous accomplishments of the city and state in challenging other sites of racial discrimination, such as segregated schools, military service, theater seating, and the like. "In this era of liberal legislation towards the colored race," the committee report continued, "surely our city does not wish to show a prejudice or deny a perfect equality."[4] In its report, the council connected its progress on civil rights locally to that of national lawmakers hoping to secure rights for African Americans broadly.

While Massachusetts officials acted during the immediate post–Civil War era "in accordance with the spirit of the times," in other ways they built upon a New England legacy of legal understandings of equality and citizenship that were ahead of their time in the 1850s. By the time the national government acted to define and guarantee African American citizenship with the Civil Rights Act of 1866, New England courts and legislatures had officially declared African Americans citizens of those states and understood that to mean reciprocity throughout the nation. Further, they crafted a definition of republican citizenship grounded in political participation and the right to vote.[5] Unlike most other states, a majority of New England governments allowed black suffrage. While southern states made states' rights arguments to uphold enslavement and inequality, New Englanders declared their rights as states to uphold black citizenship even in opposition to federal policy and legal actions, such as the *Dred Scott* decision. As New England activism provided a precursor to the Civil Rights Act, it also mobilized to press for broader civil rights protections and guarantees of American freedom.

An examination of the origins, formation, and legacies of the Civil Rights Act of 1866 in New England illuminates new knowledge about the contours of American citizenship and the struggle to achieve and maintain equality in the antebellum and Reconstruction eras. While previous scholars of the 1850s have examined New England antislavery legislation, personal liberty laws in particular, laws, along with legal opinions, defining and protecting black citizenship emerging during the same period have garnered less attention.[6] Further, scholars have neglected the influence of these statutes on the framers of the 1866 Civil Rights Act.[7]

Nearly a decade prior to the legislation, New England jurists and legislators challenged limits on African American citizenship. In response to the dire consequences of the 1850 Fugitive Slave Law and the 1857 Supreme Court decision in *Scott v. Sandford*, several New England states established legislation to protect the rights of African Americans as citizens. These laws and inherent ideas of equality influenced New England representatives' roles in the passage of the 1866 act.

The decisions, opinions, and commentaries of New England courts, legislatures, and activists make up an important yet understudied moment in the transformation of American citizenship. As scholars in this volume like Michael Les Benedict and others like William Novak have recognized, definitions of federal or constitutional citizenship were ambiguous and grounded in a diverse array of individual memberships and statuses prior to the Civil War but hardened and clarified during and after the Civil War era.[8] In the aftermath of the *Dred Scott* decision in 1857, some New Englanders increasingly spoke of a national citizenship established in the Constitution and grounded in decades of African American civic and political inclusion in their states. Yet, they still argued that national citizenship emanated from citizenship-granting authorities of each state.

In the aftermath of the Civil War, it became clear that federal power would be necessary to protect black citizenship nationally.

New Englanders were critical actors in the early years of Reconstruction and the passage of the Civil Rights Act. Antebellum antislavery activism, judicial decisions, and lawmaking shaped visions of citizenship applied to the newly emancipated and other African Americans after the Civil War. Although by 1866, New England states' laws already protected, and even expanded upon, the rights enumerated in the Civil Rights Act, local activists and office holders attempted to extend these local victories. These successes, however, were ultimately limited in scope. Although the Civil Rights Act opened the door for greater inclusion and rights for all, it failed to usher in a revolutionary era of reform and racial justice hoped for by its most radical New England advocates. Nevertheless, the fight for equality that began in the 1850s in New England judges' chambers, legislatures, and meeting halls, among black and white activists, helped shape the national debate over citizenship and built a foundation for equal rights struggles for African Americans moving forward.

AFRICAN AMERICAN CITIZENSHIP IN NEW ENGLAND

By the end of the 1850s, small but significant free African American communities settled in New England. Massachusetts had the greatest number with approximately 9,600 black residents by 1860. New Hampshire's population was the smallest with just under 500 African Americans.[9] The migration of former slaves and fugitives from enslavement bolstered these populations. Despite their small numbers, these communities formed valuable institutions and organizations and were active in struggles for civil rights and emancipation both locally and across the country.[10] Massachusetts's African American communities were especially active. Concentrated in Boston, Bay State African Americans and their white allies fought against slavery, protected fugitives from bondage, and waged local battles for civil rights, including advocating for the integration of public schools and against discrimination in public accommodations.[11]

By the beginning of the Civil War, all New England states had abolished slavery outright or enacted gradual emancipation laws.[12] Within most New England states, African Americans enjoyed basic rights protections, including rights to hold property and make contracts.[13] Some states went even further, granting African Americans suffrage and providing integrated public education. Maine, Massachusetts, Vermont, New Hampshire, and Rhode Island all permitted black voting prior to 1865, although African

Americans in these states were subject to the same restrictions on white voting such as residency and literacy requirements and poll taxes.[14] Massachusetts outlawed school segregation in public schools in 1855.[15] Despite progress, few states supported interracial marriage or prohibited public accommodation discrimination.[16] Additionally, black New England residents were often victims of private acts of prejudice and discrimination and faced dire economic circumstances.

Despite their relative expansion, prior to the *Dred Scott* decision and the Civil War, rights and privileges of New England African Americans were still rooted in state-level regimes and authority, and most rights and privileges were the product of state rather than federal citizenship.[17] The *Dred Scott* decision in 1857 was a major turning point in redefining this relationship, however, as with it the Supreme Court denied that African Americans held either state or federal citizenship.[18] As William Novak explains, majority opinion author Roger Taney's "heavy-handed and absolutist elimination of all American blacks, free as well as slave, from any past or future claim to national citizenship . . . now threatened the self-governing powers of free states to protect their own citizens and inhabitants."[19] The Supreme Court's actions prompted New England states to respond in kind, using arguments of state-level citizenship and historic recognition to promote a vision of a more inclusive national citizenship.

THE NEW ENGLAND RESPONSE TO *DRED SCOTT*

Following the 1857 decision by the Supreme Court in *Scott v. Sandford,* which declared that African Americans were not U.S. citizens and therefore not protected by the nation's courts or laws, New England states stepped in to pass citizenship laws of their own. Editors of the *Liberator,* a leading Boston antislavery press, celebrated reports from the Massachusetts legislature that showed "the utter falsity of that decision in respect to our national history, and the usages of the national government and of the several states."[20] From the outset, criticism of the decision was linked to black suffrage. Maine newspaper the *Bangor Daily Whig and Courier,* for example, called upon the state legislature to "take the necessary measures to restore, as far as possible, the rights of colored citizens who have been disenfranchised by the late atrocious decision of the U.S. Supreme Court."[21]

Along with personal liberty laws, which resisted the return of fugitives to bondage, legislation brought about by the New England states represented their attempts to not only resist the institution of slavery but also establish legal precedent for the full and equal citizenship of African Americans.

By the end of 1858, every New England state except Rhode Island issued resolutions condemning the decision.[22] These laws and the judicial opinions supporting them helped justify federal action to affirm black citizenship a decade later. They argued that the Court had overstepped its authority and that the ruling "contradicts the facts of history, is repugnant to the constitution, and subversive to the rights and liberties of the people."[23]

Striking directly at the most controversial part of the *Dred Scott* decision, many New England states passed laws and resolutions guaranteeing black residents full citizenship. For example, the New Hampshire legislature passed a law declaring "that neither descent, near or remote, from a person of African blood, whether such a person is or may have been a slave, nor color of skin, shall disqualify any person from becoming a citizen of this State, or deprive such person of the full rights and privileges of a citizen thereof."[24] The Vermont legislature passed a similar statute a year later.[25]

State lawmakers explicitly declared that state citizenship guaranteed national citizenship. The Maine legislature resolved "that it is the independent right of each state to determine who shall be admitted to political franchise and citizenship within its own limits, is clear and indisputable, and is to be exercised without question by any other state, and that persons admitted to the rights of citizenship by any state, are, by the plain letter of the constitution of the United States, 'entitled to all privileges and immunities of citizens in the several states.'"[26] Other states took on authority roles typically left to the federal government. Massachusetts, for example, filled a gap left by the annulment of citizenship in the *Dred Scott* decision when it granted authority to state officials to issue passports to "any citizen, whatever his color may be."[27]

In keeping with their vision of republican citizenship, New England states passed laws and resolutions placing suffrage as a central component of citizenship. When it passed its "Act to Secure Freedom and the Rights of Citizenship," the New Hampshire legislature made sure to emphasize that the state's voting laws would "not be so construed as in any case to deprive any person of color, or of African descent, born within the limits of the United States, and having the other requisite qualifications, from voting at any election; but such person shall have and exercise the right of suffrage as fully and lawfully as persons of the white race."[28] New England state supreme courts considered the relationship between suffrage and citizenship in their opinions as they reviewed citizenship statutes.

Unsure of the status of their black residents in a post–*Dred Scott* era, Maine and New Hampshire state legislators submitted laws related to black citizenship to their respective state supreme courts for approval. In these cases, having rejected the authority of the national court to rule, they trusted their state courts to decide cases of immediate and far-reaching consequence by defining African American citizenship not only at the state level but nationally as well. In New Hampshire, for example, the court ruled briefly that the statute affirming the citizenship of African Americans was constitutional, but it did not apply to fugitives from bondage.[29] Maine, however, took a more expansive view.

MAINE: A CASE STUDY

In Maine, state supreme court justices issued a broader review of African American citizenship, not just in their state but also in the nation. It was clear to the justices that they were living in a post–*Dred Scott* era, and they contended with what impact the decision should have on their state. The Maine legislature particularly sought the opinion of the court as to whether or not in the aftermath of the decision African Americans could continue to vote in the state.[30] Central to their question was the application of the Maine Constitution to black residents. That document provided "every male citizen of the United States" who fulfilled age and residency requirements the right to vote. "This raises for our consideration," the justices wrote in response, "the distinct question, whether free native born colored persons, of African descent, are recognized as 'citizens of the United States.'"[31]

The majority of the court agreed that African Americans in Maine had the right to vote, and in their responses the justices wrote at length about African American citizenship. In doing so, they foreshadowed many of the questions present in debates over the Civil Rights Act of 1866.[32] "We are of the opinion," the court concluded, "that our constitution does not discriminate between the different races of people which constitute the inhabitants of our state; but that the term, 'citizens of the United States,' as used in that instrument, applies as well to free colored persons of African descent as to persons descended from white ancestors."[33]

The justices focused on the major areas especially relevant for questions of black citizenship. First, they examined whether or not American birthright citizenship applied to African Americans. They also considered the legal condition of African Americans at the founding of the nation and refuted arguments that the authors of the U.S. Constitution never meant to include African Americans as citizens. Emerging from both of these issues was the question of whether the citizenship of African Americans in Maine made them full citizens across the United States.

In their opinions, the justices argued that American birth automatically conferred citizenship on a person, regardless of race. Justice Woodbury Davis argued that in the Constitution, "there is a clear recognition of the common law principle that birth makes a person a citizen by natural right."[34] African Americans were not lesser citizens just because some states restricted certain privileges. "Citizenship," Justice John Appleton explained, "as the general rule of international law, is the result of birth in the dominion of the state to which allegiance is due. It is nowhere made to depend on color or descent."[35] Therefore all free people of color born in the United States were citizens and should be granted rights bestowed to other citizens of the nation. Maine's constitution, Appleton wrote, "recognizes as its fundamental idea, the great principle upon which all popular governments rest—*the equality of all before the law*. It confers citizenship and entire equality of civil and political rights upon all its native born population."[36] Even enslavement only restricted African Americans' citizenship temporarily due to their condition, and if emancipated they returned to free status with full citizenship rights.

Laws and traditions that existed at the time of American independence, the courts argued, confirmed African Americans' status as citizens. According to the justices, African Americans were citizens at the founding of the nation, and this status could not be removed. "Before the revolution," Appleton argued, "the native born free men by the common law were subjects of the government to which they owed allegiance, irrespective of color or descent, and upon and by the revolution, from being subject they became citizens."[37]

The justices recorded a litany of examples of laws and common practices that supported the treatment of African Americans as citizens since the founding, including rights to suffrage. They found few laws containing language restricting citizenship to white Americans only. "It may be regarded as unquestionably true," Appleton concluded, "that colored freemen were regarded as citizens, and entitled to the right of suffrage, in most of the states, during the whole period of the revolution."[38] Justice Davis concurred when he affirmed, "as historical fact, that at the time when our independence was established, the white population of this country did recognize the citizenship of colored persons of African descent, and did intend to secure to them the rights of citizens."[39]

Black military service during the revolution was further evidence of African Americans' inclusion as citizens at the time of the nation's founding. "There are no historic facts more completely established," Justice Appleton argued, "than that during the revolution they were enlisted, and served as soldiers; that they were tendered and received as substitutes; that they were required to take, and took the oath of allegiance."[40] Military service was proof of African Americans' civic inclusion and thus placed them as equals among white colonists fighting for independence.

Having firmly established the stability of claims to black citizenship in Maine, the justices argued that the U.S. Constitution made all free persons equal and endowed them with federal citizenship across states. After careful analysis of the Articles of Confederation and the proceedings of the constitutional convention, Justice Appleton concluded that the authors of the Constitution deliberately meant the language of "free citizens" to include African Americans. "It is manifest, therefore," he declared, "that free persons of African descent, being native born, were regarded by those by whom the constitution was framed, as free citizens, as they had been during the revolution, and under the confederation."[41] The Constitution, by making no special restrictions based on race, not only protected the rights of African Americans in the states that enumerated their citizenship specifically but also made them full and equal citizens of the United States as a whole.

The second section of Article 4 of the Constitution was especially important. It declared, "The citizens of each state shall be entitled to all privileges and immunities of citizens in the several states." This provision, the justices argued, extended national citizenship to all free African Americans, and, once established, neither local nor state nor federal government could deny this status. As Justice Davis explained,

> All free persons, born within the limits and jurisdiction of the United States, are citizens thereof, and, as such, are citizens of the several states where they reside. . . . The citizens of each state have the right to become citizens of any other state, simply by a change of residence, without any consent, or right of refusal, on the part of such a state. . . . Neither any state, *nor the federal government*, can deprive any class of free persons, born within the United States, of their citizenship.[42]

By virtue of their native birth, all residents of the United States, regardless of race or color, were full citizens not only of their state of residence but also of all other states.

Reciprocal citizenship was the backbone of the United States, and without it national unity would crumble. "The equality of states," Appleton argued, "being the foundation upon which the Union rests, the equality of the citizens of the states, and the consequent right of general citizenship, would seem to follow as necessary consequence therefrom. Indeed, the states could hardly be regarded as equal unless equality of rights were conceded to the citizens of several states."[43] The U.S. Supreme Court ruling against African American citizenship threatened not just the rights of African Americans but, indeed, the stability of the nation itself.

Members of Maine's new Republican Party celebrated the court's opinion as a fierce rebuke of *Dred Scott* and a proud celebration of Maine and equal rights. Lot Morrill, who as a Maine senator would be a crucial New England voice in the debates advocating the Civil Rights Act in 1866, praised the court during his successful campaign for Maine governor in September 1857. Pointing particularly to Justice Appleton's comments, Morrill called the opinion "one of the most complete and best fortified arguments which has ever emanated from any bench."[44]

AFRICAN AMERICANS' RESPONSE

Questions of black citizenship were concerns not just of legislators and jurists but also of worried members of the New England public and African Americans in particular. Black activists and their allies called upon state legislatures to pass formal declarations affirming black citizenship. In Massachusetts, black and white antislavery leaders joined in a February 1858 meeting to petition the state legislature on behalf of African American rights.[45] Among the speakers and attendees were some of the most prominent black and white activists of the age, including William Lloyd Garrison, William Cooper Nell, and Lewis Hayden.

The meeting condemned the *Dred Scott* decision and declared it a representation of the growing threat against black equality. The decision had, one speaker announced, "took away citizenship, with all its rights, privileges, and immunities, at one fell blow, from every man in the land, in whose veins flows a single drop of African blood." The decision had struck at the rights of all African Americans throughout the country, even those residing in supposedly free states. The speakers called upon African Americans everywhere to mobilize. Hayden declared it a time for action and "hoped the colored people would now be fully aroused to their position and their duties, and redeem themselves from the charge of indifference to the great struggle which is going on in the land for equal rights and universal emancipation."[46] This renewed dedication was manifest in calls for legislative action.

The attendees approved a memorial to the state legislature declaring African Americans' rights as U.S. citizens and calling upon lawmakers to "declare the tyrannical decision . . . not to be binding upon the States, but utterly unconstitutional, and demand its immediate reversal." The memorial condemned the Court's ruling and, like the justices in Maine and New Hampshire, argued that it ran counter to the U.S. Constitution and the history and practices of New England states. The petitioners specifically invoked Article 4 and declared the decision "no more worthy of respect and consideration than though it denied to all the citizens of this commonwealth the privileges and immunities of citizens of the United States, and declared Massachusetts to be no longer a constituent member of the Union." They reminded the legislature of the lack of Massachusetts laws restricting rights based on race. Massachusetts law, they wrote, did not include any legislation "prejudicial to the rights or interests of any man, or class of men, on the ground of complexional differences."[47]

The petitioners recounted African American service during the American Revolution and described black people's patriotic civic service since the nation's founding as evidence of their claims to citizenship and the false basis for the Supreme Court's actions. Declaring African Americans' birthright citizenship, petitioners wrote,

> To deny that those who are native-born and personally free—whose blood has been freely poured out on every battle field, from the earliest to the latest conflict in behalf of American liberty and independence . . . by whose suffrages, in common with all others entitled to vote, the Constitution of the United States was adopted, the government brought into existence and put in operation . . . of whom allegiance and taxation are as strictly exacted as of the white inhabitants, and who have never been found wanting in the performance of their obligations and duties, but have always shown themselves to be animated by the most patriotic feelings—to deny that such are, or can be, citizens of the United States, in accordance with the plain meaning of the constitution, is to outrage the common sense of mankind, and most wickedly to pervert judgment, that the foundations of freedom may be destroyed.[48]

In response to their petition, the Massachusetts legislature joined the other New England states in decrying the *Dred Scott* decision and affirming black citizenship rights. The legislature resolved "that all citizens of Massachusetts are citizens of the United States; that all negroes, not aliens, domiciled within her limits, are citizens of Massachusetts and are entitled to all the rights, privileges, and immunities of citizenship, in the courts of the United States and elsewhere."[49]

By the end of the 1850s, in these declarations of black citizenship, New Englanders established a vision of black citizenship based in birthright, grounded in American history, and exercised through suffrage. They refused to let decisions from the Supreme Court compromise protection for African Americans in their states. In the coming years, however, questions of African American freedom and equality would shake the foundation of the Union to its core. After the Civil War, advocates of black freedom would carry antebellum ideologies of citizenship and equality as early participants in Reconstruction on the ground in the South and as formal lawmakers in the halls of Congress.

NEW ENGLAND OBSERVERS IN THE POSTWAR SOUTH

New England justifications for African American citizenship and legal protections of the region's black residents informed the vision of how black people, especially the newly emancipated, would be treated after the Civil War. As senators and representatives debated the question of postwar black rights and protections on the floor of the U.S. Congress, black and white New Englanders appeared before the Joint Committee on Reconstruction, which included several congressmen from New England, to testify as to the condition of African Americans in the South.[50] In the early years of Reconstruction, their testimony helped convince Congress of the need for affirmative legislation preserving black citizenship and that African Americans would not be protected without federal force.

Some of the most compelling testimony came from African American New Englanders who had gone south after emancipation. For example, Thomas Bain testified before the committee in February 1866. Bain, who had been enslaved in Virginia, had escaped to Massachusetts via the Underground Railroad and worked as a dentist. He returned to Norfolk after the Emancipation Proclamation, and while he sent his daughter to live in Massachusetts, he remained as a delegate to the president on behalf of the Norfolk black community.

He reported on the poor treatment of African Americans at the hands of white Virginians but also on the aspirations of the formerly enslaved. When asked about the feeling of former Confederates toward black people, Bain responded, "Their feelings are very hard—terrible."[51] Bain recounted incidents of racial violence, including rioting and regular whippings. "It is not uncommon," Bain told the committee, "to hear such threats as this: 'We will kill one negro, at least, for every rebel soldier killed by them.'" Only federal protection, Bain argued, would secure black citizenship and stop the violence. "The only hope the colored people have," Bain explained, "is in Uncle Sam's bayonets; without them, they would not feel any security." Despite the seemingly dire conditions, Bain remained hopeful and was confident in the black commitment to education. "[African Americans] are excelled by no people in an eagerness to learn," he concluded.[52]

Others supported the issues raised in Bain's testimony and argued for the need of positive federal legislation and enforcement. W. A. P. Dillingham, a treasury agent from Waterford, Maine, testified about the conditions in Mississippi. He told the committee that without interference from the national government, white Mississippians might recognize black freedom but little else. "If their own views could be carried out," Dillingham explained, "they would not allow [African Americans] to buy, hold property, or testify in course unless it was in cases between negroes, or to have schools or exercise the elective franchise, which, in their judgment, is the sum of all evils. . . . As far as they possibly could I think they would exclude them from their society, and that they would be generally under the ban of their displeasure."[53] Should military force be withdrawn, Vermont native and Massachusetts resident Lieutenant George Sanderson supposed, "there would be no hope of the freedmen's exercising any of his rights. . . . He would have no chance anywhere. His condition would be, in my opinion, worse than it was before. . . . His condition would be deplorable."[54] Colonel Orlando Brown from Massachusetts echoed this sentiment when he told the committee that rather than formal enslavement, former Confederates "would prefer to hold [African Americans], by their laws, etc., in a situation which would be slavery in effect but not in name, so as to have the benefit of his labor without the responsibility of supporting him."[55] According to Brown, Sanderson, Dillingham, Bain, and other witnesses, without federal legislation defining U.S. citizenship and enforcement power, African Americans in southern states would be in a condition little better than bondage.

THE CIVIL RIGHTS ACT OF 1866

Based in part on these complaints, confidence in black citizenship, and New England jurisprudence, representatives from New England states forcefully advocated the new Civil Rights Act and drew upon the legacy of African American citizenship and abolition in their states to protect the rights of black people nationally. They campaigned for a strong definition of national citizenship, clearly delineated rights and privileges, and federal protection of these rights for all Americans. No longer would citizenship be primarily a function of one's state-level residency.

New England lawmakers in Congress were early advocates of new legislation. In May 1865, Massachusetts senator Henry Wilson spoke before a meeting of antislavery activists in Boston. He promised that at the beginning of the next congressional session that coming December, he would introduce legislation guaranteeing protection of the rights of newly freed slaves and prohibiting infringements on liberty based on race. True to his word, in December he presented a bill declaring null and void any law "wherein any inequality in civil rights and immunities . . . is recognized, authorized, established, or maintained, by reason of, or founded upon, distinctions or differences of color, race, or descent, or upon a previous condition or status of slavery or involuntary servitude."[56] Along with Wilson, Massachusetts senator Charles Sumner introduced legislation annulling any customary or legal privileges or distinctions based on race and declaring all persons equal before the law.[57] New England newspapers praised the legislation as a rebuke to the *Dred Scott* decision. This bill, the editors of the *Vermont Watchman and State Journal* wrote, "puts free blacks where they were in the earlier and better days of the Republic, making them *citizens*."[58]

New England statesmen proudly supported Illinois senator Lyman Trumbull, who finally introduced the Civil Rights Act in January 1866. The act spelled out a new definition of who was a citizen of the United States and expressed several basic rights. Echoing language in the earlier New England laws and judicial proceedings, the act stated in part

> that all persons born in the United States and not subject to any foreign power . . . are hereby declared to be citizens of the United States; and such citizens, of every race and color, without regard to any previous condition of slavery or involuntary servitude . . . shall have the same right, in every State and Territory in the United States, to make and enforce contracts, to sue, be parties, and give evidence, to inherit, purchase, lease, sell, hold, and convey real and personal property, and to full and equal benefit of all laws and proceedings for the security of person and property, as is enjoyed by white citizens.[59]

Notably absent, however, was any mention of a citizenship right to suffrage.

Despite the lack of explicit mention of voting rights, New England legislators argued that citizenship itself guaranteed suffrage. During debates over the act, former governor and now Maine senator Lot Morrill and others pointed to transformations in both civil and political life. "Are we not," Morrill asked, "in the midst of a civil and *political* revolution?"[60] Days later, Senator Sumner, during debates over a proposed constitutional amendment addressing postwar apportionment of representatives, referred directly to the act when he made this point: "You have already in this chamber . . . decreed civil rights without distinction of color. Who can doubt that by the same title you may decree political rights also?"[61] New England congressional lawmakers rooted their understandings of postwar citizenship in antebellum concepts in which political rights, voting especially, were fundamental. "Suffrage," they argued, "is the highest element, the highest privilege, nay, the highest right of the American citizen. Without it, all other rights are of little value."[62]

Now was the time, New England representatives argued, to transform the nation and redeem the promise of American equality for African Americans. Morrill outlined the central question facing the nation after the Civil War and emancipation: "If there is anything with which the American people are troubled, and if there is anything with which the American statesman is perplexed and vexed, it is what to do with the negro, how to define him, what he is in American law, and to what rights he is entitled. What shall we do with the everlasting, inevitable negro?"[63] As governor of Maine, Morrill had dealt with the aftermath of *Dred Scott* in his state and proudly supported the opinion of his state's supreme court upholding black citizenship. Now the questions Morrill had faced a decade earlier were the questions facing a fractured nation that was attempting to rebuild.

For Morrill and other supporters, the Civil Rights Act became the most crucial legislation of the age. The act, especially its declaration of citizenship, did more than just define African Americans' legal status; it expressed central principles of equality and American freedom. The act, Morrill argued, "defines him to be a man and only a man in American politics and in American law; it puts him on the plane of manhood; it brings him within the pale of the Constitution. That is all it does as a definition, and there it leaves him." For Morrill, however, the legislation had a higher meaning. "It is not an enactment in the sense of the law, in the sense of legislation," Morrill clarified, "but a declaration of a grand, fundamental principle of law and politics . . . as such it had a transcendent importance; as such it is without parallel in the history of the legislation of this country or perhaps of any other." The Civil Rights Act, he argued, would transform the nation and inaugurate a new era of equality. The act "marks an epoch in the history of this country, and from this time forward the legislation takes a fresh and new departure."[64]

Supporters, channeling the sentiments of earlier New England jurists and lawmakers, rejected ideas stemming from the *Dred Scott* decision that the nation was founded only for the interests of white citizens. "I deny it utterly," Morrill announced; "I deny that Government was organized in the interest of any race or color, and there is neither 'race' nor 'color' in our history politically or civilly—not a bit of it. . . . 'All men are created equal' excludes the idea of race or color or caste."[65] The only relevant status, he argued, was the condition of enslavement, and with its abolition there was nothing to preclude citizenship for African Americans.

New England senators further refuted the opinion of the bill's opponents that African Americans were not citizens at the time of the founding of the nation and therefore could not be made citizens by legislation. Senator Daniel Clark from New Hampshire advocated passage of the new legislation and rooted his argument in reasoning given by New England justices in 1857 and in New Hampshire law and history to explicitly support legislation clarifying black citizenship nationwide. If African Americans could be secure in their rights as citizens in New England states, surely that citizenship extended nationwide. "In my state," Clark declared proudly, "there is not a single disqualification or discrimination between the white man and the black man."[66]

Like earlier New England jurists, Clark went on to examine the place of African Americans during the age of the American Revolution and used their role in the struggle for national independence as evidence of their citizenship. He paid special attention to black suffrage as evidence. "Before the Constitution was adopted," Clark told the Senate, "the free black man in my state was just as much a citizen as the white man; and when delegates were chosen to the Convention which adopted the Constitution he had a right to vote, and undoubtedly did vote, as well as the white man. They formed that Constitution." Any American of African descent, Clark continued, became a citizen of the United States "when he helped to achieve the independence of the country equally with the white man." He further added that under Article 4 of the Constitution, black citizens of one state were "entitled to the rights and privileges of citizens" across the country.[67] Clark and other supporters hoped black citizenship in New England would justify the amendment as a reminder to the nation that African Americans were equal to all other U.S. citizens.

If legislation alone was not enough to convince others of black citizenship, New England senators supported the use of federal force. As Michael Vorenberg makes clear earlier in this volume, the Civil Rights Act was wartime policy requiring military enforcement. New England representatives responded to the reports from New Englanders in the South that military enforcement would be necessary. Senator Wilson from Massachusetts supported the use of troops to enforce black rights. "By the will of the nation freedom and free institutions for all, chains and fetters for none, are forever incorporated in the fundamental law of regenerated and united America," he declared. Force would be required where local officials refused to abide by federal law. "Southern legislators and people must learn," Wilson demanded, even "if they are compelled to learn by the bayonets of the Army of the United States, that the civil rights of the freedmen must and shall be respected."[68]

A CELEBRATION WITH MIXED RESULTS

When the act was finally passed over President Andrew Johnson's veto in April 1866, communities across New England celebrated and heralded it as a proud moment for the nation. In Boston, the First Light Artillery, under the auspices of the Republican State Committee, fired a salute of one hundred guns in celebration.[69] The *Bangor Daily Whig and Courier* reported the celebration in that city, which included a thirty-three-gun salute, displays of flags, and a large bonfire. The streets, the paper described, "were thronged with crowds of people until a late hour, congratulating each other that Congress is firm in demanding that Right and Justice shall prevail."[70]

For African American activists and their allies, however, these celebrations in 1866 pointed to the beginning of a much larger movement to define postwar freedom. Indeed, the Civil Rights Act was a dramatic and first formal legal definition of the rights of American citizenship, but it still remained relatively limited in scope.[71] As Michael Les Benedict makes clear in this volume, the Civil Rights Act in effect limited some definitions of citizenship in play before the war. The law placed enforcement powers in the federal courts, which, while extending federal authority, did not include military policing advocated by more radical members of Congress.[72] More important for African Americans, the act said nothing about suffrage as an extension of citizenship, a major theme in the 1857 New England court opinions, nor did it prohibit racial discrimination in education or public accommodations.

Some in New England lauded the limited scope of the act and rejected continued state activism to solve the challenges African Americans would face in the coming decades. These critics, some even former antislavery activists, were part of a growing political order in the North that, while advocating civil and political equality, were fearful of broader state intervention.[73] The federal government had done its duty, they argued, in removing legal barriers to civil and political participation and defining national citizenship. It could do little, however, to guarantee economic freedom or combat individual prejudice in private businesses and public accommodations.[74]

The editors of the *Bangor Daily Whig and Courier* illustrated this sentiment. The Maine newspaper, which earlier praised the 1857 actions of the state court on behalf of black citizens, trumpeted the guarantee of civil and political rights. "[African Americans] have been made free," the editors wrote, "and the loyal people of this country are concerned that this freedom shall be a substantial fact, and not a mere shadow." Yet they reassured worried New Englanders that the law would not interfere with private acts or business. "This bill," they explained, "is intended to do justice where the state laws fail to do it, and nowhere else. . . . It leaves all merely benevolent operations where of right they belong, to private effort." The Civil Rights Act did nothing to establish schools, alleviate poverty, or regulate business and the relationship between workers and employers. "It leaves these matters," the editors continued proudly, "to regulate themselves."[75]

All African Americans were now free, opponents of state intervention argued, and must now succeed on their own effort with minimal interference from the government. From the Civil Rights Act, they concluded, "the great starting point will be gained from which the problem which now distracts the country may be left to work itself out, without further help from the Government, and with only such supplementary aid from private benevolence."[76] Now that the federal government had secured basic civil and political rights, the rest, they argued, was up to the American people themselves.

African Americans, however, believed that the federal government still held an obligation to guarantee their rights and help secure equality in all areas of public life. They called for further affirmations of citizenship through the Fourteenth Amendment and for the prohibition of racial restrictions on voting through the Fifteenth several years later. Throughout, they remained critical of moderation or patience in areas of equality. In Massachusetts, for example, many criticized the Fourteenth Amendment initially for not protecting suffrage outright and lamented the slow speed with which Congress expanded on the Civil Rights Act. While the passage of the Fifteenth Amendment relieved some of this criticism, black New Englanders faced the stark reality that citizenship, though secured by law beginning in 1866, would require persistent agitation to be made real, not only in southern states but also for black men and women in New England.

Black New Englanders and their allies worked to secure rights not specifically guaranteed by the 1866 act. Even as New England state authorities were quick to endorse equal political rights and recognized the importance of suffrage as a major component of citizenship, it would take decades of continued black activism to mobilize states to protect other African American rights, such as public accommodation access.[77] Massachusetts would pass legislation prohibiting such discrimination in the 1860s, but it remained limited and until the 1880s applied only to businesses specifically licensed by the state.[78] Other New England states would not follow suit until after the Supreme Court declared the Civil Rights Act of 1875 unconstitutional in 1883.[79] Activists in New England continued to fight for a full vision of citizenship even as the tide of Jim Crow rose into the twentieth century. Though increasingly secure in their citizenship in New England, African Americans would not be true beneficiaries of American freedom until equality was protected in all parts of the nation.

When Boston officials in 1867 responded to black claims of equality "in accordance with the spirit of the times," they drew upon much of the same sentiment behind the Civil Rights Act of 1866. If African Americans were going to be treated as equals, they required equal treatment under the law and confirmation of equal citizenship on a national level. From resistance to *Dred Scott*, to affirmative laws guaranteeing black citizenship, through the Civil War, and into the early years of Reconstruction, black and white New England advocates of full equality developed their vision of citizenship and equality, struggled for it locally, and attempted to extend it to the nation. In doing so, they played an important role in the growth and extension of American citizenship.

Yet, in other ways New Englanders represented "the spirit of the times" in a less noble fashion. In their reluctance to move quickly and mobilize an activist federal state to secure voting or economic rights or protect against private acts of discrimination, they left black citizenship compromised. Although they helped move citizenship away from inconsistent and state-centered authority, many elements of American freedom remained in state and local control. As citizens, black and white, north and south, tried to rebuild following the bloodiest conflict in American history, the limits of citizenship would continue to be tested, and many would find out that, indeed, legal definitions of citizenship and basic civil rights would be only the beginning of a much larger and longer struggle.

Notes

1. Roberts was the father of the plaintiff in the famous but unsuccessful 1850 Boston school desegregation case *Roberts v. City of Boston*, 59 Mass. 203 (1850).
2. "Petition of Benjamin F. Roberts and others that the designation of 'Colored' may be omitted on the City Tax Bills and Voting Lists," February 11, 1867, Board of Aldermen Docket Documents, City of Boston Archives, Boston.
3. "Report of the Special Committee of the Common Council of Boston," February 25, 1867, Minutes of the Mayor and Aldermen, City of Boston Archives.
4. Ibid.
5. For more on republican citizenship see, Michael Les Benedict in this volume.
6. On personal liberty laws, see Thomas D. Morris, *Free Men All: The Personal Liberty Laws of the North, 1780–1861* (Baltimore: Johns Hopkins University Press); and Norman L. Rosenberg, "Personal Liberty Laws and Sectional Crisis: 1850–1861," *Civil War History* 17 (1971): 25–44.
7. On the Civil Rights Act, see George Rutherglen, *Civil Rights in the Shadow of Slavery: The Constitution, Common Law, and the Civil Rights Act of 1866* (New York: Oxford University Press, 2013); and Robert J. Kaczorowski, "To Begin the Nation Anew: Congress, Citizenship, and Civil Rights after the Civil War," *American Historical Review* 92 (February 1987): 45–68.
8. William J. Novak, "The Legal Transformation of Citizenship in Nineteenth-Century America," in *The Democratic Experiment: New Directions in American Political History*, ed. M. Jacobs et al. (Princeton: Princeton University Press, 2003), 85–119.
9. U.S. Bureau of the Census, *Negro Population in the United States, 1790–1915* (New York: Arno Press, 1968), 57.
10. There are limited studies on African American life in New England. On African Americans in Vermont, see Harvey Amani Whitfield, "African Americans in Burlington, Vermont, 1880–1900," *Vermont History* 75, no. 2 (Summer/Fall 2007): 101–23; and Jane Williamson, "African Americans in Addison County, Charlotte, and Hinesburgh, Vermont, 1790–1860," *Vermont History* 78, no. 1 (Winter/Spring 2010): 15–42. On New Hampshire, see David T. Dixon, "Freedom Earned, Equality Denied: Evolving Race Relation in Exeter and Vicinity, 1776–1876," *Historical New Hampshire* 61 (Spring 2007): 29–47.

11. On Massachusetts African Americans, see James and Lois Horton, *Black Bostonians: Family Life and Community Struggle in the Antebellum North* (New York: Holmes and Meier, 1999); and Stephen Kantrowitz, *More Than Freedom: Fighting for Black Citizenship in a White Republic, 1829–1889* (New York: Penguin Press, 2012).
12. Leon Litwack, *North of Slavery: The Negro in the Free States, 1790–1860* (Chicago: University of Chicago Press, 1961), 3; James Horton and Lois Horton, *In Hope of Liberty: Culture, Community, and Protest among Northern Free Blacks, 1700–1860* (New York: Oxford University Press, 1997), 72–73; Paul Finkelman, "Prelude to the Fourteenth Amendment: Black Legal Rights in the Antebellum North," *Rutgers Law Journal* 17 (1985–86): 421–23.
13. Finkelman, "Prelude to the Fourteenth Amendment," 476–77.
14. Gilbert Thomas Stephenson, *Race Distinctions in American Law* (New York: D. Appleton, 1910), 282; Charles S. Mangum Jr., *The Legal Status of the Negro* (Chapel Hill: University of North Carolina Press, 1940), 371; Litwack, *North of Slavery*, 75. Connecticut prohibited black voting in 1818; see Connecticut Const. (1818), Art. 6, Chap. 2; and Finkelman, "Prelude to the Fourteenth Amendment," 423.
15. "An Act in amendment of 'An Act concerning Public Schools,' passed March twenty-fifth, eighteen hundred and forty-five," 1855 Mass. Acts 256; Litwack, *North of Slavery*, 105–6; Finkelman, "Prelude to the Fourteenth Amendment," 465–67.
16. Massachusetts allowed interracial marriage in 1843; see "An Act Relating to Marriages between Individuals of Certain Races," Chap. 5, *Acts and Resolves Passed by the General Court of Massachusetts* (Boston: Dutton and Wentworth, 1843), 4. On public accommodation discrimination, see Finkelman, "Prelude to the Fourteenth Amendment," 471–72.
17. Novak, "Legal Transformation of Citizenship," 92.
18. Ibid., 108–9.
19. Ibid., 108.
20. "Colored Citizenship," *Liberator*, April 24, 1857.
21. "Action Which Is Called for by the Slaveholders' Decision," *Bangor Daily Whig and Courier*, March 13, 1857.
22. Herman V. Ames, ed., *State Documents on Federal Relations: The States and the United States*, vol. 6 (Philadelphia: University of Pennsylvania, 1906), 55.
23. "Dred Scott Resolves," Chap. 1999, Sec. 2, *Laws of the State of New Hampshire*, June session (Concord, N.H.: John F. Brown, 1857), 1925.

24. "An Act to Secure Freedom and the Rights of Citizenship to Persons in this State," Chap. 1965, Sec. 1, ibid., 1876.
25. "An Act to Secure Freedom to All Persons within This State," No. 37, Sec. 5, *Acts and Resolves Passed by the General Assembly of the State of Vermont*, October session (Bradford, Vt.: Joseph D. Clark, 1858), 42–43.
26. "Resolves in Relation to the Decision of the Supreme Court of the United States, in the Case of Dred Scott," Chap. 112, *Acts and Resolves Passed by the Thirty-Sixth Legislature of the State of Maine, 1857* (Augusta, Maine: Stevens and Blaine, 1857), 61; "The Voice of the Republican Party in Maine," *Bangor Daily Whig and Courier*, May 19, 1857; "The State of Maine against the Dred Scott Case," *Liberator*, July 3, 1857.
27. "An Act Authorizing Passports," Chap. 224, *Acts and Resolves Passed by the General Court of Massachusetts* (Boston: William White, 1857), 558; "Colored Citizenship," *Liberator*, April 24, 1857.
28. "An Act to Secure Freedom and the Rights of Citizenship to Persons in this State," Chap. 1965, Sec. 4, *Laws of the State of New Hampshire*, June session (1857), 1876–77.
29. *Opinions of the Justices of the Supreme Judicial Court*, 41 NH 553 (1857).
30. Opinions of the Justices of the Supreme Judicial Court, On Question Propounded by the Senate, 44 Me. 505 (1857); David M. Gold, "Constitutional Problems in Maine during the Civil War Era, 1857–1872," *Maine Historical Society Quarterly* 22, no. 3 (January 1983): 127–34; "Opinion of the S. J. Court Requested," *Bangor Daily Whig and Citizen*, March 30, 1857.
31. *Opinions of the Justices*, 44 Me. at 507.
32. "Decision of the Supreme Court," *Bangor Daily Whig and Courier*, August 18, 1857.
33. *Opinions of the Justices*, 44 Me. at 515–16.
34. Ibid. at 580.
35. Ibid. at 524.
36. Ibid. at 522.
37. Ibid. at 528.
38. Ibid. at 538.
39. Ibid. at 587.
40. Ibid. at 573.
41. Ibid. at 544.
42. Ibid. at 583.
43. Ibid. at 547.
44. "Mr. Morrill's Speech," *Bangor Daily Whig and Courier*, September 7, 1857, quoted in Gold, "Constitutional Problems in Maine," 133.

45. "Important Meeting of Colored Citizens," *Liberator,* February 19, 1858; "Meeting of the Colored Citizens of Boston," ibid., February 26, 1858.
46. "Meeting of the Colored Citizens of Boston," *Liberator,* February 26, 1858.
47. Ibid.
48. Ibid.
49. "Resolve in Relation to the Decision of the Supreme Court of the United States, in Case of Scott versus Sanford," Chap. 44, *Acts and Resolves Passed by the General Court of Massachusetts* (Boston: William White, 1860), 170.
50. The committee included Senator William P. Fessenden (Mass.), Congressman Justin Morrill (Vt.), and Congressman George Boutwell (Maine).
51. *Report of the Joint Committee on Reconstruction at the First Session Thirty-Ninth Congress, Part 2: Virginia, North Carolina, South Carolina* (Washington, D.C.: Government Printing Office, 1866), 59.
52. Ibid.
53. *Report of the Joint Committee on Reconstruction, Part 3: Georgia, Alabama, Mississippi, Arkansas* (Washington, D.C.: Government Printing Office, 1866), 117.
54. *Report of the Joint Committee on Reconstruction, Part 2,* 176.
55. Ibid., 126.
56. "Senator Wilson's Bill," *Boston Daily Advertiser,* January 10, 1866; Henry Wilson, *A History of Reconstruction Measures of the Thirty-Ninth and Fortieth Congresses, 1865–1868* (Hartford, Conn.: Hartford Publishing Company, 1868), 118; *Cong. Globe,* 39th Cong., 1st Sess., 108 (December 21, 1865).
57. Wilson, *History of Reconstruction,* 117.; *Cong. Globe,* 39th Cong., 1st Sess., 2 (December 4, 1865)
58. "Protection of Civil Rights," *Vermont Watchman and State Journal,* February 9, 1866.
59. Civil Rights Act, 14 Stat. 27–30.
60. *Cong. Globe,* 39th Cong., 1st Sess., 570 (February 1, 1866).
61. Ibid., 674 (February 6, 1866).
62. Lot Morrill, ibid., appendix 154 (March 6, 1866); see also Daniel Clark, ibid., 833 (February 14, 1866).
63. Ibid., 570 (February 1, 1866).
64. Ibid.
65. Ibid., 570–571.
66. Ibid., 529 (January 31, 1866).
67. Ibid., 528.
68. Ibid., 603 (February 2, 1866).
69. "The Civil Rights Bill," *Boston Daily Advertiser,* April 9, 1866.

70. "The Passage of the Civil Rights Bill," *Bangor Daily Whig and Courier*, April 9, 1866.
71. Foner, *Reconstruction: America's Unfinished Revolution, 1863–1877* (New York: Harper and Row, 1988), 244–45.
72. Ibid., 245.
73. Ibid., 492; Heather Cox Richardson, *The Death of Reconstruction: Race, Labor, and Politics in the Post–Civil War North, 1865–1901* (Cambridge, Mass.: Harvard University Press, 2001), 122–25.
74. Foner, *Reconstruction*, 498.
75. "Public Opinion and the Civil Rights Bill," *Bangor Daily Whig and Courier*, April 2, 1866.
76. Ibid.
77. On continued activism, see Kantrowitz, *More Than Freedom;* Kazuteru Omori, "Race-Neutral Individualism and the Resurgence of the Color Line: Massachusetts Civil Rights Legislation, 1855–1895," *Journal of American Ethnic History*, Fall 2002, 32–58; Millington Bergeson-Lockwood, "'We Do Not Care Particularly about the Skating Rinks': African American Challenges to Racial Discrimination in Places of Public Amusement in Nineteenth-Century Boston, Massachusetts," *Journal of the Civil War Era* 5, no. 2 (June 2015): 254–88.
78. "An Act Forbidding Unjust Discrimination on Account of Color or Race," 1865 Mass. Acts 277; "An Act in Relation to Public Places of Amusement," 1866 Mass. Acts 252; Commonwealth v. Sylvester, 95 Mass. 247. Massachusetts enhanced its public accommodation statute in 1885. "An Act to Punish Persons Making Discrimination in Public Places on Account of Race or Color," 1885 Mass. Acts 316.
79. In 1884, Connecticut passed public accommodation protection followed by Rhode Island in 1885.

5

THE CIVIL RIGHTS ACT OF 1866 IN KENTUCKY AND MISSOURI

Aaron Astor

"The Radicals of Oregon were burning powder on last evening, in honor of the last great union victory." The *Holt County Sentinel*'s April 1866 dispatch could not resist rubbing it in. "Rebels looked blue on the occasion."[1] This last "victory" was a political one, the congressional override of President Andrew Johnson's veto of the Civil Rights Act of 1866. And the "Oregon" in question was not the state in the Pacific Northwest but a town in northwestern Missouri through which legions of pioneers had traveled in the decades before the Civil War. The "Radicals" represented the victorious faction within the state's Unionist coalition that had established effective control of Missouri after an 1865 constitution disenfranchised all of the state's former Confederate supporters.

Like the state carrying the same name, Oregon, Missouri, stood on the northwestern edge of what was once the slaveholding South. Had the war turned out differently, the town of Oregon would have marked the northwestern boundary of the Confederate States of America. This fate was not as farfetched as a cursory glance at a map would suggest. Though many of its residents had come due west from Illinois and Indiana in the 1840s and 1850s, the majority of its inhabitants came from Kentucky. This was especially true of the small slaveholding population, which held vigil along the Missouri River during the Bleeding Kansas days, jealously guarding its social system against abolitionists, Kansas jayhawkers, and runaway slaves.

Once the Civil War began, most people in Holt County sided with the Union, as did a majority of their fellow citizens across the state and in the state of their forebears, Kentucky. But most of them would have called themselves conservative Unionists, defending both the slave-based social order and the political union between slave and free states. A small minority, likely veterans of the Bleeding Kansas troubles, supported the state's secessionist governor, Claiborne Fox Jackson, and his plans for a

Confederate Missouri. On the other hand, roughly 15 percent of the population considered themselves Free-Soilers, opposing the spread of slavery into Kansas and supporting President Lincoln in the 1860 election. Most of these antislavery Unionists were either German immigrants or Yankee migrants from Illinois or Ohio.[2] For most Holt Countians, peace and stability lay with a conservative Union.

The Civil War dramatically altered Holt County, just as it did the rest of border states Missouri and Kentucky. The war unleashed both a guerrilla conflict that turned a peaceable border society inside out and a social revolution through which border slaves emancipated themselves and threatened, in the white imagination, to turn a racially hierarchical society upside down. But the political effects of the war were, on the surface at least, quite different in each state. The intense guerrilla war in Missouri left the Radical Republicans in control; they emancipated the state's slaves in January 1865 and subsequently took control of the state through a new constitution with a restrictive registration law and ironclad loyalty oath. In Kentucky, by contrast, conservative Unionist political leaders refused to embrace emancipation, even after the war ended in April 1865. Pro-slavery Unionists joined with returning Confederates to take full control of the Commonwealth of Kentucky under the auspices of the revitalized Democratic Party. Only passage of the Thirteenth Amendment in December 1865 ended slavery in the Bluegrass State, with many former Unionists feeling betrayed by the emancipationist turn of the war.

These surface differences belie an underlying shift in the sentiment of conservative Unionists in both states. In many ways, the distinction between the two states' experiences has more to do with how white Unionists felt toward white Confederates—punitive in Missouri and forbearing in Kentucky—than with white Unionist attitudes toward the freed slaves. To be sure, Missouri Unionists were more likely to embrace emancipation itself than were their counterparts in Kentucky. This was true even of key central Missourians like Congressman James Rollins, a slaveholding, conservative Unionist who came to accept emancipation as a war aim and provided a crucial vote for passage of the Thirteenth Amendment in 1865.[3] And Missouri did, in fact, establish a modicum of civil rights protections, including state-funded public education and the right to testify in court, that Kentucky rejected. But this occurred only after vigorous objection from within the Unionist coalition; enforcement of black civil rights would receive only lukewarm support at home. On black suffrage, both Kentucky Conservative Democrats and Missouri Radical Republicans opposed it.

But what of that "last great union victory" touted by the *Holt County Sentinel*—passage of the Civil Rights Act of 1866—that Missouri's congressional delegation supported in Washington? Why would passage of the act have been celebrated as such, even though the state's Radicals were never fully committed to enforcement of legal equality at home? The answer may have to do with the provenance of the Civil Rights Act nationally, which grew out of anger at passage of Black Codes by President Johnson's restored state governments in the former Confederate states of the lower South. The Black Codes signified a desire to restore slavery in all but name, which infuriated Republicans and fueled resentment against Johnson's lenient Reconstruction policy. The Civil Rights Act of 1866 provided federal protection for the legal rights of ex-slaves and defended the privileges and immunities of citizenship equally across the land.

Missouri Radicals were generally of two minds on civil rights. They supported the act as a way to counter the reemergence of the planter class that had dominant southern, and Missouri, politics for decades. But they were not as enthusiastic when it came to inscribing black Missourians' vision of a biracial republic into law at home. Controversy over the act's passage and enforcement would help fracture the Radical state coalition and would ultimately drive Missouri Radicals from power in 1870.[4] Not surprisingly, white Kentuckians who rejected emancipation as a war aim even after Appomattox found little or nothing beneficial in the Civil Rights Act. Not only did they reject the Civil Rights Act out of hand, but Kentucky U.S. senator Garrett Davis took the legislative lead in Washington in opposing the act. Returning Confederates used opposition to the Civil Rights Act and the Freedmen's Bureau as a cudgel against the state's Unionist majority. By the middle of 1866, most Unionists joined ex-Confederates in opposing the law and the principles that underlay it. But, as in Missouri, white Kentuckians found themselves in a conundrum. The act effectively removed many criminal cases from state jurisdiction, leaving Kentucky's ruling Democrats with the choice of whether to provide testimony rights to blacks—and thus relieve the state of federal interference—or to continue to resist as a matter of principle. As in Missouri, these divisions would play an important role in determining the state's future political and even economic course. "New Departure" Democrats accepted the reality of the act and sought a railroad-based development of the state's mining and manufacturing industries. At the same time, Kentucky's Bourbon Democratic leaders challenged the Civil Rights Act in a hideous racial murder case that reached the Supreme Court as *Blyew v. United States* in

1871. Conservative Democrats agreed to change Kentucky law in 1872 to allow black testimony just as the Supreme Court used the *Blyew* decision to neuter the federal Civil Rights Act.[5]

Politicians within and from Kentucky and Missouri were tasked with two interrelated considerations with respect to the Civil Rights Act. First, did the act make sense on the merits? Did African American ex-slaves deserve the same protection of the law as white citizens? The second consideration was jurisdictional: Was the federal government the appropriate vehicle for the protection of civil rights? And if so, what would that mean for former slave states that never left the Union and were not subject to "punishment" through Reconstruction legislation? Both of these considerations hinge on the nature of emancipation in the two states and the statewide political realignments that both fueled emancipation and were shaped by it. The outcome was significant for the border states and beyond. The tensions and contradictions within Kentucky and Missouri over the Civil Rights Act of 1866 revealed grassroots political tactics, rhetorical strategies, and legal maneuverings that would appear over the next ten years across the entire nation. In the end, continued white supremacist intransigence paid dividends, as white Kentuckians and Missourians showcased for ex-Confederates and racially conservative northerners and westerners how subterfuge, violence, and deployment of "states' rights" discourse could undermine any egalitarian program from Washington.

CONSERVATIVE UNIONISM AND EMANCIPATION IN KENTUCKY AND MISSOURI

The rise of conservative, proslavery Unionism in Kentucky during the late antebellum era resulted, in many ways, from the transfer of a diversified, small slaveholding class westward from Virginia. What historian Barbara Fields referred to as the "Middle Ground," a society materially based on small-scale slavery, diversified agricultural holdings, and widespread slave hiring, reemerged in large part across Kentucky and directly informed the development of conservative Unionist political culture. The local tensions and rhythms of border-state society and the national political context of late-antebellum America encouraged white Kentuckians to articulate a specific set of social values that conveyed the fears and aspirations of the small slaveholding class. These values privileged stability, pragmatism, compromise, and tradition over ideological rigidity and sectional honor and so helped solidify the region's embrace of conservative Unionism with the outbreak of the Civil War.[6]

The social structure of Kentucky and Missouri slavery facilitated such a political culture. Dispersed smallholdings, diversified farming, and slave hiring characterized the antebellum Kentucky and Missouri countryside, just as they did in much of colonial Virginia. The smallholdings consisted of farms with a mixed labor force made up of male household members, hired laborers, and slaves. The relatively dispersed slave population did not mean that white exposure to the slave system was rare. Nor did it indicate that slaveholders were statistically marginal elements among the white male voting population. To the contrary, dispersed smallholdings simply indicated a higher number of slaveholders and, more important, white family members living in households headed by slaveholders. By the time of the Civil War, Kentucky had more slaveholders than any state in the Union outside of Georgia and Virginia.[7]

Slavery imposed a distinct racial order that few in the border states dared threaten. Though some offered relatively tepid defenses of slavery, nearly all white Kentuckians and Missourians feared social chaos and the demise of white civilization if the slave population were to be liberated at once. If any ideal characterized late antebellum border-state life more than any other, it was the desire for order—social, economic, racial, and ultimately political order. The thirst for order in a region challenged by both abolitionism and secessionism stood as the central pillar to antebellum Upper South social thought. It would trump all concerns about sectional honor in the ensuing crisis, revealing a population that embraced slavery and union.

At the heart of Kentucky and Missouri values was white supremacy, or more specifically a belief that Western civilization was a product of characteristics unique to the white race and that all interracial relationships must protect the white race from subjugation or degradation by the black race. Failing to hold the line against attempts at racial equality would yield nothing less than complete reversion to barbarism, which white people believed inevitable wherever black people lived without white authority. Most white northerners and southerners agreed with this racial order, but each section preserved white supremacy differently. Northerners simply excluded African Americans outright—states like Indiana and Illinois legally banned black people from entering in 1860, and many other states placed onerous taxes on black individuals who could not prove employment or property ownership—or, failing that, they segregated black and white populations in all facets of social and economic life. White northerners protected white supremacy by monopolizing the property, power, and labor force of the northern states. White southerners, living amid populations that often included large majorities of African Americans, embraced slavery as the natural system of racial and social control. Without slavery, white southerners feared, black people would literally overrun and destroy white civilization, recreating either Haiti or Africa itself.[8]

White citizens in Kentucky and Missouri accepted a form of white supremacist ideology that fit the culture of border slave life. The slave system naturally produced excess slaves not needed to work the fields and factories, and slaveholders sought a means to control these residual slaves. Kentucky and Missouri slaveholders either manumitted or, more commonly, sold to the Deep South their excess slaves. Where manumission occurred, it took place very slowly and under the tight control of former masters. A small free black population emerged in larger towns and cities like Danville, Louisville, Columbia, St. Louis, and Lexington, but it never grew to the size it had attained in the eastern border states of Maryland and Delaware, where more than half the black population was free by 1860. Moreover, the free black population in Kentucky and Missouri remained closely tied to white patrons who posted bond for ex-slaves' rights to remain in the state. Free black persons also possessed few legal rights. In 1860 both states reaffirmed that free African Americans could not testify in court cases involving white citizens, an issue that would prove critical in the later arguments over the Civil Rights Act. The apologists and critics of slavery in Kentucky and Missouri might have differed as to the efficiency, fairness, or productivity of the slave system, but they all agreed that emancipation without complete colonization would result in total social chaos and very possibly the demise of civilization as they knew it.

The embrace of slavery and union persisted in Kentucky even as the state abandoned neutrality and entered the Civil War on behalf of the Union in September 1861. Sensitive to the demands from conservative Unionists that emancipation be forestalled in Kentucky, federal military and civilian leaders countermanded premature emancipation edicts (especially from General John C. Frémont, exempted the state from the Emancipation Proclamation, and delayed black soldier enlistment until as late as July 1864. The stakes were too high, as Lincoln believed, to risk losing his native state to the slaveholders' Confederacy. "I think to lose Kentucky is nearly the same as to lose the whole game. Kentucky gone, we can not hold Missouri, nor, as I think, Maryland. These all against us, and the job on our hands is too large for us. We would as well consent to separation at once, including the surrender of this capitol."[9]

What destroyed slavery in Kentucky, in the end, was the large-scale abandonment of farms and households by the slaves themselves. Drawing from decades of kin-based networks of resistance, slaves sensed the weak points in Kentucky's wartime slave system—patrols off duty, midwestern troops hostile to the institution, guerrilla depredations that undermined social cohesion, uncertain authority between state and military personnel—and exploited it en masse in 1864. By the end of the war, 57 percent of military-age black men in Kentucky served in the Union army, more than in any other state. Enlistment centers like Camp Nelson welcomed tens of thousands of slaves who would have found no other path to freedom.[10]

For conservative Unionist Kentuckians, emancipation unfolded like a sordid act of betrayal. Most white Kentuckians bitterly resented the implication that slavery must die if the Union were to survive. As the war came to an end and returning Confederates mocked their Unionist foes for failing to perceive Lincoln's emancipationist program, the two sides effectively reconciled on the common basis of white supremacy. They turned bitterly against the black population of the state, unleashing a wave of violence that forced thousands of black Kentuckians off their farms and into the growing cities of Lexington and Louisville. When protests against emancipation failed to stop its course and the Thirteenth Amendment headed toward ratification in 1865, many demoralized Kentucky conservative Unionists sought compensation for the loss of their slave property. By late December 1865, the Thirteenth Amendment finally ended slavery in Kentucky, and state legislators were tasked with the development of a new legal code to shape the different relationship between former slave and former slaveholder. Though the new laws would prohibit black testimony in court cases—a key provision in the federal Civil Rights Act of 1866—Kentucky legislators insisted on calling this new legal code "an act conferring certain civil rights upon negroes and mulattoes."[11] It was not exactly what the Republicans in Washington had in mind when they called their own bill by the same name. But it reflected the maximum freedom white Kentuckians would tolerate for ex-slaves, especially as many of their masters were Unionists who viewed emancipation itself as unwarranted, unconstitutional, and dangerous.

On one level, Missouri experienced a similar pattern of responses to emancipation as did Kentucky. Conservative Unionists took control of Missouri's provisional wartime government in July 1861 and attempted to forestall emancipation as long as practicable. Unlike in Kentucky, however, this conservative Unionist center could not hold out for long. It faced an increasingly vicious Confederate insurgency, based among the Little Dixie slaveholders caught behind Union lines. Failed efforts at counterinsurgency embittered much of the state's Unionist population and fueled increasing calls for total war, and even emancipation, to root out the Confederate bushwhackers once and for all. But there was a preexisting population already suspicious of the power of the Little Dixie slaveholders: the burgeoning German immigrant population along the south bank of the Missouri River, along the Mississippi River to the south of St. Louis, and in St. Louis itself. Many of them 1848 revolution émigrés, Missouri Germans formed the basis of the state's prewar Republican Party and pushed for a more radical antislavery turn in war policy shortly after the war began.[12] They, along with Missouri slaves themselves, would be instrumental in pushing the state toward emancipation.[13]

At first, Missouri flirted with outright secession. Its pro-Confederate governor, Claiborne Fox Jackson of Little Dixie's Howard County, hoped to lure the federal army to invade the state from Illinois and then to capture arms being secured from the Confederacy. This "passive-aggressive" approach nearly paid off as a "riot" in St. Louis in May 1861 touched off violence throughout the state.[14] Jackson's own militia, the Missouri State Guard, seized federal installations in preparation for secession, despite the fact that a convention called to consider secession had soundly defeated it in February. After a truce between federal and State Guard leaders failed in late May, federal General Nathanial Lyon met with Governor Jackson and General Sterling Price of the State Guard at the Planters House on June 12, 1861. Frustrated at the temerity of state leaders to resist federal authority, Lyon declared,

> Rather than concede to the State of Missouri for one single instant the right to dictate to my Government in any matter however unimportant, I would (rising as he said this and pointing in turn to every one in the room) see you, and you, and you, and you, and every man, woman, and child in the State, dead and buried. . . . This means war. In an hour one of my officers will call for you and conduct you out of my lines.[15]

The Union army proceeded up the Missouri River, captured the capitol at Jefferson City, and routed the Missouri State Guard at Boonville. Governor Jackson fled the state with his secessionist allies in tow. Despite successful Confederate military efforts at Wilson's Creek and at Lexington, the Confederate army effectively abandoned the heavily enslaved Little

Dixie region of central Missouri from the fall of 1861 onward. Secession supporters were then trapped behind Union lines and resorted to a desperate guerrilla war that quickly escalated beyond the control of Union or Confederate authorities.[16]

Meanwhile, the Missourians who had met in a February 1861 convention to consider—and soundly defeat—a secession proposal from Governor Jackson reconvened in July 1861 and declared Hamilton Gamble to be the state's new "Provisional Governor."[17] The Lincoln administration recognized this provisional government as the official state government until 1865, when a new constitution was drafted. At first, conservative Unionists, who vowed to protect slavery while authorizing several new Unionist militias to stamp out bushwhacker violence, dominated the provisional government. By late 1862, however, the center of power within the provisional government began to shift in a radical direction as the increasingly desperate guerrilla war across Missouri convinced the state's Unionists to fight the Confederate supporters more aggressively.[18] Though exempt from the Emancipation Proclamation, most Missouri Unionists recognized that slavery was doomed and so debated the best course of action to eliminate it. The "Claybank" faction around Gamble and his successor, Willard Hall, supported a gradual emancipation plan, coupled with compensation for slaveholders and colonization of freed slaves. So-called Charcoals, led by Charles Drake and many German Missourians, called for total and immediate emancipation with the hopes of eliminating the source of rebel strength once and for all. Ultimately, the Charcoal faction emerged victorious, a statewide election resulted in Radical Thomas Fletcher taking the governorship, and the state officially ended slavery on January 11, 1865.[19]

As both Claybanks and Charcoals understood, however, Missouri's slaves had played an active role in undermining the slave system. Like their Kentucky compatriots, Missouri slaves exploited weaknesses in the slave policing system, fled to provost marshal posts and to neighboring Kansas, and entered the Union army in droves in 1863. Henry Clay Bruce, a former slave in Chariton County, detailed the network of communication through which slaves living on small, scattered farms passed news of federal troop activity and the changing politics of war to fellow slaves throughout central Missouri.

> The Colored people could meet and talk over what they had heard about the latest battle, and what Mr. Lincoln had said, and the chances of their freedom. . . . When the news came that a battle was fought and won by Union troops, they rejoiced, and were correspondingly

> depressed when they saw their masters rejoicing. . . . Slaves who could read and could buy newspapers, thereby obtained the latest news and kept their friends posted, and from mouth to ear the news was carried from farm to farm, without the knowledge of masters.

This news included the prospects for emancipation as the war unfolded. "After the war commenced . . . it was not safe for patrols to be out hunting Negroes, and the system came to an end, never to be revived."[20]

In early 1865 Radical Republicans under Drake drafted a new state constitution with the hopes of altering the social structure of Missouri for good, from one based on slaveholding Little Dixie tobacco and hemp farmers to a more industrial system centered in St. Louis and the emerging livestock and railroad center at Kansas City. Radicals developed an ironclad loyalty oath and registration system that effectively disenfranchised all ex-Confederates, and they removed all non-Unionists from professions like teaching and the law. But on the racial violence exploding across the Missouri landscape in the last months of the war and the civil rights of ex-slaves in general, however, the new Radicals would pay mostly lip service.

RACIAL VIOLENCE AND BLACK TESTIMONY

In both Kentucky and Missouri, the emancipation process stimulated increasing levels of racial violence as the war drew to a close. This was especially true in Kentucky, where slaveholders held on to the peculiar institution with more vigor than anywhere else in the South. Much of the violence targeted black soldiers at first but then spread to the rest of the African American community. Because the slave code remained in full effect in Kentucky until passage of the Thirteenth Amendment in December 1865, slaves seeking the safety of enlistment camps were considered runaways under Kentucky law, regardless of the presence of Union troops or the state's official standing within the Union. As a result, slave enlistees were treated by law and by custom as runaways. Violence against them reflected the slave patrol system that governed the movement of slaves in the antebellum era. For example, near Lebanon in June 1864, two "boys" named James and Jasper Edwards walking on the road to the enlistment center in town encountered an Irish immigrant named Michael McMann, who accosted them and cut off their ears.[21] An officer at the Lebanon post immediately arrested McMann and an accomplice named William Burns, though only McMann was positively identified by the "boys" as the assailant. Mutilation of the recruits undoubtedly served to intimidate others who considered joining the military. It hardly went unnoticed that cutting off ears was an occasional punishment of slave runaways by slave patrols. McMann, who likely served as a slave patroller in the community around Lebanon, maintained full civil authority to inflict whatever punishment upon slave runaways he deemed appropriate, including bodily mutilation.

White citizens angry at black soldier enlistment also directed their violence at the families of recruits. The wife of a black recruit appeared before the office of Hiram Cornell, an assistant provost marshal in Fulton, Missouri, and reported that she and one of her children were severely beaten and driven from her home by her master. She asked to follow her husband into the army, offering to work at the camp if necessary. The black recruit, unable to protect his wife and children from the master's assault—either at home or in the army camp—faced a dilemma that would survive the war. Violence against the families of recruits continued as long as black soldiers served in the army—and in many cases these kinds of attacks lasted until late 1866. Masters also attacked slave families because the labor value of the remaining women and children did not warrant further support for them. In the Fulton case, the slave owner was an "aged man" and had already complained to the army that he could not afford to feed and clothe the remaining slaves. Ironically, earlier in the war, masters despised the Union army for luring their slaves away. Yet, once they decided to rid themselves of their remaining slave property, the army proved an inviting destination.

White individuals in central Missouri and Kentucky regularly harassed, intimidated, and attacked black recruits en route to enlistment camps to prevent them from entering the army. They also assaulted black soldiers already in uniform carrying out their duties, especially when on guard or traveling through the border countryside. In Woodford County, Kentucky, which held the largest percentage of slaves of any Kentucky county in 1860, a black soldier transporting official army dispatches was stopped by a man who stole his bridles, led him for two miles into the woods, and shot him.[22] The murderer, identified by witnesses as a man named Maddox, told the toll-keeper guarding the road that he intended to kill the black soldier. According to the toll-keeper, the only reason Maddox killed the soldier was that he was black and wearing a federal uniform. Black men in uniform, like the Woodford County soldier, represented an affront to prevailing white conceptions of citizenship.

With Missouri formally abolishing slavery in the war's final months, bushwhackers and other rebel sympathizers transformed their existing practice of threatening African Americans who joined the military into a generalized terror campaign. The purpose of this campaign was the expulsion of black people from the border states. Near Columbia, Missouri, and just days after Captain H. A. Cook found an elderly black man hanged by Jim Jackson's gang, Union troops discovered another black man murdered by Jackson. According to the Union officer present, Jackson's men had threatened "that all blacks were to leave in 10 days or be killed by them." The officer noted that most black men from the vicinity were already serving in the army, leaving behind the "unarmed and helpless" in a state of "terrible alarm."[23] With the abolition of slavery in Missouri, bushwhackers who once threatened violence against slaves escaping their masters now used terror and violence to remove all remaining African Americans from the region.

Violence in both states continued in the years following the war's completion, with so-called Regulators joining other paramilitary organizations like "Skaggs' Men" and the Ku Klux Klan to terrorize black Kentuckians and Missourians. The purpose was generally to intimidate African Americans to the point of leaving, as their labor was no longer deemed essential to the economy and their presence as freed and unsupervised people was considered threatening to the social order. Sometime the violence would take the shape of nighttime raids of black homes and other times involved very public lynch mobs. In both states it was clear that without the protection of the law, including especially the right to testify in court against white assailants, there would be no protection from racial violence. Of all the civil rights guaranteed by the federal Civil Rights Act of 1866, the right to serve as witnesses in criminal cases stood paramount in the eyes of African Americans of all classes.

Kentucky's continuing refusal to allow black testimony played a central role in the Freedmen's Bureau's presence in the state. Just after ratification of the Thirteenth Amendment in December 1865, Clinton B. Fisk, commissioner for the District of Tennessee, issued a circular declaring the bureau in force in Kentucky. The bureau established courts in the state to adjudicate all cases involving black and white individuals. Governor Thomas Bramlette responded to the bureau's circular by calling on the state legislature to repeal Kentucky's slave code and allow black people to testify against white people in court. But the legislature balked at Bramlette's request, passing instead a more conservative "Civil Rights" act that allowed African Americans to bring charges for prosecution against white citizens but prohibited them from serving as witnesses, even when a white person had committed a crime against them. Only the Freedmen's Bureau, empowered by the federal Civil Rights Act and a new bureau authorization act passed over President Johnson's veto, could provide any semblance of justice for African Americans left completely helpless by Kentucky's state law. Kentucky state courts curtailed the authority of the new bureau courts whenever possible.[24]

Lawsuits challenging the constitutionality of bureau courts when civil courts were otherwise present succeeded in driving the bureau courts out of the state. In one such case in Lexington, a white man beat a black man, William Roberts, with a gun as Roberts was returning to town. According to the victim, the white perpetrator, named Thomas Outten, told Roberts, "I have got to shoot a parcel of you God damned niggers running about all night. They have shot old Lincoln and I am going to kill about half of you damned niggers." Outten was convicted by the federal judge advocate general based on Roberts's testimony and fined ten dollars. Outten's attorney appealed, declaring that the judge advocate general had no jurisdiction in Kentucky because the civil courts still functioned; an 1866 U.S. Supreme Court ruling in the *Ex Parte Milligan* case declared all military tribunals unconstitutional so long as a functioning civil court system existed. In accordance with this ruling, the federal district court in Kentucky declared that *Milligan* prohibited the use of bureau courts in the state and that state courts remained in effect. After Outten's successful appeal of this under the *Milligan* ruling, black people could testify only in federal district court subject to the federal Civil Rights Act and in the state court of Fayette County under Republican judge William C. Goodloe.[25]

With Freedmen's Bureau military tribunals outlawed, the bureau helped remove cases from the state courts to the federal courts, but only after state courts refused to hear black testimony. Bureau commissioner Fisk initiated this policy after a highly publicized case involving a white man named James Poore who shot and killed a black man named Peter Branford in Boyle County in 1866. Before a civil trial could begin, Judge Goodloe ordered Poore to be arrested and placed in Camp Nelson for military trial. After widespread outrage and near unanimous passage of a resolution in the Kentucky legislature condemning Fisk and Goodloe, Fisk ordered that Poore be released to civil authorities but to be rearrested if the black witness's testimony was refused. "Let this be the rule in similar cases," Fisk informed the local bureau agent in Danville. Knowing that the only witness available was an African American, Governor Bramlette pardoned Poore without a civil trial. The whole affair completely soured Fisk and the bureau on the willingness of the state to budge on the testimony question. After 1867 Fisk instructed bureau agents to help hundreds of African Americans try cases against white individuals in federal courts and to initiate indictments against state judges for refusing to adhere to the Civil Rights Act.[26]

This entire sequence of events reveals precisely why Kentucky's congressional delegation opposed passage of the federal Civil Rights Act of 1866 in the first place. The act made permanent the shift of authority from state courts to federal courts, unless Kentucky's state courts adhered to federal procedures that its own citizens had rejected. That this loss of state sovereignty would befall a state that had remained loyal to the Union struck many Kentucky leaders as especially galling. To punish a rebellious state, or even rebels within a Union state, by placing criminal cases under federal jurisdiction might have made sense to conservative Unionists. Governor Bramlette had little sympathy for Confederate civilians complaining about martial law in the war's final months. But to overrule Kentucky's state courts because of restrictions against black testimony made no sense to those conservative Unionists who never believed African Americans deserved anything more than the faintest tincture of freedom.

GARRETT DAVIS AND KENTUCKY'S CONSERVATIVE UNIONISTS

No Kentucky politician better captured the spirit of conservative Unionism and subsequent opposition to the Civil Rights Act than Garrett Davis, the Bourbon Countian who became a U.S. senator and a chief opponent of the act in 1866. In fact, as historian Christopher Waldrep has suggested, Garrett Davis may signify a kind of deep-seated Constitutional, conservative Unionism that cast the entire Reconstruction project in doubt from the beginning and that was far more nationally present than historians have appreciated. What is essential about Davis is his similarity to other border South and lower North politicians until 1863.[27] A longtime Whig with a congressional career largely mirroring that of Kentucky-born Abraham Lincoln, Garrett Davis uttered some of the strongest statements in support of the Union in the state in 1861. The Union, Davis argued, provided "the freest government on earth, one that was devised by the wisest and most virtuous men, and in the full development of a glory and grandeur which the most fertile imagination could not grasp, every citizen prosperous and blessed with the mildest, happiest, and most benignant institutions ever known."[28]

Just as important, the Union allowed Kentuckians to live in peace alongside the free states of the Old Northwest, a prospect that would surely be undermined in the event of secession. "Kentucky has almost peopled the northwestern states, especially Indiana and Illinois. I have no doubt that one fourth of the people of Indiana are either native-born Kentuckians or the sons and daughters of native-born Kentuckians. They are bone of our bone and flesh of our flesh," he pointed out. The political ramifications of these kin ties across the Ohio River were clear, as one Kentuckian remarked, "What can she do by secession but make war upon the people of Indiana and Illinois many of whom Kentucky gave birth to."[29]

As the war unfolded and the Lincoln administration began the process of military emancipation, including the enlistment of African Americans in the Union army, Davis joined his fellow Unionists in condemning the move as unconstitutional, unnecessary, and revolutionary—exactly the sort of language he deployed against the secessionists. By January 1865, Davis came out strongly against the Thirteenth Amendment abolishing slavery, even as other conservative Unionists like Governor Bramlette and former governor Beriah Magoffin supported it. Davis lambasted the efforts of General John Palmer to issue emancipation papers to enslaved Kentuckians in the summer of 1865 and sought legal redress against the federal government up to the very ratification of the amendment in December. In a speech in Paris, Kentucky, in the summer of 1865, Davis warned that the amendment would "elevate the negro to all the social and civil rights of a citizen."[30] He simply never accepted the legitimacy of emancipation as a war measure, especially against a loyal state. A new "Conservative Union" Party that appeared in 1865, and that garnered support from Davis and his allies before they migrated to the Democratic Party, contained a plank that stated, "No power has been delegated by the constitution to the government of the United States to emancipate the slaves of any State."[31] Davis added that the Thirteenth Amendment was more an act of revolution than a proper amendment and so was null and void: "There is a boundary between the power of revolution and the power of amendment, which the latter, as established in our Constitution, cannot pass; and that if the proposed change is revolutionary it would be null and void, notwithstanding it might be formally adopted."[32] The new amendment had so altered the relationship between the federal and state governments on a matter of vital importance that Davis cast doubt upon the legitimacy of the amendment in American law.

Overruled in the ratification debate, Davis then assumed the leading role in the Senate debate on the newly proposed Civil Rights Act in January 1866 and again in the debates to override President Johnson's veto of the bill in April of that year. Davis's position articulated in the Senate not only reflected his oft-pronounced opinions at home but also represented quite fairly the broad opinion of white Kentuckians on civil rights and on Reconstruction as a whole.

Davis raised both structural and substantive objections to the Civil Rights Act. His structural objections matched those he raised against the Thirteenth Amendment, namely that the federal Congress simply did not have the power to redefine "citizenship" or overrule the state laws on matters of regular jurisprudence. Central to this structural argument was the insistence that the Constitution was formed solely for the benefit of white men and that "the fundamental, original and universal principle upon which our system of government rests, is that it was founded by and for white men; that it has always belonged to and been managed by white men; and that to preserve and administer it now and forever is the right and mission of the white man." Whiteness overruled every other consideration, as Davis continued: "When a negro or Chinaman is attempted to be obtruded into it, the sufficient cause to repel him is that he is a negro or Chinaman."[33]

Davis focused most of his opposition on the citizenship clause because, as he conceded, "if the proposition be true that a negro is a citizen, I concede that he is entitled to every right, every privilege, and every immunity to which a white citizen is entitled under the Constitution."[34] His objection to citizenship for African Americans, clearly stated as based in racial consideration (and not previous condition of servitude), meant that Congress could not apply a Civil Rights Act to Kentucky under the Constitution. Rejecting the argument that the enforcement clause of the Thirteenth Amendment authorized such an act, Davis proceeded to lay out the typical fears expressed by opponents throughout the country at the time: that a Civil Rights Act would lead inexorably to "social equality" and "miscegenation," that it would violate the property rights and traditions of peaceable citizens, and that it would elevate an "ignorant class of men" to the witness box where their testimony would be deemed as worthy as that of white individuals, "despite their character." Kentucky's emerging political consensus among returning ex-Confederates and conservative Unionists—coalescing behind a reinvigorated Democratic Party—supported Davis in opposition to the act. The *Kentucky Gazette* of Lexington referred to the "Negro elevation schemes of the Jacobin Congress" and hoped that the state's political leaders would emulate the old Missouri Unionist Frank Blair, who had become vehemently conservative following the war's conclusion.[35]

Kentucky's congressional delegation ultimately failed to prevent passage of the Civil Rights Act over President Johnson's veto or to hold off the subsequent Fourteenth Amendment. More important, the state legislature refused to change state law, despite increasing pressures from a business-oriented "New Departure" wing of the Democratic Party to allow black testimony. The continued presence of federal authority in a "loyal" state applied pressure on Kentucky's ruling Democrats to give in. Though some Democrats—including former Confederates like W. C. P. Breckinridge of Fayette County and J. Warren Grigsby of Boyle County—and many Democratic newspapers supported allowing black testimony, conservatives prevailed. The state legislature refused to alter its law in 1867 and then again in 1869. The federal-state crisis empowered the more hawkish conservative Democrats for the time being.

Kentucky conservatives expressed little sympathy for black victims of racial violence, choosing instead to separate out the "real" Regulators and Ku Klux Klan from the "so-called" ones who soiled the paramilitary movement's name. Even more telling was the mockery applied to black Kentuckians who sought the protections of the Civil Rights Act. Just three months after the law's passage, the *Kentucky Gazette* reported on a "negro man [who] coolly seated himself at the table of the Shelton House" in Versailles to order supper. The proprietor, "not having the fear of Charles Sumner and Thad. Stevens before him," violently ejected the man from his restaurant and threw him upon the sidewalk. Afterward, "the scene was drawn to a close by Cuffee's receiving a pretty severe drubbing, and afterwards being lodged in jail for disorderly conduct."[36] The newspaper titled the article "'Civil Rights' at a Discount," revealing the contempt white Kentuckians held for the law. The proprietor of the Shelton House executed in deed what Garrett Davis articulated in word in the U.S. Senate: that African Americans had no rights to equal justice under the law.

BLYEW AND THE CIVIL RIGHTS ACT ON TRIAL IN KENTUCKY

In 1868, Kentucky's ruling conservative Democrats finally found a case that could serve as a vehicle to challenge the constitutionality of the Civil Rights Act of 1866: *Blyew v. United States.* Considering Kentucky's steadfast refusal to allow black testimony in criminal cases involving whites, the ongoing epidemic of racial violence against African Americans in the state, and the Freedmen's Bureau's insistence upon removing racial violence cases to federal court, a Civil Rights Act test case was bound to emerge from within the Bluegrass State. In this instance, two white men named John Blyew and George Kennard brutally murdered three African Americans in Lewis County, Kentucky, in August 1868, with a fourth victim passing away a few days later.[37] The only testimony available for the case came from the dying victim and from an eight-year-old girl who had hidden from the assailants. Both were African American and thus unable to testify against Blyew and Kennard. Consequently, the U.S. district court under Judge Bland Ballard tried the case under the auspices of the Civil Rights Act. The federal court jury, though all white, accepted the black testimony and voted to convict the murderers and sentence them to death.

As R. Owen Williams discusses later in this volume, Kentucky's appeal in the *Blyew* case hinged on the question of who was an "affected party" under the Civil Rights Act. Since the victims were deceased and so could not be considered "affected parties" in the ongoing trial, the case turned on whether or not living witnesses count as "affected parties." In other words, did the Civil Rights Act of 1866 apply to witnesses in criminal cases as well as to defendants? Because of Kentucky's ban on black witness testimony in interracial criminal cases, African Americans and Freedmen's Bureau officials demanded that white-on-black murder cases in which the only available witnesses were black survivors be removed to federal court. The Supreme Court, in one of the first cases undermining the federal government's ability to protect the civil rights of African Americans, sided with Kentucky and voided the lower federal court ruling that declared Blyew and Kennard guilty. The Court stated that witnesses to crimes could not be considered under the protection of the Civil Rights Act as "affected persons," and thus Blyew and Kennard should not have been tried in a federal court.[38]

The jurisdictional argument made by the state of Kentucky is noteworthy for its utter contempt for the testimony rights of African Americans. The state legislature instructed Governor James Stevenson to employ state's attorneys to take up the appeal as a writ of error to the circuit court for the District of Kentucky on behalf of Blyew and Kennard to the Supreme Court.[39] Two attorneys, J. S. Black and I. Caldwell, were hired by the state of Kentucky to take up the appeal. They argued that if the "affected persons" clause of the Civil Rights Act were to include witnesses, then virtually every case in Kentucky where even a single African American was present could be removed to federal court.[40] In mocking tone, Black and Caldwell complained, "If a negro robbed a hen-roost, the suffering party was now obliged either to let him go unpunished or to take him for justice to wherever the Federal court sat, often hundreds of miles off."[41] Instead of providing protection to black people whose testimony was disallowed under Kentucky law, the Civil Rights Act resulted in "nine-tenths of the lower class of crimes committed by negroes" now going "unpunished in Kentucky." Alas, the Civil Rights Act had "dislocated all the machinery of the State courts and rendered them powerless to perform their duty."[42] Pushing this logic, Black and Caldwell noted that even cases involving only white citizens could easily be removed to federal courts under the Civil Rights Act. "If a fight take place between white men at a barbecue, or militia muster, or cross-roads meeting—though it concern nobody but white men—they cannot be indicted for offense in any court of Kentucky if one single negro in the whole crowd saw the thing done."[43] The logic of including all witnesses as "affected persons"—even if the affected were victims of crime—must "necessarily lead" to such an outcome. Continuing, Black and Caldwell claimed it would be an "insult" to the "dignity" of Kentucky and an "outrage on the peace of a community" if a murder trial involving a Kentucky citizen were removed from state courts. The state's attorneys suggested that the federal government had no jurisdiction whatsoever involving a murder case within Kentucky as an in-state murder was "no more an offense against the United States than it was against the republic of France or the empire of Germany."[44]

The real question, however, is why Kentucky continued to pursue this case on appeal, even though the state had finally come around to passing a black testimony law by 1872 and state prosecutors had generally accepted the principle of it as early as 1868 (even if so-called New Departure Democrats could not yet muster a majority to change the law in the state legislature). More than anything else, Kentucky's appeal of the *Blyew* case revealed the intensity of opposition to the entire Reconstruction program and the clear linkage between state sovereignty and white supremacy. So confident were Black and Caldwell in the jurisdictional argument at hand that they did not even bother to defend the 1860 state law banning black testimony. They saw no need to discuss the constitutionality of that state law because they viewed the federal government as having no jurisdiction to intervene in state laws, even though the Fourteenth Amendment had been ratified just one month prior to the murder of the Fosters. To Black, Caldwell, and the Democratic leadership of Kentucky, the scope and constitutionality of the federal Civil Rights Act of 1866 was the only issue at hand for the Supreme Court to consider, not a Kentucky law governing crimes against the state of Kentucky.

MISSOURI: SUPPORT FOR THE ACT IN D.C., LESS AT HOME

Though Missouri produced many conservative Unionists of note, like Frank Blair and James Rollins, the state's Radical Republicans sent two supporters of emancipation and black civil rights to the U.S. Senate in 1865 and 1866. John Henderson had moved from conservatism to Radicalism as a result of the war itself and even helped draft the Thirteenth Amendment. B. Gratz Brown, the other senator, had been one of Missouri's, and the nation's, signature Radical Republicans from the very beginning. A long-standing emancipationist with deep support among the German émigré community of St. Louis, Brown edited the banner Radical newspaper, the *Missouri Democrat,* and pushed for immediate emancipation, full civil rights, and black suffrage. Brown did not speak much during the debates over the Civil Rights Act of 1866, but his remarks concerning Reconstruction generally suggested his support for a far more vigorous civil rights bill than the one enacted. His commentary—"I never would vote for . . . any . . . bill that did not guaranty that class of citizens, the loyal colored population of the south, a right of suffrage"[45]—goes so far as to assume the citizenship status of African Americans, which lay at the heart of the Civil Rights Act debate. He could not have been more opposed to the principles of Kentucky's Garrett Davis.

Back in Missouri, the Drake-led Radical constitutional convention issued a Declaration of Rights, Section 3 of which read,

> No person can, on account of color, be disqualified as a witness, or be disabled to contract, or be prevented from acquiring, holding, or transmitting property; or be liable to any other punishment, for any offense, than that imposed on others for a like offense; or be restricted in the exercise of religious worship, or be hindered in receiving an education; or be subjected in law to any other restraints, or disqualifications, in regard to any personal rights, than such as are laid upon others under like circumstances.[46]

On the surface it would appear that Missouri Radicals were prepared to enact B. Gratz Brown's vision for a biracial republic into the state's new constitution. But opposition to these civil rights, not to mention suffrage, was intense, even among self-described Radicals. John Fletcher, the brother of Radical governor Thomas Fletcher, commented that he came to the convention "to represent white men, and to legislate for the benefit of the white men of Missouri." Sounding more like Garrett Davis than his own brother, Fletcher continued, "I am not here for the purpose of giving any rights to the negro further than the right of freedom." But then he settled upon a formula that had more wide-ranging appeal among Missourians than Brown's radical notions: "I desired to see every slave in the State freed, and I desire to see every slave in the country free, but when they are free, I am done with them."[47] This minimalist position regarding the rights of ex-slaves—freedom and nothing else—found support among the mass of conservative Unionists who accepted the fate of emancipation but feared a social revolution beyond that. Fletcher specifically opposed the extension of black testimony rights in interracial cases "until the Negro had at least been educated."[48] Though John Fletcher's protests were overruled and Section 3 was adopted in full, his objections revealed deep fissures within Missouri's Radical Republican coalition.

Among the majority of non-Radicals in the state, opinion was far less guarded in opposition to the federal Civil Rights Act, Section 3 of Missouri's Declaration of Rights, and the rights of African Americans generally. Fanning the flames of opposition to the Civil Rights Act provisions within Missouri were the explicitly conservative newspapers, some of them formerly Conservative Unionist like their Kentucky cousins and others outright ex-Confederate. Perhaps none betrayed a more strident tone of white supremacy than Missouri's appropriately named *Lexington Weekly Caucasian*. Its first edition appeared in April 1866, the month that the Civil Rights Act was passed over President Johnson's veto, and the paper wasted no time blasting the new measure. "The bill to dissolve the Union, debase the white man, enfranchise the negro, and perpetuate the Radical party in power *ad infinitum*, commonly called the Civil Rights Bill . . . has been carried, as it is claimed, by the Constitutional majority over the President's objections."[49] Like other opponents of the act, the *Caucasian* challenged the legitimacy of the measure as well as its substantive value.

The *Caucasian*, along with other conservative newspapers like the *Missouri Republican* and the *Fulton Telegraph*, offered continuous objections and took to mockery, as did the *Kentucky Gazette*. Repeatedly, the *Caucasian* would make light of stories of black civil rights denied and racial violence committed against blacks, with one of them under the ironic headline "And the Colored Troops Fought Nobly."[50] The net effect of the vehement opposition to black civil rights in Missouri was to persuade many African Americans to leave the rural sections of the state and to challenge the Radical Republican Party to live up to its promise spelled out in 1865. The combined pressure from white conservatives, disenchanted African

Americans, and white Republicans disillusioned by corruption under the proscriptive Drake constitution led to the emergence of the Liberal Republican movement and the downfall of Radical Republicanism in 1870.

CONCLUSION: LIMITATIONS OF THE CIVIL RIGHTS ACT IN THE BORDER STATES

African Americans in Kentucky and Missouri pressed for equal rights in the years following emancipation, regardless of the partisan or ideological leanings of the ruling parties. Groups like the Missouri Equal Rights League and Kentucky's "Colored Men's State Convention" organized grassroots efforts to agitate for legal and political rights for African Americans. These efforts paid off to some degree, especially through the construction of schools and benevolent institutions throughout Kentucky and Missouri.[51] And the lobbying efforts of black Kentuckians eventually helped convince the reform wing of the Democratic Party to accept black testimony rights in 1872.

Inspiring as the story of self-reconstruction may be, however, the real legacy of Kentucky's and Missouri's experiences with the Civil Rights Act was that persistent white supremacist agitation paid off in the American heartland and beyond. Subterfuge, violence, and the emergence of "states' rights" discourse could be employed to undermine egalitarian forces from Washington. The Civil Rights Act of 1866 may have been the first federal triumph for civil rights. But its undoing in the slave states that remained loyal to the Union throughout the Civil War showed how precarious these newly won rights really were.

Notes

1. *Holt County Sentinel*, April 13, 1866.
2. With each of the four major 1860 presidential candidates receiving votes in the county, 39 percent went to northern Democrat Stephen Douglas and 30 percent for Constitutional Unionist and former Whig John Bell. Of the remaining 31 percent of the vote, Republican Abraham Lincoln claimed 17 percent and southern Democrat John C. Breckinridge 14 percent. Election Returns, Election Division, Office of the Secretary of State, RG005: box 8, folder 15, item 12, accessed via http://www.civilwaronthewesternborder.org/content/1860-presidential-election-returns-holt-county-missouri.
3. Michael Vorenberg, *Final Freedom: The Civil War, the Abolition of Slavery, and the Thirteenth Amendment* (Cambridge: Cambridge University Press, 2004), 181–82; see also *Cong. Globe*, 38th Cong., 2d Sess., 258–59, "Mr.

Rollins," delivered January 13, 1865. He explains his support for the amendment after opposing it previously as a matter of preserving the Union. Rollins did not run for reelection in 1864; his replacement, a Radical Republican, voted for the Civil Rights Act of 1866.

4. On general Missouri Reconstruction politics, see William Parrish, *Missouri under Radical Rule* (Columbia: University of Missouri Press, 1965).
5. Aaron Astor, *Rebels on the Border: Civil War, Emancipation, and the Reconstruction of Kentucky and Missouri, 1860–1872* (Baton Rouge: Louisiana State University Press, 2012), 154–60; Victor Howard, *Black Liberation in Kentucky: Emancipation and Freedom, 1862–1884* (Lexington: University Press of Kentucky, 1983).
6. Astor, *Rebels on the Border*, 15–32.
7. On the slave system in central Missouri, see R. Douglas Hurt, *Agriculture and Slavery in Missouri's Little Dixie* (Columbia: University of Missouri Press, 1992).
8. On racial ideologies within each section, see Leon Litwack, *North of Slavery: The Negro in the Free States, 1790–1860* (Chicago: University of Chicago Press, 1965); and George Fredrickson, *The Black Image in the White Mind: The Debate on Afro-American Character and Destiny, 1817–1914* (Middletown: Wesleyan University Press, 1987).
9. Lincoln to Orville Browning, September 22, 1861, in *Collected Works of Abraham Lincoln*, ed. Roy P. Basler, 9 vols. (New Brunswick, N.J.: Rutgers University Press, 1953–55), 4:531–33.
10. Ira Berlin et al., *The Destruction of Slavery*, Freedom: A Documentary History, ser. 1, vol. 1 (Cambridge: Cambridge University Press, 1982).
11. *Journal of the House of Representatives of the Commonwealth of Kentucky, 1865–1866* (Frankfort, Ky.), 602.
12. For German Missourian attitudes toward slavery, see Alison Clark Efford, *German Immigrants, Race, and Citizenship in the Civil War Era* (Cambridge: Cambridge University Press, 2013).
13. Diane Mutti Burke, *On Slavery's Border: Missouri's Small-Slaveholding Households, 1815–1865*, Early American Places (Athens: University of Georgia Press, 2010).
14. Christopher Phillips, *Missouri's Confederate: Claiborne Fox Jackson and the Creation of Southern Identity in the Border West* (Columbia: University of Missouri Press, 2000).
15. Quoted in John McElroy, *The Struggle for Missouri* (Washington, D.C.: National Tribune Company, 1909).

16. Michael Fellman, *Inside War: The Guerrilla Conflict in Missouri during the American Civil War* (New York: Oxford University Press, 1989).
17. Dennis K. Boman, *Lincoln's Resolute Unionist: Hamilton Gamble,* Dred Scott *Dissenter and Missouri's Civil War Governor* (Baton Rouge: Louisiana University Press, 2006).
18. William E. Parrish, *Turbulent Partnership: Missouri and the Union, 1861–1865.* (Columbia: University of Missouri Press, 1963).
19. William Parrish, *Missouri under Radical Rule,* 3.
20. Henry Clay Bruce, *The New Man: Twenty-Nine Years a Slave, Twenty-Nine Years a Free Man* (York, Pa.: P. Anstadt and Sons, 1895), 100.
21. James Fidler to J. Sidell, June 9, 1864, Letters Received, box 2 F-178, ser. 3967, KY Assistant Adjutant Provost Marshal Guard, RG 110, National Archives, Washington, D.C.
22. *Lexington National Unionist,* October 4, 1864.
23. Thomas Russell to Clinton B. Fisk, February 21, 1865, Letters Received, box 16, ser. 3537, District of North Missouri, 393/2, National Archives.
24. Astor, *Rebels on the Border,* 155–56.
25. Reporting on the Outten and Poore (next paragraph) cases can be found in J. W. Cardwell to Colonel W. H. Coyl, Registered Letters Received, F-18, ser. 1068, Kentucky Assistant Commissioner; and Clinton Fisk to Ely, February 13, 1866, Registered Letters Received, F-18, ser. 1068, RG 105, National Archives.
26. Johnston to Bourne, Lexington Chief Superintendent, April 30, 1867, Unregistered Letters Received, Ser. 1186, RG 105, National Archives.
27. Christopher Waldrep, "Garrett Davis and the Problem of Democracy and Emancipation," *Register of the Kentucky Historical Society* 110, nos. 3 and 4 (Summer/Autumn 2012): 363–402.
28. *Paris Western Citizen,* March 22, 1861.
29. Quoted in E. Merton Coulter, *Civil War and Readjustment in Kentucky* (Chapel Hill: University of North Carolina Press, 1926), 15.
30. *Paris Western Citizen,* June 9, 1865.
31. Ibid., June 16, 1865.
32. Garrett Davis speech, March 30, 1864, Debates on Adoption of Thirteenth Amendment, *Cong. Globe,* 38th Cong., 1st Sess., appendix, 104 (1864).
33. *Cong. Globe,* 39th Cong., 1st Sess., 575 (1866).
34. Ibid., 595.
35. *Kentucky Gazette,* July 11, 1866.
36. Ibid.

37. "The Family of Jack and Sally Foster," entry in *Notable Kentucky African Americans Database*, ed. and comp. Reinette Jones and Rob Aken, University of Kentucky Libraries (retrieved January 2016).
38. Blyew v. United States, 80 U.S. 581 (1872).
39. Blyew v. United States, 80 U.S. 13 Wall. 581 581 (1872), error to the circuit court for the District of Kentucky.
40. *Reports of Cases Argued and Adjudged in the Supreme Court of the United States*, December term, 1871, reported by John William Wallace (Washington, D.C.: W. H. and O. H. Morrison Law Publishers and Booksellers, 1872), 80:585–88.
41. Ibid., 587.
42. Ibid.
43. Ibid., 588.
44. Ibid., 586.
45. *Cong. Globe*, 39th Cong., 1st Sess., 1804 (April 6, 1866).
46. *Journal of the Missouri State Convention Held at St. Louis* (St. Louis, January 6 to April 10, 1865).
47. Quoted in Parrish, *Missouri under Radical Rule*, 115–16.
48. Ibid., 116.
49. *Lexington (Mo.) Weekly Caucasian*, April 25, 1866.
50. Ibid., May 16, 1866.
51. Lorenzo J. Greene, Gary R. Kremer, and Antonio Holland, *Missouri's Black Heritage* (Columbia: University of Missouri Press, 1980), 88–103.

6

THE CIVIL RIGHTS ACT OF 1866 IN SOUTH CAROLINA

Jeff Strickland

Following the Civil War, the overwhelming majority of white South Carolinians maintained allegiance to the Democratic Party, and they refused to accept African Americans as their social, economic, and political equals. State legislators, all of them white, formulated and eventually passed the so-called Black Codes, an extensive series of laws aimed at controlling freedmen and freedwomen that resembled the antebellum slave code in many respects. Black South Carolinians organized politically in an effort to block the legislation, and they protested when the legislature enacted the law. Although the federal government failed to intervene with the machinations of the South Carolina legislature and U.S. military officials in South Carolina refused to enforce the law, congressional Republicans successfully passed the Civil Rights Act of 1866 over President Andrew Johnson's veto, requiring southern states to provide certain civil protections to African Americans.

Historians have tended to focus on the popular reaction to the passage of the South Carolina Black Code, and they have paid less attention to the reaction of South Carolinians, both black and white, to the passage of the Civil Rights Act of 1866. In particular, they have largely ignored the efforts of Governor James L. Orr and the South Carolina legislature to rescind the Black Code and provide civil rights protections in the state constitution.[1] The state government was motivated, of course, to earn readmission to the Union and end the federal occupation, especially the military courts, and reinstall the South Carolina judiciary. In this essay, I focus on white South Carolinians' rejection of the Civil Rights Act of 1866 and the South Carolina state legislature's rapid acceptance of the federal law, necessitated by their desire to earn readmission to the United States.

White South Carolinians disagreed wholeheartedly with the Civil Rights Act, decrying it as an unnecessary and unconstitutional federal intervention into states' rights. Nowhere in the South was the Civil Rights

Act of 1866 more revolutionary than in South Carolina. The law increased the power and role of the federal government, something white southerners opposed. White South Carolinians claimed that race relations should remain the domain of the state, and they passed state laws aimed at subjugating African Americans. Congressional Republicans passed the Thirteenth Amendment, Civil Rights Act, and later the Fourteenth Amendment with the understanding that the legislation "represented a revolutionary change in American constitutionalism."[2] The Civil Rights Act of 1866 required "states to impartially protect the personal rights and safety of all persons through systems of civil and criminal justice" and provided "a cause of action for those unable to enjoy rights as white citizens enjoyed them." Congress allowed the states "to decide for themselves the conditions under which civil rights were to be exercised and enjoyed, as long as the conditions were reasonable."[3] South Carolina soon relented and passed a series of laws in September 1866 that adhered to the requirements outlined in the Civil Rights Act.

WHITE RESISTANCE

In the wake of the war, former Confederates continued to support state sovereignty and limited federal authority, and many former secessionists resided in South Carolina.[4] In December 1860, South Carolina had seceded from the United States following the election of Abraham Lincoln to the presidency. South Carolina legislators felt compelled to preserve chattel slavery and its extension into the western territories and states. At minimum, white South Carolinians understood that Lincoln's election meant slavery would no longer extend into the West, while many people believed his election was a mandate for the abolition of slavery. Ten southern states would eventually join South Carolina in forming the Confederate States of America. On April 12, 1861, Confederate forces in Charleston began the Civil War when they demolished Fort Sumter with cannon fire. Nearly four years later, the U.S. military, including U.S. Colored Troops (USCT), occupied the city on February 18, 1865. White Charlestonians resisted the occupation, especially because the USCT maintained a strong presence in the city.

White southerners in the former Confederacy resisted emancipation following the Civil War. White South Carolinians, many of them slave owners, had long argued that slaves would not work as free people, and they concentrated their efforts on passing laws that would control the labor of newly freed black southerners and restrict their civil rights. In rural and urban areas throughout South Carolina, white citizens used violence, intimidation, and murder to impose the color line that the slave code had long imposed. In Charleston and Columbia, white Union army troops and former Confederates fought with freedmen and the USCT. Small riots took place in Charleston but nothing on the scale that occurred in Memphis and New Orleans in 1866. White South Carolinian Augustine Smythe, in a letter to his brother, expressed anxiety about his failure to hire enough labor during harvest time, and he worried that freedmen would resort to violence if they could not obtain enough food. "My stock man talking to me the other day, told me to look out, for there was to be trouble," Smythe wrote. He continued, "The negroes were making nothing [and] selling all they drew, [and] when 'hungry came,' there would be a contest between those who had corn & those who had not that[,] they were talking of it. And unless we have some strict rule it will come. Strict rule we have not, [and] I do not see how we shall soon."[5] A week later, Smythe wrote his mother,

> The poor negro, besotted with ignorance, [and] so full of freedom, looking forward to January as to some day of Jubilee approaching, with all the difficulties [and] dangers of a free man's life to encounter, [and] none of the experience or sense necessary to enable him successfully to battle with them, thinking only that freedom confers the privilege of going where & doing as they please, work when they wish, or stop if they feel disposed, and yet be fed, supported & cared for by his Master, lazy, trifling, impertinent! Mother they are awful!

Smythe expressed his disapproval of the presence of the USCT because, in his view, the soldiers incited local black southerners to crime and insolence. Smythe concluded the letter with expressions of fear similar to those mentioned in the letter to his brother a week earlier. "I am very blue about the future Mother," Smythe wrote. "What shall we do? Here am I, with not enough to feed half my people next year & must turn some off, others all around in the same way. What will those expected do with themselves? Some are already predicting a struggle between those who have, [and] those who have not corn, [and] I fear it will come to it."[6] On October 24, 1865, Eliza Fludd, a native white Charlestonian and former slave owner, wrote Margaret Worrell,

> Both ladies and gentlemen have been dragged through the streets of Charleston by insolent negro guards in U.S. uniform, for some trifling false charges made by negroes, and there is not a single Provost Marshal that has been in Charleston, who has not encouraged the

> negroes in this insolence by invariably preferring negro evidence and deciding in their favour. And every officer that has been in command in Charleston, has done the same. I could tell you of outrages of this kind that would make your blood boil with indignation.[7]

Both Fludd and Smythe embellished the current state of political affairs while demonstrating a lack of empathy for the plight of African Americans.

Some white Charlestonians bent on restoring the prewar order attempted to shape Reconstruction policy in Washington, D.C. On September 4, 1865, Christopher Memminger, a successful lawyer and former slave owner, wrote President Johnson, "I take it for granted that the whole Southern Country accepts emancipation from Slavery as the condition of the African race; but neither the North nor the South have yet defined what is included in that emancipation." He added, "The boundaries are widely apart which mark on the one side, political equality with the white races, and on the other a simple recognition of personal liberty." Memminger believed that it would take time for African Americans to deserve equality, and he contended that freed slaves would not work. "The Northern people seem generally to suppose that the simple emancipation from slavery will elevate the African to the condition of the white laboring classes, and that contracts and competition will secure the proper distribution of labor," Memminger wrote. "In the present case, to these general causes, must be added the natural indolence of the African race, and the belief now universal among them, that they are released from any obligation to labor. . . . The effect will be the abandonment of the negro to his indolent habits."[8] Many white southerners agreed.

Julius J. Fleming, a white South Carolinian and former slave owner, did not believe freed slaves would work unless the law compelled them. "The planters generally entertain but little faith in their ability to make a crop next year under the present system of labor," he wrote. "As to cotton, it is out of the question. The Negroes exhibit growing indisposition to work." Fleming offered his opinion about the Black Code:

> What Judge Wardlaw's code will do, if the legislature adopts and the government allows it to be enforced, remains to be seen. But something must be done to enforce and secure regular, systematic, and reliable labor, or this fine country becomes a wilderness. The Negroes are at present . . . in a very restless condition; groups of them are seen at our street corners unemployed, and the devil's workhouse (and idle mind) is in full blast.[9]

Thousands of white southerners were also unemployed, yet Fleming did not perceive them as a threat. He did not expect them to work in the fields, of course. Most white South Carolinians believed the Black Code was necessary because, as the editor of the *Charleston Courier* determined, "a large portion of her population suddenly emerged from a state of dependence and slavery, into one of complete and unrestrained freedom, both for the security of the latter, and for the well being of society, and for the harmony and adjustment of these new relations."[10]

White southerners had long relied on slave labor, and they had implemented an oppressive slave code that regulated nearly every aspect of slave life. South Carolina had been a slave society since the early eighteenth century, and Charleston had served as the most important slave trading port in the South. As the war ended, most white South Carolinians expressed strong antiblack sentiment, and they shared a profound commitment to white supremacy. During the summer of 1865, many white South Carolinians, including several town councils, wrote President Johnson that they worried the economy of the state would not recover if the government did not compel emancipated African Americans to work.

THE BLACK CODE

White supremacists, including former slave owners, understood that the Thirteenth Amendment abolished slavery, and they sought ways to implement a legal code based on the former slave code. In June 1865, President Johnson appointed Benjamin F. Perry, a proslavery Unionist who had served in the Confederate state legislature, as provisional governor of South Carolina. Perry called for an election to select delegates for a state constitutional convention, held in Columbia on September 13. Delegates included James L. Orr, a Confederate senator; F. W. Pickens, South Carolina Confederate governor; several Confederate generals; various Confederate officers; and twelve former members of the secession convention.[11] At the convention, white South Carolinians elected a state legislature that convened without African American representation, and they quickly moved to enact social controls on black South Carolinians.

When the state legislature convened in September, Governor Perry advised the legislators to enact a legal code that would control black South Carolinians and maintain the caste system that existed under slavery. In his opening address, Governor Perry declared, "In making this unavoidable change in your Constitution, abolishing slavery, and which will require the substitution of hired labor for that of slave labor, it is to be hoped that one of those evils will be experienced which some have anticipated. By a wise, just and humane treatment of your 'freedmen' and women, you may attach them to you as strongly in their new condition as they were whilst your slaves."[12] He added, "The 'freedman' will soon find out that he must work or perish. Legislation will necessarily be required to regulate the relative duties of the employer and employee." Perry expressed concern that Republicans in the North wanted to enfranchise African Americans, and they were paying close attention to developments in the South, particularly in South Carolina. "They forget that this is a white man's government, and intended for white men only; and that the Supreme Court of the United States has decided that the negro is not an American citizen under the Federal Constitution," Perry defiantly declared. He further argued it was the "unquestioned right" of each state to make suffrage laws.[13] The editor of the *New York Tribune* responded to the election of former Confederates to the South Carolina state legislature: "Rebellion, its birthplace in Charleston, having failed to save their cause, they have carried to Columbia and seek to preserve it there."[14]

In his message to the South Carolina state legislature, Governor Perry asserted,

> It becomes your urgent duty, gentlemen, to make immediate provision for the protection and government of the freemen and colored people who have been so suddenly released from slavery in their ignorance and destitution. . . . The Convention ordered the Provisional Governor to appoint a Commission for the purpose of preparing and submitting to the Legislature, for their adoption, a code of laws for the protection and government of the freedmen and colored persons.[15]

In October, the all-white South Carolina legislature formed a committee to create a Black Code, and the proposed legislation threatened to impose strict limitations on African American freedom. Black South Carolinians found the vagrancy provision particularly offensive because it not only criminalized unemployment but also legalized forced labor as punishment. White southerners implemented the vagrancy provision to restrict migration from the countryside into towns and cities. In addition, African American shopkeepers and peddlers were required to pay $100 for operating licenses, and many skilled trades were reserved for white citizens only.[16] Moreover, the code contained an apprenticeship provision that would force black children to work for white employers at low wages. The editor of the *Courier* believed the code necessary to maintain order: "The sudden change of a large portion of the population from a condition of slavery to that of freedom required, for the security of society and the happiness of all races, the restraint of wise and just laws, so that liberty might not generate into license, violence and anarchy."[17] The *Columbia Daily Phoenix* wrote that the Black Code, "induced by the emancipation of slaves, requires no comment."[18] For white southerners, the maintenance of the old order meant the rejection of the new order and all that it entailed: emancipation, civil rights, and the right to vote.

On November 13, 1865, the South Carolina House of Representatives voted to accept the Thirteenth Amendment that abolished slavery and involuntary servitude. The Senate passed the bill 68 to 35.[19] The editor of the *Newberry Herald* determined, "It is considered very important, in view of the early restoration of the State to her former status in the Union, that there should be legislation on this subject, showing that the State has not only acquiesced in the abolition of slavery but that it has enacted a code of laws for the protection of civil rights of freedmen, and adapted in all respects to the new order of things."[20] Surprisingly, the editor considered the Black Code a necessary condition for readmission of South Carolina to the Union and the withdrawal of federal troops. The *Edgefield Advertiser* believed the Black Code necessary to deal with the labor "emergency" now that slavery had been abolished.[21]

White South Carolinians determined the code did not restrict African American freedom and equality. Instead, they argued that it merely maintained racial harmony between white citizens and African Americans. The *Charleston Courier* concluded that the code, "as a whole, . . . may be regarded as a safe and wise system of laws, oppressing none, and affording guarantees to all. To have no laws would be merely to encourage license and misrule, in all the relations of life." The editor added, "The code is intended for the benefit of the two races. It attacks the rights of neither. It regulates and harmonizes the intercourse of both. . . . To designate it an endeavor to revive slavery, is simply absurd."[22] As the South Carolina legislators mulled over the bill, the *Courier* concluded, "Upon a careful review we cannot perceive that they are inconsistent with the principles of right, justice or equity. We believe their enactment will prove beneficial to the common welfare. We are not wedded to the particular sections introduced, in fact to some there may be objections; but it is evident that new relations require laws, so that there may be security, repose and prosperity to all."[23] An opponent of the legislation determined that the South Carolina congressmen wanted to pass the Black Code because they were "awfully afraid of being put 'on a footin'" with their late emancipated slaves, and cannot afford to be governed by the same laws." The author added that white southerners were "not yet prepared to confess that the negro is a free man, and should be governed, protected, and punished by the legally constituted authorities of the country."[24]

On December 5, Governor Orr issued a message regarding the current economic condition of South Carolina, arguing that the state could not take any loans and that the "only recourse" entailed raising revenue through taxation. Orr declared,

> Our policy toward the freedmen should be kind and humane. If his rights of person and property are not fully and effectively secured by our local legislation, we can not hope to be relieved from the presence of the Military and the Provost Courts. The authorities of the United States will not remove their protecting hand from the negro whom they have manumitted, and in whose freed we have acquiesced, until we provide by our laws to give him full protection in all his civil rights. His labor is necessary for the successful prosecution of the agriculture of the State, and it will be best commanded by making him cheerful and contented.[25]

Orr indicated that he wanted the legislature to enact laws that were "kind and humane" to the freed people and would guarantee their civil rights. Yet he did not discourage the labor provisions of the Black Code, because that was the overwhelming concern of white southerners.

White South Carolinians worried about more than just labor control of the freed people, however. Many white southerners feared freed slaves would resort to violence and perhaps revenge. Rumors of insurrection, the same that pervaded South Carolina since the Stono Rebellion of 1739, circulated throughout the summer and fall of 1865. Not surprisingly the several rumors coincided with the passage of the Black Code. The editor of the *South Carolina Leader*, a Republican newspaper, considered the rumors "groundless fears." White planters near Santee, on the Cooper River, had notified the military that local freedmen and freedwomen planned to rebel against the landowners. Yet when General James C. Beecher arrived on Edisto Island, he found no evidence of insurrection. Indeed, he found the freedmen engaged in work and politics, the likelier cause of white alarm.[26]

On December 21, 1865, the South Carolina legislature passed the Black Code, and it resembled the antebellum slave code in many respects. The legislature did include a declaration of rights that recognized the Thirteenth Amendment had abolished slavery. Governor Orr signed the Black

Code into law, but he soon called for its suspension. On December 23, Orr wrote President Johnson, "Some of the provisions are objectionable but as a whole I think ample & complete protection is given to the present property of the negro." Orr continued,

> The vagrant Laws are stringent but necessary but they will only be enforced against the idle & dissolute and many of them you know will not work without the compulsion of law. . . . I hope that our legislation with reference to the freedmen may be satisfactory to you and that it will suit your views at an early day to remove the troops and turn over all our people to our state laws.[27]

Judge F. J. Moses gave a speech concerning the Black Code to a meeting of several thousand freedmen and freedwomen and white landowners at Sumter. Moses indicated that white planters should obey the federal government and that the code was an experiment that the legislature could modify if necessary.[28] The *Edgefield Advertiser* announced it would print copies of the "Negro Code" for twenty-five cents each or five for one dollar.[29]

Some white South Carolinians feared the fallout from the legislation, especially when they considered the progress that had been made between freedmen and planters. Fleming believed the South Carolina legislature would need to revise the code because it conflicted with the Freedmen's Act. He thought "it would have been better" for the legislature "to have made no such ostentatious legal and judicial distinction between the races, but to have slightly modified the common law and left the law to cover and regulate the entire population. This would have been less expensive and onerous to the people and certainly less offensive to those whose renewed antagonism it were folly to invoke."[30] Fleming concluded, "The less is done in the way of special legislation, either by Congress or the state, the better it will be for them and the country. They are free, and if labor is left to regulate itself all will be well."[31]

By the end of 1865, the constitutional and political process of restoring the southern states to the Union had become the problem of preserving the principles for which the war had been fought.[32] Jacob Schirmer wrote the following diary entry:

> Congress has convened but our members are not admitted. We were first state to abolish slavery, thus the correction done. Now we are told to repudiate our debt, neither the Convention or Legislature has acted upon the requirements and therefore here we stand in status

> quo, the next move will be to give the "Nigger" free suffrage. Our hot secessionists and Fire Eaters have become the most abject submissionists and appear to be ready to do any thing our infernals say we must and shall do.[33]

The Freedmen's Bureau agents, along with military officials, had been making progress in negotiating labor contracts between agricultural workers and landowners. On December 25, Fleming revealed that planters and freedmen had attended mass meetings to reach labor agreements for the following calendar year. "The planters have conferred together, in conjunction with the military authorities and the officers of the Freedmen's Bureau, and have agreed upon a form and the terms of contract for another year," Fleming wrote. He portrayed the freedmen as passive agents in the negotiation process, but they were heavily involved in the contract dealings.[34] On January 18, 1866, Fleming wrote, "A great change has come over the freedmen since the Christmas holidays. They very generously evince a willingness to work and are making arrangements to do so."[35] Freedmen demonstrated a strong desire to return to work as sharecroppers because it afforded greater independence than wage labor.[36]

AFRICAN AMERICAN POLITICAL ORGANIZATION

Although black South Carolinians had been denied direct political participation, they organized politically and called for federal protection. Black South Carolinians had served meritoriously in the Union army during the Civil War, and African American participation on behalf of the Union served as the basis for constitutional reforms following the war. African Americans organized politically before they earned the right to vote. African American leaders, many of them Union veterans, worked tirelessly to gain a political voice. They called for passage of the Thirteenth, Fourteenth, and Fifteenth Amendments and for Congress to resist the transparent attempts of white South Carolinians to control their labor and deny them civil equality. Black South Carolinians in Charleston and Columbia paraded through the streets, danced, and feasted on the Fourth of July in 1865. African Americans also organized elaborate Emancipation Day celebrations to take place on January 1, 1866.[37]

In addition, black South Carolinians organized against the Black Code.[38] The editor of the *South Carolina Leader* determined the proposed legislation was "perfectly atrocious, and worse than slavery." He revealed that the law required African Americans "to make contract for labor; to remain on the plantation; the hours for work are from sunrise to sunset and those having horses to care for must do so that they may be ready to go to work at daylight. The act is interspersed freely with punishment for offenses not now known to any criminal code in the North."[39] The editor contended the code "expresses an average of the justice and humanity which the late slaveholders possess. Its advocates, however, seem to have talked themselves out and gone to sleep. It is well not to disturb it. Let it lie." The paper was incensed that President Johnson did not support protective legislation for African Americans in the South.[40]

In November 1865, African American activists had organized a convention at Charleston's Zion AME Church, where they demanded full equality.[41] Participants sent a petition to the South Carolina legislature, but its contents were ignored because they contradicted the intentions of the white legislators. In fact, the petition was never presented to the legislature.[42] African Americans used the convention to pressure military authorities and protect civil rights, while white southerners sought to maintain their position at the top of the racial hierarchy. Activists listed six demands and addressed them to white South Carolinians. They desired citizenship, the right to testify in court, an end to restrictions on black businesses, access to agricultural land, an end to the claims that freedmen were destroying the countryside, and equality under the law.[43] The *South Carolina Leader* was particularly impressed by the following statement written at the convention: "You have given us little or no encouragement to engage in agricultural pursuits, by refusing to sell us lands, while you are organizing societies to bring foreigners into the country, the clear intent of which is to thrust us out, and reduce us to a serfdom intolerable to us, and as you will find in the end, ruinous to your own prosperity."[44]

Black South Carolinians' desire for access to land led to their petitioning President Johnson and Congress to make land available at low or no cost.[45] Many former slaves continued to work their own plots on the South Carolina Sea Islands and along the coast, and they hoped to obtain title to the land. On Edisto Island, freedmen and freedwomen had taken control of sixteen thousand acres with the approval of the U.S. military. It was their hope that they would continue to farm the land. The federal government, however, had begun to restore the land to its original owners. Black Edisto Islanders wrote President Johnson on October 28, 1865, requesting "that some provisions be made by which every colored man can purchase land, and hold it as his own." They continued, "We therefore look to you in this trying hour as a true friend of the poor and neglected race for protection and Equal Rights, with the privilege of purchasing a Homestead."[46] Fleming revealed that some freed slaves had entered into wage contracts with planters for the next year, while others hoped to farm their own land.[47] "There is one great difficulty in the way of the country's hope and the freedmen's success: it is the idea which has been insidiously and sedulously instilled into the blacks that the government would give them lands and that each family should have its freehold possession—an idea which the military authorities have earnestly endeavored to remove, but which still pervades the mass and is cherished with a tenacity which nothing can overcome," Fleming determined.[48] In a racist diatribe, Jacob Schirmer wrote, "Our Nigger Population have not yet realized the full extent of their freedom, they feel no inclination or desire to work and still are under the impression that lands and property are to be given to them."[49]

THE CIVIL RIGHTS BILL

White and black Republicans in the North found the Black Code wholly objectionable, and congressional Republicans moved to remedy the situation. The *Philadelphia Inquirer* and the *Chicago Tribune* argued that South Carolina was "attempting to legislate the colored race again into a condition of slavery."[50] By 1866, Radical Republicans had enlisted the support of moderate and conservative Republicans in their civil rights efforts.[51] On January 5, 1866, Illinois senator Lyman Trumbull introduced a cautious and conservative civil rights bill designed to set aside the Black Codes and codify the basic notion of equal rights under the law. The measure contained no provision for black suffrage, but it did empower the federal government to guarantee the newly emancipated slaves the right to make and enforce contracts, to sue and give evidence in court, and to inherit, hold, and sell real estate. States needed merely to end legal discrimination in their own state laws to avoid enforcement.

Many white South Carolinians felt the military authorities sufficient to "to enforce an observance of the established relations between the whites and the freed people."[52] In particular, they approved of labor regulations that appeared to protect both landowner and laborer and banned agricultural laborers from unionizing.[53] In March 1866, Major General Daniel E. Sickles issued General Order No. 7 that asserted the authority of federal military courts in all legal matters related to African Americans.

Initially, white South Carolinians followed the Freedmen's Bureau Bill more closely than the Civil Rights Bill. Indeed, Section 8 of the Freedmen's Bureau Bill contained a civil rights provision that white southerners found threatening: it imposed a fine on anyone that deprived African Americans "any civil right secured to white persons." That meant jury duty, intermarriage, and suffrage.[54] In the view of most white southerners, the federal Constitution delegated the power to legislate social issues to the states. Furthermore, white South Carolinians denied they were racist and guilty of oppressing African Americans. The *Columbia Daily Phoenix* contended that Republicans were wrong in their assessment that white southerners wanted to subjugate black southerners. "There is no feeling of resentment or hatred against the colored people in any of the Southern States, that we know of; on the contrary, the best sympathies of the Southern people are with them in their new position," the editor wrote.[55] A month later, the *Daily Phoenix* added, "The Southern States 'lately in rebellion' lost by the results of the war about two thousand millions in slave property alone. . . . One would suppose that this were sufficient to appease the anger of the men at the North who are still trying further to persecute us."[56]

White South Carolinians opposed the Freedmen's Bureau, and they hoped President Johnson would veto congressional legislation to renew the agency. In the main, white southerners believed the states should handle their own affairs and viewed the bureau as an intrusion of federal authority. The editor of the *Charleston Courier* argued that without the Freedmen's Bureau "as a general rule, we believe the States themselves, exercising civil authority, will be found to be the best and most humane guardians of the freed people."[57] The *Courier* rejoiced at President Johnson's veto of the Freedmen's Bureau Bill: "To the veto of the so-termed Freedmen's Bureau Bill, the voice of the patriotic country has responded, and its ringing notes may be heard from the Atlantic to the Pacific, and from the Penobscot to the Rio Grande, with its grand utterances on behalf of the defender of the Constitution and the guardian of the rights and liberties of the people."[58] The *Daily Phoenix* wrote, "In the Southern States, we are of the opinion the bureau to supervise the interest of the freedmen will be all sufficient to attend to the education of the colored children, and as to the whites, the States have all made annual and ample appropriations for common schools. . . . Constitutional amendments and the establishment of bureaus all look to the centralization of power—a dangerous tendency in a republican form of Government."[59] Two days later, the editor of the *Daily Phoenix* declared, "The veto is one of the most important that has ever been issued from the Executive chair. . . . He is opposed to it on constitutional grounds, and holds that there is not authority for the measure—no justice in it to the States directly interested, and no necessity for it."[60]

White South Carolinians turned their attention to the Civil Rights Bill in early March. One observer wrote, "The sympathies of the masses are on the side of the struggle for freedom and equal rights" and felt confident the Republican Congress would pass the bill.[61] In fact the Civil Rights Bill passed the Senate 33 to 12 on February 2, and the House voted 111 to 38 on March 13. On March 27, however, President Johnson vetoed the bill, sending it back to the Senate. In doing so, Johnson declared, "In all our history, in all our experience as people living under Federal and State law, no such system as that contemplated by the details of this bill has ever before been proposed or adopted." Johnson claimed the congressional protections elevated the status of black people above white people and interfered with the rights of states. In a telling prediction, Johnson concluded, "The tendency of the bill must be to resuscitate the spirit of rebellion and to arrest the progress of those influences which are more closely drawing around the States the bonds of union and peace."[62]

White South Carolinians agreed with President Johnson's decision to veto the Civil Rights Bill. The *Charleston Courier* editor wrote, "It will be hailed as an additional evidence of his devotion to the great cause of public justice. The South never can sufficiently estimate the measure of the great deliverance which he has affected for them. Standing, as it were, over the brink of the precipice, we now begin to see the immense gulf of oppression, deprivation of right and misrule into which the Radicals, by their illegal measures, sought to plunge the liberties and rights of these States." Johnson was determined to leave civil rights legislation to the states.[63] "The objections of the President are to the whole tenor and scope of the Bill," wrote the *Courier*.

> He not only regards it as unconstitutional, but inexpedient and fraught with evil. . . . It infringes, and, in fact, destroys the rights of the States. It concentrates all power in the central Government and converts it into a consolidated domination. It sets at naught the judiciary of the States and renders them amenable and subservient to the Federal authority. It attempts by legislation the impossible task of enforcing the equality of variant races.[64]

Many white South Carolinians believed the Civil Rights Act of 1866 would lead to heightened violence between white citizens and freedmen and freedwomen. On March 30, 1866, the editor of the *Charleston Daily News* wrote, "The veto of the Civil Rights Bill by the President is a fact of which it were not too much to say that it has given satisfaction here. In the ground of his objection we, of the South, of course, concur. We know the evils of the system to have been inaugurated; we have dreaded the terrible evils of that estrangement between the races which must have been its necessary results."[65]

On April 6, congressional Republicans passed the Civil Rights Act over Johnson's veto, effectively nullifying the Black Code and granting federal citizenship rights and protection to African Americans.[66] The *Charleston Daily News* made it clear, however, that the legislation did not authorize African Americans to vote.[67]

WHITE SOUTH CAROLINIANS' RESPONSE

White South Carolinians refused to admit they had continued to oppress black South Carolinians, and they objected to northern newspapers that portrayed them in a negative light. In a *Charleston Courier* editorial, the author implicitly recognized the reasons Congress passed the Civil Rights Act but denied white South Carolinians had done anything wrong. "There seems to be a persistent, determined effort, on part of several Radical papers at the North to persuade their readers that the rebellion still exists in certain of the Southern States," the editor opined. "We believe the citizens of this State have not the slightest idea of ever again inaugurating a revolutionary movement against the established General Government," he added.[68] Fleming believed that the *Courier* had done much to vindicate white Southerners. Yet, he determined that "in some places we are still regarded as semibarbarous, that ruffians abound in this country, and the lawless spirit of the people is only restrained by the presence of the military, and that the removal of the latter would be at once the signal for a reign of violence and outrage."[69] The editor of the *Lancaster Ledger* considered the Civil Rights Bill "a measure of vast significance to the Southern people. The principle of 'equality before the law,' seems to be the determined policy of the party in power, and we presume it will come to that sooner or later."[70]

The *Lancaster Ledger* reported that the bill had passed over Johnson's veto "and resulted in the most uproarious demonstrations of delight by the Republicans. When Mr. Morgan announced the vote, it was greeted with applause and he was congratulated by many Senators and members of the House."[71] The editor called it an "odious and revolutionary measure," and he thought that the Supreme Court would rule on its constitutionality.

> It will be remembered that it obliterates all distinctions between classes, confers the right of citizenship and places all persons upon

> an equality before the law—negroes, Indians, Chinese, paupers, &c. It is a wicked and detestable measure, and we hope will, in some way or either, ultimately recoil upon the heads of those, who, actuated by the worst feelings of hatred and revenge, have attempted to saddle it upon a subdued and powerless people, with no representation in the councils of the nation to interpose their objections and make known their wants.[72]

The editor believed it would take a year to eighteen months for the law to appear before the Supreme Court.[73] In response to the passage of the Civil Rights Act, the editor of the *Columbia Daily Phoenix* hoped for redemption:

> All the South needs now is to be let alone. Let alone in the management of her labor—let alone in her efforts to develop her resources. With her civil and political rights guaranteed to her, with no obstacle or obstruction to the energies of her people, we believe, today, she could work out her own redemption, retrieve her shattered fortunes, and start on a career of prosperity that she has never yet enjoyed.

In his view, the Republicans opposed readmission of the former Confederate States to the Union. "They keep her out of the Union—out of the fraternity of States which constitute the republic; they regulate her system of labor; and do this by military rule," he wrote. The editor concluded that "all the South needs now is to be let alone in the management of her affairs, to be restored to full equality and communion with her co-States of the Union, and the best interests of the whole people, North and South, will be advanced and promoted."[74] One week later, the paper declared, "The civil rights bill has been passed over his veto since his proclamation restoring the Southern States was issued," and predicted that Johnson might argue that the two-thirds majority did not include southern states and decline to execute it.[75] Senator Willard Saulsbury of Delaware called the Civil Rights Act "an inauguration of revolution." "Attempt to execute this law within any State of this Union, and, in my judgment, this country will again be plunged into all the horrors of civil war," he argued.[76]

The editor of the *Charleston Courier* also decried the Civil Rights Act. "The agony is over," the editor determined.

> The Civil Rights Bill, so called, has become a law. It has been driven through both branches of Congress by a two thirds majority. The President's veto has been cast aside. His constitutional objections

> have been ignored. His views as to the dangerous tendencies of the doctrines therein enacted, have been utterly disregarded. It therefore becomes a part of the statute law of the land. The vote thus announced does not make the Act constitutional.[77]

The *Courier* believed the Senate vote did not reflect the will of the people and entertained the prospect that the House of Representatives would not approve the Senate's override.[78]

Some leading white South Carolinians understood the implications of the Civil Rights Act for the Black Code. Fleming determined that South Carolina would have soon repealed the Black Code and that the Civil Rights Act was unnecessary. The former slave owner wrote, "South Carolina is the only state which has pursued a distinct legislation for the Negroes. No other state has followed her example. And it is very probable that the freedmen's code and district courts which thus far are entirely inoperative will be abolished when the next legislature meets."[79] He was not wrong, as the third section of this essay reveals. Fleming observed, "The Bill has passed. In vain the president's veto. In vain the voice of reason and the protest of patriotism. It has become a law—a law specially obnoxious and known to be so to the very states excluded from representation and allowed no voice in its passage. A measure pronounced by prominent statesmen to be most fatal to liberty and certainly most damaging to our great unrepresented southern domain." Fleming believed the law was likely to be found unconstitutional, noting,

> This will necessitate additional state legislation. Our own legislature must undo much of its last winter's work. The freedmen's code and its adjunct machinery, considered by some at the time an abortion, must be decently buried. Under the high pressure now brought to bear, we have no option. Not state law must be left on the statute which does not accord with the express will and decree of Congress. There must be no more class legislation, no discrimination in codes or courts on account of color, but equality before the law must be everywhere.[80]

On April 21, Fleming wrote the *Charleston Courier*, "In this state there is no operative law for the freedmen, except that of the bureau, and a citizen may be arrested on information or complaint made before the provost." He determined that planters were called away from their plantations to answer charges that were ultimately dropped for lack of evidence.[81]

White southerners expressed their dismay with the passage of the Civil Rights Act in letters to ex-governor Benjamin Perry. A. C. Garlington wrote Perry that President Johnson did "not properly estimate the strength of the opposition." M. L. Brinkley determined that the state was "now powerless in the hands of a set of unprincipled bad men whose sole aim is how much they can oppress and degrade us." David Milling opined that the "political horizon seems cloudy, and not much appearance of a clear atmosphere while the Radicals have the control" and maintained "hellish and evil designs."[82] In late April, Schirmer wrote, "Our political affairs I do not think are in any manner improved. A civil rights bill has been passed over the President's veto and what effect that will have is yet to be realized."[83] In May, Schirmer determined, "In our political affairs there is nothing encouraging. Our Hell Hounds are endeavoring to go to every extremity to degrade and crush us and were it not for the occasional interposition of the President's veto, God knows where we should now be. They are still at work endeavoring to pass every obnoxious law in their power, trampling the Constitution under their feet and probably drunk all the time."[84]

The *New York World* declared, "The real obstacle to the success of the law is the repugnance of the Southern people to its provisions, and their disbelief in its constitutionality."[85] A correspondent to the *New York Times* wrote that most white Charlestonians were upset with the federal government because they viewed the federal government as oppressive. "Nevertheless the spirit of submission still pervades the entire mass. They will never again take up arms in any wide-spread organization, and they can be led to love the Government as dearly as it is loved in the North, with proper treatment."[86]

White southerners continued to believe that African Americans would not work unless the law compelled them. In June, the editor of *DeBow's Review* wrote a story titled "What's to Be Done with the Negroes?" "We of the South would not find much difficulty in managing the negroes, at least tolerably well, if left to ourselves, for we would be guided by the lights of experience and the teachings of history, sacred and profane." The editor continued, "We should be satisfied to compel them to engage in coarse, common manual labor, and to punish them for dereliction of duty or nonfulfillment of their contracts with sufficient severity, to make the great majority of them useful, productive laborers."[87] Fleming determined that planters now found difficulty securing a full labor force on their plantations. "Kind and experienced planters declare that while the freedmen generally behave well," Fleming revealed, "they do not exhibit the energy or industry which would entitle them to rate as full hands; and, as the temperature rises with the advancing season, it is apprehended that in many places the crops will suffer from their indifference and neglect."[88]

On June 6, 1866, General Sickles wrote Governor Orr and asked whether the courts of South Carolina could "entertain jurisdiction of the following cases":

> 1. Criminal proceedings against persons for offences affecting the persons, property or other civil rights of persons of color, as such civil rights are defined and established by the recent acts of Congress known as the "Civil Rights Bill," and by the laws of the State not inconsistent therewith. 2. Whether, in the administration of justice in South Carolina, the laws relating to the rights of persons and property and the remedies for injuries are the same, as regards the definition of offences, the mode of arrest, indictment and trial, and as to the nature and character of the proofs admissible, without distinction or difference as to the color of the parties or their witnesses. 3. Whether persons of color are competent to testify before Grand Juries and Magistrates in the character of complainants in criminal cases, as well as witnesses therein. 4. Whether the pains and penalties imposed by the laws of the State are identical for offences committed by white persons and persons of color. I have also to request that your Excellency will designate the capital felonies on the trial of which, when committed by white persons against the rights and properties of persons of color, the testimony of persons of color is entitled to be received under sections 29 and 30 of the Act to establish District Courts.

Governor Orr responded that he had consulted with Chief Justice Benjamin F. Dunkin, and Dunkin affirmed that all of those equal protections had been established.[89]

On June 26, 1866, General Sickles issued Special Order No. 19, which called for equal treatment in the courts for white citizens and African Americans. In Part 4 of the order, "the refusal or neglect of any civil officer to perform an official act, properly required of him, by an aggrieved party seeking redress in the civil tribunals, whereby a failure of justice ensues in the prosecution of the class of offenders remitted to the civil jurisdiction by this order, will be promptly reported by any officer cognizant of the same."[90]

In the summer, white South Carolinians remained fixated on the passage of the Civil Rights Act, and Governor Orr, understanding that the state would need to adhere to the act to earn readmission to the Union, called the legislature to an extra session to repeal the Black Code. The editor of the *Keowee Courier* declared, "That 'nigger institution'—Congress, before its adjournment, passed an amendment to the act creating the 'Freedmen's Bureau,' continuing it for the space of two years. As we are all—black and white—'beholden' to the *Bureau*, we publish on our first page the 'so-called' act, in full."[91] The *Keowee Courier* wrote, "The immediate measure for consideration will be, probably, the amendment of the 'negro code,' giving the negro the right to testify in all our courts, with his other rights as guaranteed by Congress. The sooner this is done the better for all parties."[92] On August 22, 1865, Orr issued a proclamation convening the General Assembly because it had become "necessary that the laws of this State with reference to persons of color should be materially modified, and that the Courts for their enforcement should be re-organized, so that jurisdiction in all cases, civil and criminal, may be exercised by the Courts, and under the Statutes" of South Carolina.[93] On September 4, 1866, Governor Orr declared in a message to the state senate and House of Representatives: "In the series of Acts, passed in December last, known as the Code, there are various discriminations against freedmen, which should be repealed, and civil rights and liabilities as to crime should be accorded to all inhabitants alike." Orr observed that the provost courts imposed penalties on freedmen that were "much lighter than punishments imposed by State Courts upon white men for the same offences" and focused on revision of the act to establish district courts. The governor also indicated that persons of color must be allowed to testify in court. "If the rules of evidence in all the Courts were so modified as to make all persons and parties competent witnesses in their own and all other cases, no possible danger could result from it," he wrote.[94]

The South Carolina legislature moved to implement the Civil Rights Act when it convened its extra session in September. At the extra session, Senate Bill No. 1, intended to define the term "persons of color and to declare the rights of such persons," received considerable attention. On Friday, September 7, 1866, the state senate passed the bill with a vote of 19 to 9. The Low Country appeared to favor the revision, while the Up Country opposed it.[95] The House of Representatives read Senate Bill No. 1 for the first time on Saturday, September 8, and members referred it to the Committee on the Judiciary. That committee made a report on the bill on September 10, and the House planned to consider the bill the following day. The second reading occurred on September 11, and the House made it the special order of the following day. The House delayed the second reading until Saturday, September 15, when legislators changed the title to "A Bill to declare the rights of persons lately known as slaves and free persons of color" and returned it to the Senate. On Thursday, September 20, the Senate returned the bill to the House, and it passed on the third reading, therefore becoming an act.[96] The South Carolina legislature then passed laws that afforded African Americans the same rights outlined in the Civil Rights Act. Yet even though African Americans had earned access to the courts, courts were controlled by white supremacists.[97] A special dispatch to the *New York Times* summarized the act declaring the rights of persons formerly known as slaves and as free persons of color. It provided freedmen and freedwomen "the right to make and enforce contracts, to sue and be sued, to give evidence, to inherit, purchase, lease, sell real and personal property, to make bills, enjoy full and equal benefit of personal security, personal liberty, and private property, and of all legal remedies the same as whites."[98] In October 1866, the military authorities returned the civil courts to the state, and African Americans served as witnesses for the first time.[99]

On September 11, Fleming seemed to accept the impending legislative changes to the Black Code. He wrote about African Americans,

> They form a large and important part of the state. Are jails cheaper than school houses? Is ignorance the prolific source of crime? While learning may have been prudently debarred the slave, will it be wise to neglect and discourage this in the freedman? . . . These people are our neighbors, and for years will doubtless be found in our midst; and, if we allow them to create around them a malarious and tainted atmosphere, the infection will spread to our own habitations. Hence, to improve their condition is to benefit ourselves.[100]

CONCLUSION

Following the Civil War, white South Carolinians, most of them Democrats, attempted to maintain the racial caste system. Although they accepted the Thirteenth Amendment that abolished slavery, they sought to maintain a dependent labor force of African American men and women.

Black South Carolinians resisted those attempts and organized politically in efforts to achieve equality. When the all-white South Carolina legislature assembled at its constitutional convention in September 1865, black South Carolinians called upon Congress to grant them suffrage rights. In early November, a legislative committee began to outline a Black Code, and again, African Americans protested. The legislature passed the Black Code in late December, drawing the ire of congressional Republicans, including radicals, moderates, and even some conservatives.

The U.S. Congress began discussing the Civil Rights Bill in early January 1866. White South Carolinians argued the proposed legislation was unnecessary because race relations in the state were generally positive. Moreover, they believed the legislation was unconstitutional because it intruded upon the state's rights. The Senate and House of Representatives passed the bill, but President Johnson vetoed the proposed law. Congress overrode the president's veto, and the legislation passed in April. White South Carolinians continued to express their displeasure with the perceived federal intrusion upon their rights, but they were more upset with the notion of African American equality. Regardless, Governor Orr and the South Carolina state legislature adhered to the requirements of the Civil Rights Act, repealing the Black Code in September. It would take white South Carolinians a mere ten years to convince congressional Republicans that they should leave race relations to them.

Notes

1. Dan T. Carter, *When the War Was Over: The Failure of Self-Reconstruction in the South, 1865–1867* (Baton Rouge: Louisiana State University Press, 2003); James Alex Baggett, *The Scalawags: Southern Dissenters in the Civil War and Reconstruction* (Baton Rouge: Louisiana State University Press, 2003); Bernard E. Powers, *Black Charlestonians: A Social History, 1822–1885* (Fayetteville: University of Arkansas Press, 1994); Julie Saville, *Work of Reconstruction: From Slave to Wage Laborer in South Carolina, 1860–1870* (Cambridge: Cambridge University Press, 1994); Leslie A. Schwalm, *A Hard Fight for We: Women's Transition from Slavery to Freedom in South Carolina* (Urbana: University of Illinois Press, 1997).
2. Robert J. Kaczorowski, "To Begin the Nation Anew: Congress, Citizenship, and Civil Rights after the Civil War," *American Historical Review* 92, no. 1 (1987): 45–68, quote on 47.
3. Ibid., 56.

4. Ibid., 51.
5. Augustine Smythe to Brother, December 5, 1865, Smythe Family Papers, South Caroliniana Library, University of South Carolina.
6. Augustine Smythe to Mother, December 12, 1865, ibid.
7. Eliza Fludd to Margaret Worrell, October 24, 1865, Eliza Fludd Papers, Duke Special Collections, Duke University.
8. Christopher Memminger to Andrew Johnson, Memminger Family Papers, Duke Special Collections, Duke University.
9. Julius J. Fleming and John Hammond Moore, *The Juhl Letters to the Charleston Courier: A View of the South, 1865–1871* (Athens: University of Georgia Press, 1974), 52–53.
10. *Charleston Courier,* December 1, 1865.
11. Herbert Aptheker, "South Carolina Negro Conventions, 1865," *Journal of Negro History* 31, no. 1 (January 1946): 91–92.
12. *Columbia Daily Phoenix,* September 15, 1865.
13. Ibid.
14. *New York Tribune,* October 17, 1865.
15. *Journal of the Senate of the State of South Carolina* (Columbia, S.C., 1865), 10.
16. Wilbert L. Jenkins, *Seizing the New Day: African Americans in Post–Civil War Charleston* (Bloomington: Indiana University Press, 1998), 53.
17. *Charleston Courier,* November 4, 1865.
18. *Columbia Daily Phoenix,* November 3 and 4, 1865.
19. *Journal of the House of Representatives of South Carolina* (Columbia, S.C., 1865), 91.
20. *Newberry Herald,* November 8, 1865.
21. *Edgefield Advertiser,* November 22, 1865.
22. *Charleston Courier,* November 29, 1865.
23. Ibid., December 1, 1865.
24. *Christian Advocate and Journal,* November 23, 1865.
25. Governor Orr's Message, December 5, 1865, in *Journal of the Senate of the State of South Carolina* (1865), 40.
26. *South Carolina Leader,* December 9, 1865.
27. Quoted in Andrew Johnson, *The Papers of Andrew Johnson,* ed. LeRoy P. Graf, Ralph W. Haskins, and Paul H. Bergeron (Knoxville: University of Tennessee Press, 1967), 9:538.
28. Fleming and Moore, *Juhl Letters,* 56.
29. *Edgefield Advertiser,* December 27, 1865.

30. Fleming and Moore, *Juhl Letters*, 59–60.
31. Ibid., 59.
32. Kaczorowski, "To Begin the Nation Anew," 51.
33. Schirmer Diary, December 1865, Schirmer Family Papers, South Carolina Historical Society, Charleston.
34. Fleming and Moore, *Juhl Letters*, 55.
35. Ibid., 68.
36. Ibid., 72.
37. *South Carolina Leader*, December 9, 1865.
38. Jenkins, *Seizing the New Day*, 53.
39. *South Carolina Leader*, December 16, 1865.
40. Ibid.
41. Jenkins, *Seizing the New Day*, 54.
42. State Convention of the Colored People of South Carolina, *Proceedings of the Colored People's Convention of the State of South Carolina* (Charleston: South Carolina Leader Office, 1865).
43. *Liberator*, December 9, 1865.
44. *South Carolina Leader*, December 9, 1865.
45. Ibid.
46. *Papers of Andrew Johnson*, 9:296–97.
47. Fleming and Moore, *Juhl Letters*, 56–57.
48. Ibid., 73.
49. Schirmer Diary, December 1865.
50. Cited in *Charleston Courier*, December 1, 1865.
51. Kaczorowski, "To Begin the Nation Anew," 49.
52. *Charleston Courier*, February 9, 1866.
53. Ibid., February 12, 1866.
54. Ibid., February 27, 1866.
55. *Columbia Daily Phoenix*, January 14, 1866.
56. Ibid., February 15, 1866.
57. *Charleston Courier*, February 22, 1866.
58. Ibid., March 1, 1866.
59. *Columbia Daily Phoenix*, February 22, 1866.
60. Ibid., February 24, 1866.
61. *Christian Advocate and Journal*, March 22, 1866.
62. Andrew Johnson, "Veto Message," March 27, 1866, The American Presidency Project, http://www.presidency.ucsb.edu/ws/?pid=71978.
63. *Charleston Courier*, March 29, 1866.

64. Ibid., April 2, 1866.
65. *Charleston Daily News,* March 30, 1866.
66. Kaczorowski, "To Begin the Nation Anew," 49; *Charleston Courier,* April 7, 1866; Carter, *When the War Was Over,* 235–36.
67. *Charleston Daily News,* March 14, 1866.
68. *Charleston Courier,* April 18, 1866.
69. Fleming and Moore, *Juhl Letters,* 79.
70. *Lancaster Ledger,* April 4, 1866.
71. Ibid., April 18, 1866.
72. Ibid.
73. Ibid.
74. *Columbia Daily Phoenix,* April 7, 1866.
75. Ibid., April 14, 1866.
76. Ibid., April 19, 1866.
77. *Charleston Courier,* April 13, 1866.
78. Ibid., April 9, 1866.
79. Fleming and Moore, *Juhl Letters,* 82.
80. Ibid., 89.
81. Ibid., 91.
82. Quoted in Richard Zuczek, *State of Rebellion: Reconstruction in South Carolina* (Columbia: University of South Carolina Press, 1996), 33.
83. Schirmer Diary, April 1866.
84. Ibid., May 1866.
85. *New York World,* April 17, 1866.
86. *New York Times,* June 2, 1866.
87. *DeBow's Review* 1, no. 6 (June 1866): 576–77.
88. Fleming and Moore, *Juhl Letters,* 93.
89. *New York Times,* July 8, 1866.
90. Ibid.
91. *Keowee Courier,* August 4, 1866.
92. Ibid.
93. *Journal of the Senate of the State of South Carolina* (1866), 3–4.
94. Ibid., 9, 10
95. Ibid., 11. Boozer, Bratton, Buist, Davant, Frierson, Grisham, Hemphill, Kershaw, McDuffie, McQueen, Reid, Sullivan, Thomson, Townes, Weatherly, George W. Williams, J. H. Williams, Wilson, and Winsmith voted in favor. Beaty, Dozier, McCutchen, Richardson, Shingler, Skipper, Tillman, Townsend, and Tracy voted against it.

96. *Journal of the House of Representatives* (1866), 37, 43, 52, 64, 70, 105.
97. Zuczek, *State of Rebellion*, 33.
98. *New York Times*, September 23, 1866.
99. Powers, *Black Charlestonians*, 85–86.
100. Fleming and Moore, *Juhl Letters*, 64.

7

THE CIVIL RIGHTS ACT OF 1866 AT THE SUPREME COURT

R. Owen Williams

There is no more significant federal legislation—historically, politically, or legally—than the Civil Rights Act of 1866. It set the stage for the mighty "equal protection" clause of the Fourteenth Amendment by providing for the "full and equal benefit of all laws and proceedings for the security of person and property." Yet, despite the first official use of the cherished concept of "civil rights," the act is mentioned so infrequently in the U.S. Supreme Court record that one might assume it never existed.[1] The act did not go before the Supreme Court until 1872, by which time the Fourteenth Amendment completely overshadowed it and, just as important, most Americans had lost any enthusiasm they previously claimed for civil rights.

The perplexing issue of "civil rights" precipitated a new constitutional order, one that solidified the shift from antebellum values of voluntary association, individual freedom, and a republic led by virtuous elites, to an America in which nationhood, equality, and popular democracy prevailed. No longer a loose confederation of similarly situated sovereign democracies, the United States became just that, namely, a nation of inextricably linked states, with the emphasis on "nation" rather than on "states."[2] As this new nation shifted from an economy predicated upon slavery to one of free labor, the need to protect civil rights became immediately evident. Yet none of these changes happened all at once—far from it; the Reconstruction amendments to the Constitution, Thirteen through Fifteen, altered American notions of federalism and equality before the law. Theoretically, states' rights diminished as central authority increased; in reality, states' rights took on a more subdued yet still hale form. Practically, Section 1 of the Fourteenth Amendment gave us the most important and most adjudicated clauses of the Constitution.[3] That amendment simultaneously constitutionalized the Civil Rights Act of 1866 and revolutionized American culture.

Scholars disagree about the political activism of the Supreme Court during this period, just as they disagree on the timing of or extent to which the justices unraveled the positive achievements of the Reconstruction Congresses.[4] Those debates are far too substantial to be resolved in this short essay. The intent here is to examine the few Supreme Court cases pertaining to the Civil Rights Act of 1866 and to demonstrate that, despite a little known flicker of support the act got from the justices when on circuit, it received very little attention from the nation's highest tribunal.

FROM THE BATTLEFIELD TO CONGRESS

It is almost impossible to fathom the death toll. The Civil War claimed the lives of some 700,000 soldiers, more than 2 percent of the entire American population, or "the total American fatalities in the Revolution, the War of 1812, the Mexican War, the Spanish-American War, World War I, World War II, and the Korean War combined." One in five white southern men did not survive.[5] On top of all that suffering, almost four million freed slaves, 13 percent of the U.S. population, somehow needed to be assimilated after the war.[6] So Americans took their battles to the floor of Congress, giving rise to a period of unparalleled political contest.

The most significant legislation of the period was the Civil Rights Act of 1866, which made citizens of all persons born in the United States, "excluding Indians," and ensured that people of "every race and color" would have "full and equal benefit of all laws . . . as is enjoyed by white citizens."[7] The act's ten sections focused largely on the legal process by which citizens could protect their "civil rights."[8] Congress intended to provide practical effect to the Thirteenth Amendment (thus also reversing the Supreme Court's 1857 *Dred Scott* finding that black people were not and never could be citizens of the United States)[9] while simultaneously eradicating the rash of southern legislative assaults on that amendment through Black Codes. Any violations of the act based on race, private or public, would be punished as a crime.[10] To suggest that this was radical legislation is to traffic in gross understatement.

The very notion of "civil rights" was quite new.[11] In his *Virginia Statute for Religious Freedom* (one of only three accomplishments he selected for his gravestone), Thomas Jefferson claimed, "Our civil rights have no dependence on our religious opinions, any more than our opinions in physics or geometry." In *The Rights of Man,* Thomas Paine distinguished civil from natural rights, insisting, "Natural rights are those which appertain to man in right of his existence. . . . Civil rights are those which appertain to man in right of his being a member of society. Every civil right has for its foundation some natural right pre-existing in the individual."[12] Yet those and other early references to civil rights lacked specificity and typically conflated them with the more fundamental "natural rights." Even by the time Congress passed the Civil Rights Act, there was no consensus whatsoever as to the content of "civil rights," which were then little more than an extension of the common law. Actually, the Reconstruction era represents America's first attempt to define the concept of civil rights; legislatures and courts expended great energy parsing "civil" rights from "political" and "social" rights, though to little definitive effect.[13] It is important to recognize that the Civil Rights Act of 1866, though broad in scope, did not attempt to extend political rights (for example, the right to vote) or social rights (such as the right to marry) to black people. Rather, it protected "equal rights," which were primarily those rights enumerated in Section 1 of the act.[14]

Given the lack of definition, it is not surprising that the concept of "civil rights" came under great scrutiny and endless attack. Delaware senator Willard Saulsbury, a Democrat, found the Civil Rights Act "flagrantly unjust, so oppressive in its character" as to be "one of the most dangerous bills, as well as one of the most unconstitutional bills" Congress had ever considered. Saulsbury also insisted that "the time for shedding tears over the poor slave has well nigh passed."[15] Even Ohio Republican representative John Bingham, principal author of the Fourteenth Amendment, believed that, before ratification of that amendment, Congress lacked the necessary power to pass the act.[16] Many critics accused Congress of "reverse discrimination"—generations before that particular slant became a popular tool of twentieth-century conservatives—none more vociferously than President Andrew Johnson, who vetoed the act when it first passed Congress.[17] Johnson argued that Congress ought not to act before southern states were readmitted and properly represented. Importantly, the fact that Congress overrode Johnson's veto, on April 9, 1866, demonstrates an unprecedented congressional power, a power already augmented by Section 2 of the Thirteenth Amendment and shortly thereafter reinforced by Section 5 of the Fourteenth Amendment and Section 2 of the Fifteenth Amendment.[18]

Congress passed the Fourteenth Amendment on June 13, 1866—in order to bolster, or constitutionalize, the Civil Rights Act—and the amendment was ratified and adopted by the states on July 9, 1868. Section 1 of the amendment was a streamlined version of the act, articulating the litany of new rights in three key clauses of one extraordinary sentence: "No State shall make or enforce any law which shall abridge the *privileges or immunities* of citizens of the United States; nor shall any State deprive any person of life, liberty, or property, without *due process of law;* nor deny to any person within its jurisdiction the *equal protection of the laws.*" That has certainly become the most important sentence of the entire U.S. Constitution. The majority of all cases that go before the Supreme Court are at least partially grounded in one of those clauses; the same clauses have also been used to incorporate, or apply, most of the Bill of Rights against the states.[19] The Fourteenth Amendment, and by extension the Civil Rights Act, is central to all debates relating to individual rights and the power of Congress relative to the states. Those debates played out in the U.S. federal court system.

FROM CONGRESS TO THE CIRCUIT COURTS

As much as anything, it was Section 3 of the Civil Rights Act that distinguished it from the eventual Fourteenth Amendment. Explicit within the full name of the Civil Rights Act—*An Act to protect all Persons in the United States in their Civil Rights, and furnish the Means of their Vindication*—was that it furnished citizens, black people most notably, the "means of their vindication." That vindication came from access to federal courts.

Through Section 3, Congress substantially strengthened the terrain for black persons: "The district courts of the United States . . . shall have, exclusively of the courts of the several States, cognizance of all crimes and offenses committed against the provisions of this act, and also, concurrently with the circuit courts of the United States, of all causes, civil and criminal, affecting persons who are denied . . . the rights secured to them by . . . this act." Allowing cases to be heard in federal courts, as opposed to state courts, represented a significant jurisdictional shift.

Prior to the Civil War, most Americans had little interaction with the federal government, except perhaps through the postal service. And most Americans did not distinguish between state and federal courts; yet black people quickly saw that the federal courts were more likely to hand down decisions favorable to their plight. Actually, African Americans turned first to the Union military commanders and the Freedmen's Bureau—established in 1865 by Congress to assist and protect former slaves and poor white individuals—even before the Civil Rights Act granted jurisdiction to the federal courts.[20] The Civil Rights Act and the second Freedmen's Bureau Bill were closely related, in purpose and language, as Representative Bingham explained from the floor of Congress: "The seventh and eighth sections of the Freedmen's Bureau bill enumerate the same rights . . . that are enumerated in the first section of this [Civil Rights] bill."[21] But it was the right to choose federal courts, or remove cases from state to federal courts, that gave African Americans the prospect of "vindication."

The federal court system contains three levels, all of which altered the course of justice and assimilation for black people: district courts, circuit courts, and the Supreme Court. Federal courts have limited jurisdiction, which is to say they can adjudicate only those cases authorized by the U.S. Constitution or by Congress.[22] A district court is the general trial court for any legal case arising under federal statutes, the Constitution, or treaties; its authority is known as "original jurisdiction."

Once a district court hands down a decision, it can be appealed to a U.S. court of appeal, also called a circuit court. Today there are twelve federal circuits (covering variously sized geographic regions), consisting of six (First Circuit) to twenty-nine (Ninth Circuit) judges; cases are typically tried before a bench of three judges, though they can also be appealed, in rare instances, to the entire slate of circuit judges (called "en banc" appeals).[23] Prior to the Judiciary Act of 1891, one of those three judges was actually a Supreme Court justice appointed from that specific region of the country. For most of the year, the justices were expected to "ride circuit" in their home region; they literally rode through a predetermined string of towns (circuit), by horseback and later by train, hearing cases as part of a panel with two district judges.[24] The fact that a few of the justices weighed over three hundred pounds may explain why they hated traipsing around on horseback to hear an ever-growing docket of cases, though just how many cases is difficult to determine since the federal government started to collect data on caseloads only after Congress created the Department of Justice in 1870.

While on circuit, the justices heard many sorts of cases. In those instances when civil rights came before circuit courts, some of the participating Supreme Court justices supported black individuals in a manner that may surprise readers familiar with subsequent Supreme Court decisions.[25] Consider for example the pro–civil rights decision from Associate Justice Noah Swayne in *United States v. Rhodes* (1866),[26] or the most promising civil rights decision of the period, written by Chief Justice Salmon Chase in *In re Turner* (1867).[27] Almost as encouraging for African Americans was Associate Justice Joseph P. Bradley's opinion in *Live-Stock Dealers & Butchers Association v. Crescent City Live-Stock Landing & Slaughterhouse Co. et al.* (1870). Judge (soon to be Justice) William Burnham Woods wrote a seemingly auspicious circuit court opinion in *United States v. Hall* (1871), and Justice William Strong offered something hopeful in *United States v. Given* (1873).[28] Only the first three of these cases pertain to the Civil Rights Act of 1866; the later two were grounded in the Fourteenth Amendment.

The first Supreme Court justice to opine on the Civil Rights Act, somewhat appropriately, was President Lincoln and the Republicans' first appointee to the bench, Noah Swayne. Justice Swayne addressed the constitutionality of the Civil Rights Act of 1866 in a relatively obscure case from the U.S. Circuit Court of Kentucky, a white-on-black burglary case where the victims were prevented from testifying because they were black.[29] Prosecuted under the Civil Rights Act of 1866, the three defendants were found guilty by the jury, giving rise to an appeal on the grounds that the indictment was not within the Civil Rights Act and that the act was unconstitutional in any event. Swayne, with Judge Bland Ballard concurring, penned a forceful opinion that favored both civil rights and the national government like few decisions of the era.

Swayne's opinion examined each section of the Civil Rights Act and then emphatically struck down a Kentucky law[30] barring black testimony: "Congress met these evils by giving to the colored man everywhere the same right to testify 'as is enjoyed by white citizens.'" In his effort to validate the Civil Rights Act, Swayne pointed to Section 2 of the Thirteenth Amendment, which granted Congress the power to support the freedom of black persons through "appropriate legislation." He reiterated Chief Justice Marshall's claim in *McCullough v. Maryland* that the word "appropriate" was equivalent to "necessary and proper." So, "who will say [the Civil Rights Act] is not an 'appropriate' means of carrying out the first section of the amendment, and a necessary and proper execution of the power conferred by the second?"[31]

But there were limits to Swayne's support of Congress and civil rights. After insisting, "We entertain no doubt of the constitutionality of the [Civil Rights] act in all its provisions," Swayne toed the line with this: "It gives only certain civil rights." It is important to recall that *civil* rights in 1866 did not mean *equal* rights. The Civil Rights Act in its original form extended suffrage to black people, but Congress dropped political rights from the legislation's final version. Most Reconstruction era Americans viewed voting as a privilege, not as a right.[32]

One very important justice, however, was determined to expand the American concept of rights. When Chief Justice Roger Taney died, late in 1864, President Lincoln tried to appease the radical wing of the party by appointing Salmon Chase—the former senator and governor from Ohio who stridently opposed the "slave power conspiracy"—to be the new chief justice. The Senate confirmed Chase the very day Lincoln nominated him. If any of the Supreme Court justices could be counted on to support civil rights, it would be Chase, which certainly pleased Radical Republicans even as it concerned many more. The Columbus, Ohio, antiwar newspaper *Crisis* mocked Chase in a poem titled "Nigger at the Bar" for almost immediately admitting John Rock to practice before the Supreme Court (the first African American afforded that privilege).[33]

On October 16, 1867, Chase wrote a circuit court opinion that confirmed his critics' fears and suspicions. Though surprisingly brief (only one page of the court record) and typically ignored, Chase's decision is among the more important and unusual of the postwar period.[34] It has appropriately been called "the most powerful antislavery statement ever given by a Chief Justice" and neatly summarizes Chase's values and ambitions for the nation, for which he believed the Civil Rights Act provided tremendous support.[35] The case, *In re Turner*, involved a prejudicial labor contract between a former slave, Elizabeth Turner, and her former master. Chase ruled that the Thirteenth Amendment and the first clause of the Civil Rights Act (granting white and black people "full and equal benefit" of the law) prohibited that sort of contract.[36] Chase intended his decision to disrupt only those private contracts that, because of race, unfairly reduced a person to involuntary servitude; he also probably hoped his decision would be appealed to the Supreme Court, where he could then cajole his colleagues into widely applying his principles and elevating the moral rectitude of the post–*Dred Scott* Court.

Chase offered five propositions that he believed were "sound law" and would "decide the case," all of which he actually numbered. The power of this decision resides in its succinctness: "1. The first clause of the thirteenth amendment . . . interdicts slavery." Second, "The alleged apprenticeship in the present case is involuntary servitude." Third, while the Civil Rights Act was not yet established as good law, Chase proceeded as if it were; he claimed that, if Elizabeth's apprenticeship were not involuntary servitude, it would have required (and Chase quoted the Civil Rights Act directly) "full and equal benefit of all laws and proceedings for the security of person and property, as is enjoyed by white citizens." The only problem with that particular proposition was that there was, at that time, no constitutional prohibition against a state's ability to legislate differential indenture, even on the basis of race. Since the Fourteenth Amendment had yet to be ratified, Turner's contract was probably valid and deserving of judicial protection.

Nevertheless, in his fourth proposition, Chase settled the matter by ruling, "This law [Civil Rights Act of 1866] having been enacted under the second clause of the thirteenth amendment, in enforcement of the first clause of the same amendment, is constitutional, and applies to all conditions prohibited by it."[37] This was Chase at his boldest. He surely knew of the tremendous resistance and skepticism regarding the constitutionality of that act, a matter of great debate in and around Congress.[38] Chase's final proposition spoke to his predecessor's *Dred Scott* decision (holding that black people were not and never could be American citizens) by underscoring black citizenship: "Colored persons equally with white persons are citizens of the United States." The chief justice staunchly supported civil rights, though he later sang a very different tune as he attempted to secure the Democratic nomination for president.[39]

Another member of the Court who supported the Civil Rights Act while riding circuit was Associate Justice Joseph P. Bradley,[40] a conservative Republican appointed to the bench in 1870 by President Ulysses S. Grant, who probably did not anticipate that Bradley would eventually write Supreme Court opinions opposing the Enforcement Act of 1870, the Civil Rights Acts of 1871, and the Civil Rights Act of 1875.[41] As it turns out, Bradley's opinions are riddled with challenging contradictions that tend to tie historians in knots. Whatever inconsistency exists between Bradley's early circuit decisions and his later Supreme Court opinions, one can hardly doubt the pro–civil rights potential in *Live-Stock Dealers & Butchers Association v. Crescent City Live-Stock Landing & Slaughterhouse Co. et al.* (which later became part of the *Slaughterhouse Cases* at the Supreme Court).[42]

In this case Justice Bradley insisted that the Fourteenth Amendment enhanced the Civil Rights Act, as regards both the power of Congress and the expansive rights due all Americans. Although the Civil Rights Act was "intended merely to secure to citizens of every race and color the same civil rights and privileges as are enjoyed by white citizens," Bradley observed, "the Fourteenth Amendment is much broader in its terms." All of the postwar amendments were "intended to protect the citizens from oppression by means of state legislation and to confer upon congress the power by appropriate legislation to carry the amendments into effect," and "it is to be presumed that the American people . . . understood what they were doing," which was prohibiting any state "from abridging the privileges or immunities of the citizens of the United States, whether its own citizens or any others." The rights of "all citizens shall be absolutely unabridged, unimpaired," and "there is no more sacred right of citizenship than the right to pursue unmolested a lawful employment."[43] Bradley remained true to his *Crescent City* decision, dissenting (with Swayne and Chase) in the *Slaughterhouse Cases* of 1873, though by 1883 (with Swayne gone from the Court and Chase from this world), Bradley led the Supreme Court's anti–civil rights majority in the *Civil Rights Cases*.[44]

Important as these early pro–civil rights circuit court decisions obviously were, they stand in stark contrast to subsequent Supreme Court opinions that constricted civil rights. The justices must have appreciated that they could be more aggressive and experimental while riding circuit since their decisions could always be appealed. As Justice Swayne circumspectly concluded in *Rhodes*, "If we [the circuit court] have erred the supreme court of the United States can revise our judgment."[45] Whether or not the circuit courts erred, the Supreme Court certainly revised.

FROM THE CIRCUIT COURTS TO THE SUPREME COURT

Whereas circuit courts are required to take all appeals from the district courts, the Supreme Court maintains complete flexibility and authority to decide whether or not to accept appeals from the circuit courts. After the Civil War, the Supreme Court's caseload ballooned to more than 114 cases every year (save one) and reached 193 in 1873, for a total of 1,226 cases in the eight years Chief Justice Salmon Chase presided—December 15, 1864, to May 7, 1873—as compared with an average annual caseload of 61 cases under Chief Justice Taney.[46] The Court's load picked up even more during the fourteen years under Chief Justice Morrison Waite (1874–88). One might expect that, given the significance of the issue, civil rights would have factored prominently on the Supreme Court docket. One might also expect that, given the trend at circuit courts, these decisions would bode well for African Americans. Yet, neither was true.

The Civil Rights Act rarely came before the Supreme Court. There were good reasons for this. It usually takes years before any issue percolates through the U.S. legal system, so ratification of the Fourteenth Amendment (the constitutional version of the act), on July 9, 1868, greatly reduced the likelihood that the act could or would be constitutionally challenged. Nevertheless, the Supreme Court heard a great many cases grounded in the Fourteenth Amendment.[47]

Since the justices decide which cases they will hear, the political predilection of the bench does factor prominently in case selection. The Republicans generally shared Chief Justice Chase's antislavery, pro–civil rights positions, yet, ironically, at the very time when Republicans achieved a majority on the bench—in 1870, six Republicans (Noah Swayne, Samuel Miller, David Davis, Salmon Chase, William Strong, and Joseph Bradley) and three Democrats (Stephen Field, Samuel Nelson, and Nathan Clifford) sat on the bench—the Court began to narrow the boundaries of civil rights.

Consider this case, one of the first instances in which the full Supreme Court analyzed the Civil Rights Act of 1866. On August 29, 1868, two young white men, John Blyew and George Kennard, hacked a black family to death with carpenter's tools as retaliation for the Civil War. The victims included Jack and Sallie Foster and Jack's ninety-seven-year-old grandmother, Lucy Armstrong. All three died immediately. Sixteen-year-old Richard Foster died two days later, after crawling to safety and giving written testimony.[48] Richard's sisters, Laura and Amelia, both survived without injury. Blyew and Kennard were indicted by an all-white jury and sentenced to hang by the U.S. Circuit Court of Kentucky. "With a view to test the constitutionality of the Civil Rights bill [of 1866] this case was taken to the Supreme Court," claimed the *Louisville Courier-Journal*.[49]

The central question in *Blyew v. United States*, which did not reach the Supreme Court until 1872, was whether federal or state courts had jurisdiction over the prosecution of John Blyew and George Kennard for the brutal ax murders in Lewis County, Kentucky.[50] The U.S. government claimed jurisdiction under a provision of the Civil Rights Act whereby "affected persons" who had been denied their rights in state courts could remove to federal courts.

Also among the issues tested was whether black individuals like Richard and his sister Laura could provide evidence—a right specifically granted them by Section 1 of the Civil Rights Act—since Kentucky barred African Americans like the Fosters from giving evidence against white citizens. Normally, murder cases are tried in state courts, but this would appear to be exactly the sort of case the act of 1866 targeted for removal to federal courts.[51] The critical question pertained to whether Section 3 of the Civil Rights Act legitimately granted the circuit court jurisdiction in the first place, the answer to which might render the other issues moot. And if the Supreme Court found the bill unconstitutional, black people would thereafter have to rely on state courts in criminal cases. The decision hinged on whether persons called to testify were "affected" parties under the act; the Court decided that only the government (prosecutor) and defendant were affected parties.

According to the justices, if witnesses could be affected parties, then federal courts would end up with jurisdiction in far too many cases. Justice William Strong, on behalf of the Supreme Court, ruled that Civil Rights Act of 1866 did not permit the federal courts to take jurisdiction since Kentucky law prohibited black people from testifying unless they were parties in a case. As to victims, well, according to the Court, "Manifestly the act refers to persons in existence."[52] Since she was deceased, Lucy Armstrong was, Justice Strong insisted, "beyond being affected."[53] Justice Bradley, joined by Justice Swayne, dissented vehemently against the Court's majority opinion, insisting that the Civil Rights Act was precisely intended "to counteract those unjust and discriminating laws of some of the States."[54]

It is important to note that even Bradley and Swayne changed their minds, deciding instead that states' rights mattered more than civil rights. In the Court's 1876 decision in *United States v. Cruikshank*—a case emanating from the gruesome Colfax Massacre, where white rioters murdered 105 African Americans—both Bradley and Swayne joined a unanimous majority that expounded at length on the rights of states, concluding,

> The government of the United States is one of delegated powers alone. Its authority is defined and limited by the Constitution. All powers not granted to it by that instrument are reserved to the States or the people. No rights can be acquired under the constitution or laws of the United States, except such as the government of the United States has the authority to grant or secure. All that cannot be so granted or secured are left under the protection of the States.[55]

The *Cruikshank* case was grounded in the Civil Rights Act of 1870 (also called the Enforcement Act),[56] and the decision mentions the Civil Rights Act of 1866 only enough to dismiss it:

> No question arises under the Civil Rights Act of April 9, 1866 (14 Stat. 27), which is intended for the protection of citizens of the United States in the enjoyment of certain rights, without discrimination on account of race, color, or previous condition of servitude, because, as has already been stated, it is nowhere alleged in these counts that the wrong contemplated against the rights of these citizens was on account of their race or color.

That the Court saw no reason to suspect 105 black people were killed "on account of their race or color" tests the limits of credulity. In *Cruikshank*, as in *Blyew*, the Supreme Court demonstrated clear resistance to the Civil

Rights Act of 1866. In both cases, vicious white murderers of black southerners were released on the basis of legal technicalities. In *Blyew,* the state of Kentucky challenged the Civil Rights Act of 1866 as a congressional encroachment upon its sovereignty, and the Court took the state's side. Ironically, while the Supreme Court deliberated, Kentucky legislators, fearing the Court's wrath, repealed their state law proscribing black testimony, whereupon the Lewis County court indicted Blyew and Kennard.[57]

In the period just after *Blyew,* it became increasingly difficult to enforce (or even define) federally protected civil rights, a difficulty magnified by the 5-to-4 *Slaughterhouse Cases* decision in 1873 that narrowly read the Fourteenth Amendment as protecting the "privileges and immunities" only of national rather than state citizenship.[58] That landmark decision left African Americans at the mercy of southern states and, though grounded in the Fourteenth Amendment rather than in the Civil Rights Act, is clearly among the most important civil rights decisions ever handed down by the Supreme Court; indeed, the case has received a small library's worth of attention that need not be rehashed here.

Suffice it to say that the *Slaughterhouse Cases* decision represents the Supreme Court's first step on the road toward abandonment of black people and civil rights. For various reasons, the Civil Rights Act of 1866 largely disappeared from view, but there were a few cases where the Court found an obligation of the federal government to protect individual rights, as in *Railroad Company v. Brown,* a case concerning discrimination and segregation on railroads.[59] Keep in mind, the anti-segregation legislation that gave rise to this case, passed in 1863,[60] could not be called "civil rights" legislation, not in the way we know civil rights after the Civil Rights Act of 1866. As historian John Frank long ago observed, "That [pre-1866] generation thought of race relations as a series of separate problems—a transportation problem, an education problem, a marriage problem. There was then no generalized conception of a broad principle of race relations" as only began to take shape in the Civil Rights Act of 1866.[61]

In 1863, Congress granted the Alexandria & Washington Railroad Company the power to extend its railroad northward, providing "that no person shall be excluded from the cars on account of color."[62] Violating the terms of its arrangement, Alexandria & Washington segregated black and white passengers. Catherine Brown, a black woman, bought a train ticket on February 8, 1868, and entered a railcar that was designated for white women, though an employee of the railroad removed her by force. Brown filed a discrimination suit against the railroad company, and the U.S. Supreme

Court ruled in her favor and declared that the railroad company was clearly not permitted to separate its passengers. Justice David Davis, on behalf of the majority, held, "It was the discrimination in the use of the cars on account of color where slavery obtained which was the subject . . . and not the fact that the colored race could not ride in the cars at all."[63] That the Court flipped to the opposite view more than twenty years later in *Plessy v. Ferguson* (a subsequent racial segregation case that gave us the infamous "separate but equal" doctrine) does not alter the fact that the Chase Court demonstrated at least some concern for civil rights.[64]

Throughout the remainder of the nineteenth century, the Court infrequently opined on the Civil Rights Act of 1866, yet one such instance came in a personal property case emanating from the state of Virginia in 1885. Samuel C. Carter, a resident and property owner in Richmond, Virginia, sued the city and its treasurer, Samuel C. Greenhow, for refusing to accept coupons from Virginia bonds as satisfaction for property tax assessments, a right that lawyers for Carter claimed were guaranteed by both Virginia statute and the U.S. Constitution. While Carter looked to a Virginia statute, "An Act to provide a plan of settlement of the public debt," dated March 28, 1879, Greenhow acted under a later Virginia statute, "An act to provide for the more efficient collection of the revenue," dated January 26, 1882. In *Carter v. Greenhow*, the Court looked to "the provisions of the act of the ninth of April, eighteen hundred and sixty-six, entitled 'An act to protect all persons in the United States in their civil rights,'" to determine jurisdiction for this case and decide whether Virginia subjected Carter to "the deprivation of any right secured or protected by this act" and the Constitution, specifically Article 1, Section 10, which forbids any state from passing laws that impair the obligations of contracts. Contracts are sacrosanct in America, of course, but Justice Stanley Matthews discoursed in this way for the Court:

> That constitutional provision, so far as it can be said to confer upon or secure to any person any individual rights, does so only indirectly and incidentally. It forbids the passage by the states of laws such as are described. . . . The individual has a right to have a judicial determination declaring the nullity of the attempt to impair its obligation. This is the only right secured to him by that clause of the constitution. But of this right the plaintiff does not show that he has been deprived. He has simply chosen not to resort to it. The right to pay his taxes in coupons, and the immunity from further proceedings,

> in case of a rejected tender, are not rights directly secured to him by the constitution.

In what appears to be a legal technicality, the Court found against Carter—and the spirit of the Civil Rights Act—when affirming the decision of the lower court.[65]

Another instance where the Court addressed the Civil Rights Act, repeatedly, came in a prolix citizenship decision, *United States v. Wong Kim Ark*, where the justices exhaustively interrogated historical notions of "natural born" citizenship. Wong—born in San Francisco, California, in 1873 to parents of Chinese descent and subjects of the emperor of China—lived his entire life as a U.S. resident but was refused reentry after a short trip abroad. Writing on behalf of the Court, Justice Horace Gray looked to the record: "The Civil Rights Act, passed at the first session of the Thirty-ninth Congress, began by enacting that all persons born in the United States, and not subject to any foreign power, excluding Indians not taxed, are hereby declared to be citizens of the United States." Gray continued, "The same Congress, shortly afterwards, evidently thinking it unwise, and perhaps unsafe, to leave so important a declaration of rights to depend upon an ordinary act of legislation, which might be repealed by any subsequent Congress, framed the Fourteenth Amendment of the Constitution," which stated, "All persons born or naturalized in the United States, and subject to the jurisdiction thereof, are citizens of the United States." The Court proceeded to examine every word and clause of Section 1 of the Civil Rights Act and Section 1 of the Fourteenth Amendment, as well as a great many legal cases relating to those words.[66] It was, however, the language of the Civil Rights Act that proved dispositive:

> By the first section of the bill, all persons born in the United States, and not subject to any foreign power, excluding Indians not taxed, are declared to be citizens of the United States. This provision comprehends the Chinese of the Pacific States, Indians subject to taxation, the people called Gypsies, as well as the entire race designated as blacks, persons of color, negroes, mulattoes, and persons of African blood. Every individual of those races, born in the United States, is, by the bill, made a citizen of the United States.[67]

And, if that were not enough, Justice Gray recalled Congress's deliberations on the Civil Rights Act, when the Senate debated the specific issue of Chinese citizenship and resolved that even "children born here of Mongolian parents shall . . . be entitled to civil rights and to equal protection before the law with others."[68] As such, the Court found on behalf of citizen Wong.

Come the twentieth century, the Supreme Court referenced the Civil Rights Act of 1866 far more often than at the time of the act. Some cases that mentioned the act were rather substantive, none more so than *Hodges v. United States* in 1906, which involved a violation of the civil rights found in Section 1977 of the U.S. Revised Statutes (granting all persons the same contract rights "as is enjoyed by white citizens") and enumerated in the act. Specifically at issue was violence by three white men against the contract rights of eight black men working at a sawmill in Arkansas.[69] Writing for the Court, Justice David Brewer did not directly mention the Civil Rights Act but focused instead on whether Section 1977 was justified by the Thirteenth Amendment (since "the Fourteenth and Fifteenth Amendments . . . are restrictions upon state action, and no action on the part of the state is complained of"), which he insisted was not limited to race cases, such that the federal government had no jurisdiction in this instance. The Court remanded the case to the state tribunals. In a dissenting opinion, Justice John Marshall Harlan directly referenced the Civil Rights Act of 1866 by quoting, "Citizens, of every race and color, without any regard to any previous condition of slavery or involuntary servitude, should have *the same right,* in every state and territory, *to make and enforce contracts*" (Harlan's italics).[70]

In the 1968 case of *Jones v. Alford H. Mayer Co.*, for example, the Court addressed a complaint by Jones and his wife that a housing developer refused to sell a residence to them on account of their race. The Court held that the legislative history tied to the Civil Rights Act of 1866 and carried through to Title 42 of the U.S. Code prohibited "all racial discrimination private as well as public in the sale or rental property and that the statute thus construed is a valid exercise of the power of Congress to enforce the 13th amendment."[71] This decision is significant for having found against "private" discrimination, thus reversing many precedents; according to Justice John Marshall Harlan II in dissent, it was "ill considered and ill advised to apply the act to private discrimination, rather than solely to state action."[72] Less than a decade later, the majority opinion from *Jones* was extended to include another federal statute, 42 U.S.C., Section 1981, in *Runyon v. McCrary* (1976), which held that the Civil Rights Act of 1866 as codified in the U.S. Code also prohibits racial discrimination in the making and enforcing of private contracts. That the Civil Rights Act of 1866 prohibits private racial discrimination was expressly reaffirmed in

Paterson v. McLean Credit Union (1989).[73] As recently as 2010, in *McDonald v. City of Chicago*, the Court held that the Fourteenth Amendment incorporates the Second Amendment right to keep and bear arms for purposes of self-defense. In delivering the opinion, Justice Samuel Alito referenced the Civil Rights Act, stating, "It is generally accepted that that [Fourteenth] Amendment was understood to provide a constitutional basis for protecting the rights set out in the Civil Rights Act."[74] As is to be expected, the act lives in the shadow of its extraordinary offspring.

FROM THE SUPREME COURT TO THE AMERICAN ELECTORATE

In the years after the Civil Rights Act of 1866, America's highest bench repeatedly took a conservative stance toward civil rights. Few of the justices of the Supreme Court shared Justice Noah Swayne's enthusiasm for civil rights, particularly after the death of Chief Justice Salmon Chase in 1873.[75] Yet Republicans in Congress continued the fight, passing three more civil rights acts in 1870 and 1871, variously called Enforcement Acts, Force Acts, and Ku Klux Klan Acts, which were designed to protect the rights of black people to vote, hold office, serve on juries, and receive equal protection of the laws.[76]

Although Republicans in Congress supported civil rights, the American public lost interest. General support for civil rights, probably never that great, virtually disappeared during the Panic of 1873. Already exhausted by Reconstruction, Americans suffered an enormous economic disruption that lasted for many years—the Panic of 1873 was commonly referred to as the Great Depression until the 1930s—which further tested the nation's commitment to civil rights.

The congressional elections of 1874 brought forth one of the most dramatic democratic revolts in history: the composition of Congress shifted from 68 percent Republican to 62 percent Democrat. Thus it was a lame-duck Congress that passed the last civil rights legislation of the era, the Civil Rights Act of 1875, which passed partly to honor Massachusetts senator Charles Sumner, whose dying wish just months earlier was that this legislation be approved.[77] Few in Congress expected the bill to endure the inevitable assault from the Supreme Court or the Senate's recently elected Democratic majority. Republican fears were realized on both counts: Democrats passed several measures intended to reverse substantial portions of Republican legislation, and in 1883 the Supreme Court ruled the Civil Rights Act of 1875 unconstitutional. As historian Peter Magrath so aptly observed, "1876 was an era—not a decade—removed from 1866."[78] If the earlier period can be remembered for its economic opportunity, racial justice, and high idealism, the later was marred by its financial panic, runaway corruption, and harsh pragmatism. It was in that later, far different, era that the Supreme Court adjudicated Reconstruction and the rights of black citizens. It could not have been hard to predict which way the Court would go, since, as Yale political scientist Robert A. Dahl once observed, "the policy views dominant on the court are never for long out of line with the policy views dominant among the lawmaking majorities of the United States."[79] As became increasingly evident, neither the majority of Americans nor the Supreme Court was ready for civil rights.

Notes

1. I am indebted to my research assistants, Lindsey Hale and Clark Murray, for their efforts to identify Court cases, newspaper articles, and congressional records pertaining to the act. On the significance of the Civil Rights Act of 1866, George Rutherglen has offered perhaps the best monograph: *Civil Rights in the Shadow of Slavery: The Constitution, Common Law, and the Civil Rights Act of 1866* (New York: Oxford University Press, 2013). See Civil Rights Act of 1866, 14 Stat. 27; the text is reproduced in the appendix to this volume and is quoted throughout this essay.
2. It has become commonplace to observe that Americans no longer said of themselves, "The United States are . . . ," preferring instead the language "The United States is . . ."
3. This may not have been the intent of Republicans in Congress. Mark Graber makes the convincing case that Republicans were more interested in creating a new constitutional politics, as opposed to articulating the rights of citizens, such that Sections 2 through 4 (constitutional politics that limited the reach of former Confederates) of the Fourteenth Amendment mattered more than Section 1 (citizens' rights). See Mark A. Graber, "Constructing Constitutional Politics: Thaddeus Stevens, John Bingham, and the Forgotten Fourteenth Amendment," University of Maryland Francis King Carey School of Law, Legal Studies Research Paper No. 2014–37.
4. There is general agreement among historians that the Supreme Court "abandoned" black people and the cause of civil rights, though little consensus as to when, and to what extent, that occurred. The scholarship on these issues is vast. The traditional view was that the process of abandonment began with the *Slaughterhouse Cases* and fully materialized during the Waite Court, 1874–88, following the death of Chief Justice Salmon Chase, whose

pro–civil rights leadership was sorely missed. See, for example: Kermit L. Hall, ed., *The Oxford Companion to the Supreme Court of the United States*, 2d ed. (New York: Oxford University Press, 2005), 828. More on Chase below. Challenging the traditional view, Pamela Brandwein contends, quite compellingly, that "definitive judicial abandonment" did not take place until the Fuller Court (1888–1910). See Pamela Brandwein, *Rethinking the Judicial Settlement of Reconstruction* (New York: Cambridge University Press, 2011), 184, 186–92. My own view, which is slightly more developed below, is that the Panic of 1873 deserves more attention than it gets in the story of Reconstruction. The very name of this event, the Panic of 1873, quite misleadingly understates the significance of what was one of the most significant financial setbacks of the entire nineteenth century. Prior to the 1930s, Americans referred to the Panic, which actually lasted for several years, as "the Great Depression." It contributed mightily to the massive defeat of the Republican Party in the congressional elections of 1874, which further accelerated America's abandonment of black people. For more of a general sort on Reconstruction and the law, see, among others, Pamela Brandwein, *Reconstructing Reconstruction: The Supreme Court and the Production of Historical Truth* (Durham: Duke University Press, 1999); George P. Fletcher, *Our Secret Constitution: How Lincoln Redefined American Democracy* (New York: Oxford University Press, 2001); Barry Friedman, *Will of the People: How Public Opinion Has Influenced the Supreme Court and Shaped the Meaning of the Constitution* (New York: Farrar, Straus and Giroux, 2009); Robert Kaczorowski, *The Politics of Judicial Interpretation: The Federal Courts, Department of Justice, and Civil Rights, 1866–1876* (New York: Fordham University Press, 2005); Stanley L. Kutler, *Judicial Power and Reconstruction Politics* (Chicago: University of Chicago Press, 1968); and Frank J. Scaturro, *The Supreme Court's Retreat from Reconstruction: A Distortion of Constitutional Jurisprudence* (Westport, Conn.: Greenwood, 2000).

5. Drew Gilpin Faust, *This Republic of Suffering: Death and the American Civil War* (New York: Alfred A. Knopf, 2008), xi, xiii; David J. Hacker, "A Census-Based Count of the Civil War Dead," *Civil War History* 57, no. 4 (2011): 307–48, doi:10.1353/cwh.2011.0061.
6. For the total number of slaves in the United States and the percentage of the total American population, see the Civil War Home Page, http://www.civil-war.net/census.asp?census=Total.
7. All told, there were four civil rights acts passed by Congress during Reconstruction, in 1866, 1870, 1871, and 1875: Civil Rights Act of 1866, 14 Stat. 27, passed April 9, 1866; Civil Rights Act of 1870 (the Enforcement Act),

16 Stat. 140; Civil Rights Act of 1871, 17 Stat. 13; Civil Rights Act of 1875, 18 Stat. 335. After these acts, Congress enacted no further civil rights bills until 1957, though several states did pass their own civil rights laws.

8. Civil Rights Act of 1866, 14 Stat. 27–30.
9. Scott v. Sandford, 60 U.S. 393 (1857). Congress addressed black citizenship and reversed *Dred Scott* in Section 1 and Black Codes in Section 2 of the Civil Rights Act.
10. It is a subject of some debate as to whether the Civil Rights Act prohibits private as well as public discrimination. The Thirteenth Amendment did not limit itself to "state action," whereas the Fourteenth Amendment did. The Civil Rights Act emanated from the Thirteenth Amendment but was the model for the Fourteenth Amendment, to which the Court has tended to associate it.
11. See G. Edward White, "The Origins of Civil Rights in America," 64 *Case W. Res. L. Rev.* 755–816 (2014).
12. Thomas Jefferson, *Virginia Statute for Religious Freedom* (Virginia General Assembly, 1779); Thomas Paine, *The Rights of Man* (London: J. S. Jordan, 1791).
13. On civil rights as "part of the natural law tradition," see Pamela Brandwein, *Rethinking the Judicial Settlement of Reconstruction*, 96. On the distinction among civil, political, and social rights, see Harold Hyman and William Wiecek, *Equal Justice under Law: Constitutional Development, 1835–1875* (New York: Harper and Row, 1982), 394–99. More on both below.
14. The final sentence of Section 1 reads as follows: "to make and enforce contracts, to sue, be parties, and give evidence, to inherit, purchase, lease, sell, hold, and convey real and personal property, and to full and equal benefit of all laws and proceedings for the security of person and property, as is enjoyed by white citizens, and shall be subject to like punishment, pains, and penalties, and to none other, any law, statute, ordinance, regulation, or custom, to the contrary notwithstanding."
15. Delaware senator Willard Saulsbury, *Cong. Globe*, 39th Cong., 1st Sess., quotes taken from pages 481, 478, and 477 (January 29, 1866).
16. Not only would it appear that Congress had the authority to pass the act, but the final sections of each Reconstruction amendment simultaneously granted Congress the authority to interpret, along with the Supreme Court, what those amendments mean. See Rutherglen, *Civil Rights in the Shadow of Slavery*, 10.
17. George Rutherglen, "The Origins of Arguments over Reverse Discrimination: Lessons from the Civil Rights Act of 1866," University of Virginia

School of Law, Virginia Public Law and Legal Theory Research Paper No. 2014-14.

18. While this was not the first time Congress overrode an executive veto, as is sometimes reported, it was probably the most substantial override up to that point. Congress overrode President John Tyler on March 3, 1845.
19. The Bill of Rights was not known by that name until the Reconstruction era, an innovation attributed to Ohio representative John Bingham. See Gerard N. Magliocca, *American Founding Son: John Bingham and the Invention of the Fourteenth Amendment* (New York: New York University Press, 2013), 114–15.
20. Laura Edwards, *A Legal History of the Civil War and Reconstruction: A Nation of Rights* (New York: Cambridge University Press, 2015), 129. Congress established the U.S. Bureau of Refugees, Freedmen, and Abandoned Lands, popularly known as the Freedmen's Bureau, on March 3, 1865. For more on the bureau, see Paul A. Cimbala, *The Freedmen's Bureau: Reconstructing the American South after the Civil War* (Huntington, N.Y.: Krieger, 2005).
21. *Cong. Globe*, 39th Cong., 1st Sess., 1292 (March 9, 1866). President Andrew Johnson vetoed the original second Freedmen's Bureau Bill, on February 19, 1866, various subsequent versions of which worked their way through Congress throughout the spring and summer months of that same year. Johnson has been called the "Veto President" because of the vast number of times (twenty-nine) he overrode Congress, over half of the combined number of times all presidents before him had exercised this power.
22. U.S. Const., Art. 3, Sec. 1.
23. The information in this paragraph is intended as a broad stroke; there have been many changes to the federal court system over the years and, as is so often the case in legal matters, there are exceptions to every rule. For example, in some district court cases, it is possible to intervene before a decision is handed down through an action known as "interlocutory appeal." Also, there were originally nine circuit courts. And the three judges at circuit have, at various times, included either a Supreme Court justice or a district court judge. Congress passed several acts of legislation reconfiguring the federal court system, including the Judiciary Act of 1891.
24. 26 Stat. 826. Also known as the Everts Act and/or the Circuit Court of Appeals Act, the Judiciary Act of 1891 created the U.S. Court of Appeals that we know today and that did away with circuit riding.

25. As will be seen below, the Supreme Court did grave damage to Reconstruction and the first Civil Rights Movement.
26. Legal scholars tend not to regard Justice Swayne very favorably. University of Chicago Law School professor David Currie claimed, for example, "[Justice Nathan] Clifford and Swayne, for perfectly adequate reasons, were never assigned anything of importance; they were two of the worst opinion-writers to ever sit on the Court." "The Constitution in the Supreme Court: Civil War and Reconstruction, 1863–1873," 51 *U. Chi. L. Rev.* 361 (1984).
27. Though less known for his legal acumen than someone like Justice Stephen Field, Chase was the most politically astute and motivated member of the bench. To the extent anyone from the Court could be said to have protected or salvaged the many Reconstruction acts of Congress, it was Chief Justice Salmon Chase.
28. Justice Swayne in United States v. Rhodes, 27 F. Cas. 785 (C.C.D. Ky. 1866) (No. 16,151); Chief Justice Chase in In re Turner, 24 F. Cas. 337 (C.C.D. Md. 1867) (No. 14,247); Justice Bradley in Live-Stock Dealers & Butchers Association v. Crescent City Live-Stock Landing & Slaughterhouse Co. et al., 15 F. Cas. 649 (C.C.D. La. 1870) (No. 8,408); Justice Woods in United States v. Hall, 26 F. Cas. 79 (C.C.S.D. Ala. 1871) (No. 15,282); and Justice Strong in United States v. Given, 25 F. Cas. 1324 (C.C.D. Del. 1873) (No. 15,210).
29. In his enormous opus (1,540 pages in the first of two volumes) on the Reconstruction era Supreme Court, Charles Fairman mentioned this case only once, in a single fleeting comment. See Charles Fairman, *Oliver Wendell Holmes Devise History of the Supreme Court of the United States*, vol. 7, *Reconstruction and Reunion, 1864–1888* (Cambridge: Cambridge University Press, 2010), 1309. As often happened with federal court cases, even Supreme Court cases, the facts of the case were sometimes reported incompletely, inconsistently, or incorrectly. The facts as reported by the *New York Times*, for example, are not the same as those reported to the Senate by Kentucky's senator Garrett Davis, who criticized Swayne's decision at some length, on January 14, 1868. See *New York Times*, "A Case in Kentucky under Civil Rights Bill—Negro Witnesses," October 18, 1866, 5. See also *Cong. Globe*, 40th Cong., 2nd Sess., 492–99 (January 14, 1868).
30. The law struck down was Section 669 of the 1854 Code of Civil Practice of Kentucky, which denied "Negroes, Mulattoes, and Indians" the right to testify against white defendants.

31. *Rhodes*, 27 F. Cas. at 787. On Swayne's antislavery credentials, see Michael Vorenberg, "The Chase Court, 1864–1873: Cautious Reconstruction," in *The United States Supreme Court*, ed. Christopher Tomlins (New York: Houghton Mifflin, 2005), 115.
32. *Rhodes*, 27 F. Cas. at 794. On the difference between civil and political rights, and the debates over the reach of the Civil Rights Act of 1866, see Hyman and Wiecek, *Equal Justice under Law*, 394–99.
33. *Columbus Crisis*, January 15, 1865. This was an antiwar paper published by Sam Medary from 1864 to 1871; it is available online at http://www.columbuslibrary.org/ebranch/index.cfm?pageid=96&parentid=481.
34. *In re Turner*, 24 F. Cas. 337, 339. It was customary for circuit court decisions to be brief, almost as if to underscore their finality. Any appeals tended to be on points of law, not on the facts of the case.
35. Vorenberg, "Chase Court," 118. See Jonathan Lurie, *The Chase Court: Justices, Rulings, and Legacy* (Santa Barbara, Calif.: ABC-CLIO, 2004), 26. As Lurie states, "Perhaps the best example of a decision that clearly reflected Chase's values is the little-known case of *In re Turner*."
36. *In re Turner*, 24 F. Cas. 337.
37. Ibid.
38. Justice Swayne took the same bold position in *Rhodes*. Although many politicians questioned the constitutionality of the law at the time, Swayne and Chase treated it as constitutional. The 1866 act declared that "all persons born in the United States and not subject to any foreign power, excluding Indians not taxed," were citizens of the United States. Such citizens were "of every race and color" and "without regard to any previous condition of slavery or involuntary servitude." As citizens they could make and enforce contracts, sue and be sued, give evidence in court, and inherit, purchase, lease, sell, hold, and convey real estate and personal property. Persons who denied these rights to former slaves were guilty of a misdemeanor and upon conviction faced a fine not exceeding $1,000 and/or imprisonment not exceeding one year.
39. Salmon Chase was among the most ambitious politicians of his day, so much so that he would change parties to secure a nomination. Chase ran for president many times, once from the Court.
40. The initial P. in Bradley's name was an affectation he added as a boy, perhaps in honor of his father, Philo, a farmer.
41. See Bradley's opinions in United State v. Reese, 92 U.S. 214 (1876); United States v. Cruikshank, 92 U.S. 542 (1876); United States v. Harris, 106 U.S. 629 (1883); and the Civil Rights Cases, 109 U.S. 3 (1883).

42. *Crescent City*, 15 F. Cas. at 653. Bradley would later change his opinion about civil rights but not before exhibiting yet more progressive thinking, as we will see below, as a dissenter in *Blyew v. United States*.
43. Ibid. at 649, 651, 652. Sitting alongside Justice Bradley at the circuit court for the Fifth Circuit that decided *Crescent City* was Judge William Burnham Woods, appointed by President Rutherford B. Hayes to the Supreme Court in 1880. When writing his decision in *United States v. Hall*, just a few months after *Crescent City*, Judge Woods appears to have been persuaded again by his good friend Bradley, as he had been in *Crescent City*. Evident from the many letters to Bradley from Woods and other judges, Bradley was very respected and often regarded as the Supreme Court authority on the Reconstruction amendments. Bradley's brethren often sought his advice on both philosophical and procedural matters. The Bradley Papers contain multiple examples from Ward Hunt, William Woods, Horace Gray, and even the equally august Samuel Miller. See Bradley Papers, New Jersey Historical Society, Manuscript Group 26, box 3, files 1870–74, 1875–78, and 1879–82, Newark.
44. Bradley wrote the infamous majority opinion in the *Civil Rights Cases*, decided 8–1, joined by Chief Justice Waite and Associate Justices Miller, Field, Woods, Matthews, Gray, and Blatchford. Only Justice John Marshall Harlan had the courage to dissent.
45. *Rhodes*, 27 F. Cas. at 794.
46. Lee Epstein, Jeffrey A. Segal, Harold J. Spaeth, and Thomas G. Walker, eds., *The Supreme Court Compendium: Data, Decisions, and Developments* (Washington, D.C.: Congressional Quarterly, 1994), 227. During the fourteen years under Waite, the Court heard a total of 3,445 cases.
47. Even today, over two-thirds of all Supreme Court cases contain at least one claim grounded in either the "due process" or the "equal protection" clauses of Section 1 of the Fourteenth Amendment.
48. R. D. Goldstein, "Blyew: Variations on a Jurisdictional Theme," 41 *Stan. L. Rev.* 469–566 (1989). The *Louisville Democrat* incorrectly reported the details of the crime, on October 3, 1868, stating that only three people had died, including one of the children who actually escaped death.
49. *Louisville Courier-Journal*, April 20, 1869.
50. Blyew v. United States, 80 U.S. 581 (1872).
51. Several cases between 1866 and 1870 took advantage of Section 3 of the Civil Rights Bill of 1866 in order to gain access to federal courts. See Goldstein, "Blyew," 473.
52. *Blyew*, 80 U.S. at 594.

53. Ibid.
54. Ibid. at 596.
55. United States v. Cruikshank, 92 U.S. 542, 551 (1876).
56. 16 Stat. 140.
57. Notable Kentucky African Americans Database, University of Kentucky Libraries website, http://www.uky.edu/Libraries/NKAA/subject.php?sub_id=99.
58. Slaughterhouse Cases, 83 U.S. 36 (1873).
59. Railroad Company v. Brown, 84 U.S. 445 (1873).
60. Statutes at Large of the United States of America 12:805 (March 3, 1863).
61. John P. Frank, "Can the Courts Erase the Color Line?," 2 *Buff. L. Rev.* 28, 29 (1952–53).
62. 10 Stat. at Large, 810, Sec. 3.
63. *Railroad Company*, 84 U.S. at 452–53.
64. Plessy v. Ferguson, 163 U.S. 537 (1896).
65. Carter v. Greenhow, 114 U.S. 317 (1885).
66. United States v. Wong Kim Ark, 169 U.S. 649 (1898) at 675.
67. Ibid. at 682.
68. *Cong. Globe*, 39th Cong., 1st Sess., pt. 4, 2890–92; 169 U.S. at 698–99.
69. Hodges v. United States, 203 U.S. 1 (1906).
70. Ibid. at 29.
71. Jones v. Alford H. Mayer Co., 392 U.S. 409 (1968). See 42 U.S.C., Sec. 1982.
72. Ironically, Harlan's grandfather Justice John Marshall Harlan penned the famous dissent in *Plessy v. Ferguson*, claiming, "Our constitution is color-blind, and neither knows nor tolerates classes among citizens. In respect of civil rights, all citizens are equal before the law." *Plessy*, 163 U.S. 537 at 559.
73. Runyon v. McCrary, 427 U.S. 160 (1976); Paterson v. McLean Credit Union, 491 U.S. 164 (1989).
74. McDonald v. City of Chicago, 561 U.S. 742 (2010).
75. For more on Salmon Chase, see Harold Hyman, *The Reconstruction Justice of Salmon P. Chase:* In re Turner & Texas v. White (Lawrence: University Press of Kansas, 1977); Jennifer M. Lowe, *The Supreme Court and the Civil War* (Washington, D.C.: Supreme Court Historical Society, 1996); Brian McGuinty, *Lincoln and the Court* (Cambridge, Mass.: Harvard University Press, 2008); and John Niven, *Salmon P. Chase: A Biography* (New York: Oxford University Press, 1995).

76. 16 Stat. 140, enacted May 31, 1870; 16 Stat. 433–40 and 17 Stat. 13, passed the Senate April 14, 1871.
77. 18 Stat. 335 (1875).
78. The Democrats were especially eager to reverse the Enforcement Acts. *Civil Rights Cases,* 109 U.S. 3 (1883). For quote, see C. Peter Magrath, *Morrison R. Waite: The Triumph of Character* (New York: Macmillan, 1963), 131.
79. Robert A. Dahl, "Decision-Making in a Democracy: The Supreme Court as a National Policy-Maker," 6 *J. Pub. L.* 279, 285 (1957).

8

THE CIVIL RIGHTS ACT OF 1866 AND THE RIGHT TO CONTRACT

Richard L. Aynes

BACKGROUND AND CONTEXT

This chapter discusses the right to make and enforce contracts under the Civil Rights Act of 1866. Though the federal protection of contract rights was prompted by the Black Codes enacted after the Civil War, one can trace the need for the act back to slavery itself.

One of the most common rights that white people took for granted was the right to make contracts. Contracts were seen as important to people even at the founding of the nation, as exemplified by Article 1, Section 10, of the U.S. Constitution prohibiting states from "impairing the Obligations of contracts."[1]

Contracts are essential for living in a free society. Indeed, descriptions of the importance of contracts in modern times, such as the following from John D. Calamari and Joseph M. Perillo, give us an analogous view of what was true in the 1860s: "The law of contracts permeates every aspect of our society. Every day it reaches into the life of the individual, governing to some extent the individual's employment, purchase and sale of land and goods, the insuring of the individual's possession and the financing of these transactions. On a vaster scale, it enters into practically every aspect of domestic and international trade."[2] These concepts have been referred to as the right of "freedom of contract."[3] Freedom of contract goes hand in hand with the nineteenth-century Republicans' advocacy of "free labor" and "free men" and is completely antithetical to slavery. In writing about contracts, Theophilus Parsons, a professor at Harvard Law School in the nineteenth century, stated that "all social life presumes it and rests upon it."[4]

For this reason, these same rights were denied to those held in slavery. Thomas R. R. Cobb's famous (or infamous) treatise on slavery[5] devotes a whole chapter on the topic of contracts.[6] Among the commonly accepted "rights" that white people took for granted but were denied to people held in slavery was the right to enter into contracts and enforce them.

Cobb was purportedly writing to state the law and not to change it. Thus, as one might expect, there are many court decisions supporting the views he expressed.[7] Cobb began with the idea that a person held in slavery had many disabilities, one of which was "his inability to contract or to be contracted with."[8] Given the fact that any such contract would be void, it necessarily followed that it could not be enforced.

Besides the fact that those held in slavery had no legal right to enter or enforce contracts, they also had no access to the courts, could not be a party to a suit, could not be a witness to a signed document, such as a promissory note, and could not give testimony in court.

Part of the reason for the ban on making and enforcing contracts was to implement the American form of slavery. In the words of North Carolina chief justice Thomas Ruffin, the "power of the master must be absolute, to render the submission of the slave perfect."[9] If people held in slavery had the right to enter into contracts, to enforce those contracts, and to have contracts enforced against others, this would directly undermine the "absolute" power and control of the slaveholder. Of course, slavery itself was abolished during the Civil War era through what had been called the "friction" of the war, the First Confiscation Act, the Second Confiscation Act, the Emancipation Proclamation, and ultimately the Thirteenth Amendment to the U.S. Constitution.

Senator Lyman Trumbull's (R-Ill.) draft of the Thirteenth Amendment, ratified by the states on December 6, 1865, was based on language from the Northwest Ordinance. The Civil Rights Act of 1866 was passed pursuant to that amendment and used the enforcement power given by the amendment to enact it.[10] In 1870, this statute was amended so that all persons were given the same right to contract as white persons.[11]

As articulated by Representative William Lawrence (R-Ohio), a former judge, in the debates over the Civil Rights Bill, "In law the incident always adheres to and accompanies the principles. It is idle to say that a citizen shall have the right to life, yet to deny him the right to labor, whereby he can live. It is a mockery to say that a citizen shall have a right to live, and yet deny him the right to make a contract to secure the privilege and the rewards of his labor."[12] Over and over again the proponents of the bill argued that it simply outlined the rights of every free man.[13] In the words of Senator Jacob Howard (R-Mich.), a member of the Joint Committee on Reconstruction and the floor manager of the Fourteenth Amendment in the Senate, the Civil Rights Act was designed to "secure the ordinary rights of a freeman."[14] Hence, the inability to make and enforce contracts was not just a "badge" of slavery but one of slavery's key elements.

Many thoughtful people believed that if one were freed from slavery, such as happened with the adoption of the Thirteenth Amendment, the people formerly held in slavery would be free citizens and have the same rights as other citizens.[15] For example, even before the war, northern legal theorists such as one-time House of Representatives judiciary chairman John A. Bingham (R-Ohio) maintained that people held in slavery were citizens of the United States but did not have full rights because they were subject to the disability that came with being held in slavery.[16] Under this view, once the disabilities of slavery were removed, all the rights of a citizen would accrue to those previously held in slavery.[17]

Another group of respected legal thinkers reached the same result without looking at the status of people when held in slavery. As early as 1840, James Kent, former chancellor of New York, wrote, "If a slave born in the United States, be manumitted or otherwise lawfully discharged from bondage, or if a black man be born within the United States and born free, he becomes thence forward a citizen."[18] Similarly, Timothy Walker, one-time law partner of future U.S. Supreme Court chief justice Salmon Chase, one of the founders of the University of Cincinnati Law School, and the publisher of the *Western Law Journal,* wrote that "native citizens include . . . all persons born within the jurisdiction of the United States since our Independence."[19] He made no distinction based upon race.[20] Again, if the Thirteenth Amendment gave freedom from slavery, under the Kent/Walker view, this would have made them citizens and given them the same rights as white people in making and enforcing contract rights.

Finally, if one credits Cobb's statement that "unless restricted by statute," African Americans who were free could contract with "any free person capable of contracting,"[21] then this is a third principle that should have given former slaves the right to make and enforce contracts after the ratification of the Thirteenth Amendment.

Thus, under any one of the above legal approaches, there should have been no need for much of the Civil Rights Act, including the guarantee for contract rights. The problem was that while the former Confederates and former slaveholders said they accepted the end of slavery, they wanted to maintain a modified type of state-slavery for all African Americans after the war through the use of Black Codes. White resisters who refused to accept any of the legal theories that would have provided a smooth transition to becoming members of the community for people formerly held in slavery created the Black Codes to take the place of the slave codes, largely performing the same function. It was to counteract these Black Codes and to sweep away this important part of slavery that Congress enacted the 1866 Civil Rights Act, which protected, in part, the right of free people to make and enforce contracts.

Senator Henry Wilson (R-Mass.), later vice president of the United States, introduced legislation, on the first day of the Senate session of the Thirty-Ninth Congress, to declare null and void all laws in the insurrectionary states that discriminated based on distinctions of race, color, descent, or previous condition of or status of slavery or involuntary servitude.[22] A December 13, 1865, discussion ensued, in part, over the prudence of voting upon such a bill before the Thirteenth Amendment was ratified. Among those urging postponement was Senator John Sherman (R-Ohio), who nevertheless proclaimed, "I believe it is the duty of Congress to give the freedmen of the Southern States ample protection in their natural rights."[23] During this debate Senate Judiciary Committee chairman and former Illinois Supreme Court justice Lyman Trumbull gave notice of his intention to introduce legislation to "secure to those men every one of these rights; they would not be freemen without them."[24]

Indeed, W. E. B. DuBois found that the public debates between 1864 and 1868 demonstrated that "a large majority" of the people supported the "public opinion" that "[a] legal status of freedom without actual civil rights would mean almost nothing."[25] These sentiments were expressed during the 1866 debates. Even conservative senator James Doolittle (R-Wisc.), in opposing making American Indians citizens, said that to do so would both give them the ability to make contracts and bind them to perform duties under contracts.[26]

Senator Trumbull introduced the Civil Rights Act of 1866 early in the January 1866 session.[27] Historian Michael Les Benedict termed the act "a brilliant piece of legislation" because "Trumbull had found a way to force the states themselves to alter their discriminatory laws."[28] One approach that could have provided a smooth path to freedom was outlined by Senator James Guthrie (D-Ky.), a former U.S. secretary of the Treasury, who indicated that there were laws for white citizens, free African Americans, and those people held in slavery. He admitted the laws concerning slavery had died with the Thirteenth Amendment and seemed to concede that the laws applying to free black people now applied to those formerly held in slavery.[29] In the debates over the Freedmen's Bureau, Representative

Charles E. Phelps (Union War–Md.) argued that the freedmen "ought to be protected in the rights under contract."[30]

After the Civil War, white southerners were resistant to entering into contracts with people who had formerly been held in slavery. For people who had always lived in a culture in which African Americans "had no rights which the white man was required to respect,"[31] it was more difficult to accept the fact that people formerly held in slavery had rights than it was to accept the fact that they were no longer physically held as slaves. Many white people felt they were not obligated to honor any contract made with an African American. This is consistent with a type of aristocratic culture white slaveholders had developed. They might well issue a challenge to or accept a challenge from another "gentleman" of their own class to a duel. But they would never make or accept a challenge from someone they considered their inferior such as a small farmer, a common laborer, or even a U.S. senator such as Charles Sumner.[32] Rather, they would simply proceed to beat or shoot the allegedly inferior person. Similarly, they felt no obligation to keep their word to an individual who was not a "gentleman" of their own class.

Even when contracts were made, post–Civil War enforcement was often a great difficulty. The Bureau of Freedmen and Refugees spent a considerable amount of time hearing disputes over contracts and their enforcement.[33] These attitudes, when mixed with overt racism and armed struggle over political control, deprived the former slaves both of economic stability and of an enforceable right to contract as enjoyed by white citizens.

Michael Les Benedict has indicated that the Freedmen's Bureau was intended to "aid the transition from slave to free labor."[34] Part of the way it did this was by mediating disputes on contracts. Many white southerners attempted to keep conditions as they were before the war. They refused to make contracts with African Americans or, if contracts were made, would break them to the detriment of the African Americans.

To take one common example, they might "discharge" a sharecropper before the crop was sold and refuse to give that sharecropper any share of the crop. The Freedmen's Bureau devoted much time and energy in trying to support the Thirteenth Amendment and the concept of free labor by enforcing such contracts. In another example, a planter refused to pay the amount due under a contract unless the worker signed a contract for life. Further, a report from Mississippi indicated that freedmen who did not sign a contract for at least a full year's labor were judged to be vagrants. Consequently they were arrested and sold to private parties for whom they were required to labor to work off their fine.[35]

Such was the understanding of the key importance of the ability to make and enforce contracts in the nineteenth century that during the debates on the act only one lone congressman, Representative Edgar Cowen (R-Pa.), raised any objections to that individual provision.[36] First, Cowen argued that the "equality" requirement of the act would allow married women, minors, "idiots," and "lunatics" to make and enforce contracts. Second, he argued it would void laws such as Pennsylvania's law that a contract made on a Sunday was void, as were contracts "against chastity."[37]

In theory, these provisions should have brought individual and economic stability to the former slave states as well as to those formerly individually held in slavery. In practice, the same terrorism and violence that was used to deprive African Americans and white unionists of political rights were also used to deprive them of their contract rights. Further, even in normal business transactions, the continuing economic and aristocratic institutions favored former slaveholders in disputes over contracts with former slaves. Indeed, historian Eric Foner, quoting with approval an unnamed congressman, indicated that the act was "to secure to a poor, weak class of laborers the right to make contracts for their labor, the power to enforce the payment of their wages, and enjoying proceeds of their toil."[38]

The political changes caused by the "long depression" of 1873,[39] the "retreat from reconstruction,"[40] and the use of violence and fraud that deprived unionists, black and white, of their right to vote all resulted in the stunted judicial interpretation of the Civil Rights Act and its contract provision. Volume 10 of the *Century Edition of the American Digest* included cases from 1866 to 1895 and covered the words "citizens" to "contractors."[41] In it, some 401 pages of digests of cases concern "collisions"[42] and 180 pages concern "continuances,"[43] but only 23 pages address "civil rights."[44] This is analogous to the lack of full-fledged application and exploration of the contours of the Fourteenth and Fifteenth Amendments until the 1940s and, indeed, the advent of the later Civil Rights Movement.

This lack of early cases can be explained by the fact that not only were attorneys sometimes risking their lives in bringing actions under Section 1981 (the modern codification of the 1866 Civil Rights Act), but also it was not until 110 years later, in 1976, that 42 U.S.C. 1988 was amended to provide for the award of attorneys' fees to the prevailing party. Only after this change was it practical for attorneys to take the cases of low-income plaintiffs.[45]

Some people worry about the right not to extend an offer or accept an offer if discrimination in forming contracts is prohibited.[46] But this concern is overstated. Following an analogy to *Batson v. Kentucky*[47] (peremptory challenges), one could say that a contractual relationship can be denied for a good reason or for no reason but not for a "bad" or illegal reason such as race. Indeed, the making of the prima facie case and the shifting of the burden to the state to demonstrate a race-neutral reason for disputes over peremptory challenges is very similar to what happens in Title VII sex discrimination cases. This solution is the one most consistent with the statutory language, the legislative history, and the purpose of abolishing the "badges and incidents of slavery."[48]

MODERN ISSUES

In one of the few books with a focus upon Section 1981, George Rutherglen, after referring to what he terms "expansive decisions," states, "Thus, section 1981 was interpreted to support claims by whites as well as blacks and to support claims on the basis of national original as well."[49] Yet, the decisions to which he refers, discussed below, seem to be consistent with the plain meaning of the statute and the legislative history.

In advocating the Civil Rights Act, Senator Trumbull declared that the act would apply "to white men as well as black men" and that "all persons" would be "entitled to the same civil rights."[50] Trumbull played an unusually large role in speaking on the bill, and his views are consistent with the current law. Some members of both the House and Senate opposed his views on the need for the adoption of the act, but no one rose to oppose his interpretation of the act itself.

Because of the stunting of the determination of Section 1981's meaning in its early days, we have to look to the Court's cases since the 1960s to "recover" what was lost. In doing so, three key Supreme Court cases and a congressional response warrant discussion: *Jones v. Alfred H. Mayer Co.*,[51] *Runyon v. McCrary*,[52] and *Patterson v. McLean Credit Union*.[53]

Theodore Eisenberg points out that "together, *Jones* and *Runyon* establish Sections 1981 and 1982 as broad federal antidiscrimination provisions covering most contractual and property relationships."[54] Though *Patterson* limited Section 1981 to the formation of contracts, Congress functionally overruled that limitation by amending the section in passing the Civil Rights Act of 1991. The 1991 act, in Section 2, defined the "making and enforcement of contracts" to include the "making, performance, modification, termination of contracts, and the enjoyment of all benefits, privileges, term, and conditions, of the contractual relationship."[55]

This amendment, in turn, led to *CBOCS West, Inc. v. Humphries*, decided in 2008. The first paragraph of the Court's opinion indicates, "The basic question before us is whether the provision encompasses a complaint of retaliation against a person who has complained about a violation of another person's contract-related 'right.' We conclude that it does."[56]

An amicus brief filed by forty-eight historians, citing the lengthy 1865 report of the Freedmen's Bureau director and former general, Oliver Otis Howard, concluded that after "the Civil War [there were] regular reprisals by white landowners and others against former slaves who sought to exercise their contractual rights."[57] Indeed, "regular reprisals" also followed efforts to report contract violation to the authorities.[58] Such reprisals led this group of scholars to conclude that "the right to 'make and enforce contracts' is appropriately understood to include protection against retaliation for seeking to assert contract rights."[59]

The Court concluded, by a 7-to-2 majority, that the statute as amended in 1991 did prohibit retaliation against an individual who successfully vindicated his or her rights under the statute.[60] It relied, in part, upon the decision of *Sullivan v. Little Hunting Park, Inc.*,[61] where an implied right to be free from retaliation was found under the companion statute, Section 1982. While it appears unlikely the current Court would have reached this conclusion without the amended statute, such a conclusion could be reasonably reached by implication in the original statutory language giving "persons" the right to "make and enforce contracts." Further, the act guarantees the "full and equal benefit of all laws and proceedings for the security of person and property" as enjoyed by white citizens. One can reasonably conclude that being able to enforce the right to contract without retaliation is necessary for there to be a "full" benefit and an "equal" benefit. Thus, it would seem that the normal rules of legislative construction support the conclusion in *Jones*, *Runyon*, and *CBOCS West*, with or without the aid of the 1991 amendment.

There are possible advantages in using Section 1981 in litigation or negotiation. Justice Felix Frankfurter noted that there are not only "simple-minded" but also "sophisticated . . . modes of discrimination."[62] The nineteenth-century attempts to discriminate by legislatively making African Americans incapable of entering into contracts or certain types of contracts are simple-minded examples. The cases from *Jones v. Mayer* to *CBOCS West* represent several levels of the "sophisticated" type of discrimination. Because of the early stunted growth of litigation under the statute, one would expect to see competing lawyers raising more and more issues about its application so that a mature body of law emerges.

Though the act has a "citizenship" clause, it is not linked to the rights protected by the statute like it is in the Fourteenth Amendment, so there is no state action requirement. Thus, one advantage of using Section 1981 is that it applies to everyone, including state and private individuals.[63] In the words of its chief sponsor, Senator Trumbull, the act pertained "not [to] State officers especially, but [to] everyone who violates the law. It is the intention to punish everyone who violates the law."[64] Further, unlike statutes based upon the interstate commerce clause, the Civil Rights Act of 1866 applies to everyone and not simply to employers with a certain number of employees or with a direct effect upon interstate commerce.

Indeed, the lower courts have applied Section 1981 to a broad spectrum of race-based behavior, including security deposit requirements, admissions to educational institutions, supply contracts, admissions to amusements parks, the sale of insurance, and dealing with mortuaries.[65] Further, the lower courts have held that if a Section 1981 violation is to be processed in courts, the remedies for the right should be brought under Section 1983 and not directly through Section 1982, *if* the defendant is a state actor. This implies, as well, that a 1981 action can be brought directly against a private party.

The contracts provision of Section 1981 overlaps with Title VII of the Civil Rights Act of 1964 prohibiting discrimination based upon race and gender. The provisions of Title VII require that a complaint be filed with the Equal Employment Opportunity Commission and that remedy be exhausted before one can proceed to court. Depending upon the nature of the case, the less formal proceedings and the possibility of an expedited decision under the EEOC may be attractive. In other instances plaintiffs may prefer to go directly to court under Section 1981. In some instances individuals may take the first course and, if no remedy is forthcoming, pursue the complaint in court under both Title VII and Section 1981.

Further, Section 1981 has a longer statute of limitations than does Title VII. Title VII requires that a charge of discrimination generally be filed "within 180 days from the day the discrimination took place."[66] This time period is extended so that a complaint has a total of 300 days if "a state or local agency enforces a law that prohibits employment discrimination on the same basis."[67]

In contrast, the statute of limitations for Sections 1981 and 1982 borrows from the most relevant state statute.[68] This creates the possibility of the statute of limitations varying state by state. But whatever the statute used, it will almost always be longer than under Title VII.[69]

CONCLUSION

The Civil Rights Act of 1866 is an important part of our history and the current legal landscape. In seeking to implement the meaning of a viable Thirteenth Amendment abolishing slavery and involuntary servitude, it helps us to understand what freedom means beyond the lack of physical restraint and self-ownership. Though it is clear that the Freedmen's Bureau spent a considerable amount of time in mediating and making decisions concerning contracts made pursuant to the act, it is unclear to what extent that bureau developed a comprehensive body of "law" that fleshed out the act and to what extent it was or was not reasonably effective.

The ratification of the Fourteenth Amendment in 1868 both supported the act and at the same time overshadowed it. The amendment and the act overlapped but were not identical, as shown by the fact that Congress reenacted the act after the Fourteenth Amendment was passed.[70] This reenactment would not have been necessary if the Fourteenth Amendment was identical to the act. Given the conditions of Reconstruction, especially when the transition to free labor was being made and after the depression of 1873, which brought a dramatic shift in attitudes,[71] there were few reported contract cases under the act in the nineteenth century. The act remained largely, though not entirely, dormant until the 1960s.

This period of dormancy saw the rise of what has been termed the *Lochner* era, 1897–1937. It has been suggested that the contracts clause of the 1866 Civil Rights Act was related to and supported the expansive liberty and substantive due process decisions of the *Lochner* era.[72] Though some respected scholars argue the 1866 Civil Rights Act is supportive of the *Lochner* era cases,[73] they are few and far between. While one can understand the argument, there are at least three reasons to consider it anachronistic.

First, though one has to be cautious about claiming to have proved a negative, in my reading of the debates and literature about the debates, I found no instance in which the framers of the act expressed a view that the right to contract was thought to be met even if large disparities occurred between the parties to the contract. Indeed, if the parties had had equal bargaining power, no need would have existed to enact a provision guaranteeing the right to "make and enforce" contracts. Further, this view is supported by the Anti-peonage Act of 1867, which indicates one cannot voluntarily contract to enter into binding servitude, and by the fact that the Thirteenth Amendment prohibits all slavery, not just involuntary slavery.[74]

Second, in spite of the claim that the act was to prevent "freedom of contract without government interferences," it is not supported by any contemporaneous legislative history or court decisions. Indeed, the guarantee of the right to contract was itself a government interference, as was the contemporary legislation creating the Freedmen's Bureau. The very purposes and later actions of the bureau were, contrary to *Lochner* era cases that assumed equality between an employer and his or her employees, to enforce the contract because of the lack of equality and the use of the employer's economic power to coerce unfair contracts.

Further, law professor Wilson R. Huhn has indicated that Republican goals and theory were just the opposite:

> In advocating "Free Labor" Republicans were fighting against "the Slave Power," whose essence was exploitation of workers. In this the slaveholders had much in common with the laissez faire capitalists of the Robber Baron era. For example, James Henry Hammond's "mudsill" theory of labor or John C. Calhoun's description of the role of the slaveholder as the director of both labor and capital, expressed perfectly the notion that workers exist to serve the owners and have no legal rights that need to be recognized. Lincoln responded to Hammond beautifully in 1859 in his address at the Wisconsin Agricultural Fair, stating that labor is prior to capital and is much the superior. Lincoln wanted opportunity for all to rise by their own efforts, and that was a constant theme of the early Republicans. Freedom of contract originally meant that no-one owns another person and the fruits of one's labor were owned by the one doing the labor. This message was distorted and perverted in the rise of the great corporations to mean that owners of factories and mines should be free to crush workers. . . .
>
> Slavery is the absence of law, an absence of any legal protection on behalf of the working class and the ordinary person. The 39th Congress believed profoundly that the states had a duty to extend the protection of law to every person—equally. The Whig Republicans believed in the power of government to improve the life of the ordinary citizen through taxation and public works. When the time came they would have supported legislation to protect ordinary people from business corporations as well.[75]

This same view was advanced by Fourteenth Amendment coauthor John A. Bingham. In 1860, while campaigning in Philadelphia for Abraham Lincoln, the Ohio congressman argued that the prohibition of nobility in the Constitution was because "there should be no nobility, except the nobility of merit."[76] In further speaking of the Constitution, Bingham said that it was the "object of this instrument, among other things, to secure a fair day's wages for a fair day's work," to which there was "applause."[77] At late as 1885, at the age of seventy, Bingham was still condemning the Democratic *Dred Scott* decision as oppressing millions of workers.[78] During the great national coal strike of 1894, Bingham's life-long supporter, the *Cadiz (Ohio) Republican*, supported the workers against the owners.[79]

In one of the very first cases upholding the constitutionality of the 1866 act, Chief Justice Chase, on the circuit, held the pre–1866 civil rights apprentice contract invalid, upholding the act and voiding the contract.[80] Further, as far as I can determine, no *Lochner* era cases occur in which the Court cited the 1866 Civil Rights Act in support of its decision.[81] There is nothing to suggest that the 1866 Civil Rights Act was to protect the citizens against state regulations of contract terms or the type of remedies that existed for breach or similar contract matters regulated by the state. Thus, while one can follow the logic of the argument for using the Civil Rights Act to advance *Lochner*-type goals, the fact of the matter is that no contemporary did so and such an argument today is anachronistic.

As a result, many of the issues that could have been litigated and resolved in the nineteenth century remain open today. This explains, for example, why there was no discussion of retaliation until *CBOCS West, Inc. v. Humphries* was decided by the Supreme Court in 2008.

There are also those who are concerned with overlapping provisions. However, as Jacobus tenBroek pointed out in his landmark *Equal under Law*, "The three clauses of the Fourteenth Amendment are mostly but not entirely duplicative."[82] By analogy, a similar claim can be made of the provision of the Civil Rights Act, its parts, and the Fourteenth Amendment. Sometimes such provisions are in the nature of what Thirty-Ninth Congress member Martin Thayer (R-Pa.) called "double security" in relying upon multiple sections of the Constitution or law to protect a right.[83]

The concepts of free labor and a democratic nation are protected, in part, by the overlapping provisions of the Civil Rights Act of 1866 and the Fourteenth Amendment. For this we all owe a debt to Senator Trumbull and the members of the Thirty-Ninth Congress.

Notes

1. To some extent, this clause both assumes and implies the existence of a general right of contract. The Supreme Court has essentially changed the clause to read, "No State may [unreasonably] impair the Obligations of Contracts." See Calvin Massey, *American Constitutional Law: Powers and Liberties*, 3d ed. (New York: Aspen Publishers, 2009), 593.
2. John D. Calamari and Joseph M. Perillo, *Calamari and Perillo on Contracts*, 5th ed. (St. Paul, Minn.: West Group, 2003), 4.
3. Robert A. Hillman, *Principles of Contract Law*, 2d ed. (St. Paul, Minn.: Westlaw, 2011), 2.
4. Amy Dru Stanley, *From Bondage to Contract: Wage Labor, Marriage, and the Market in the Age of Slave Emancipation* (New York: Cambridge University Press, 1998), 3, quoting Parsons's *The Law of Contracts*, 3 vols. (1873). Stanley's book is both interesting and important in illustrating that the act still left black women with many challenges and problems. One insight into the situation of black women was the view expressed by a wife of those times, that her husband had replaced the "master" once slavery was abolished. Yet it is anachronistic to think that the act should have given black women or all women the rights we associate with citizenship today, imperfect as our present society is.

   In reading the act in the context of its time, it did elevate black women to the same status as white women under the law. While, by modern lights, this was insufficient for black women, as it was for white women, the act was a step forward that established equality for black women with white women and secured for them basic civil rights.

   Some people want to read modern views into the "should" of the 1866 act. They fail to realize that it was Ben Wade's advocacy (in a Kansas speech) of women voting that helped defeat the impeachment of President Johnson because people thought Ben Wade was too radical to be president. Had Johnson been impeached, Wade would have been president, and by working with Congress, the loss of thousands of lives and some of the struggles of Reconstruction might have been avoided. Further, he might have advanced women's rights far more than any other president in the nineteenth century. Even Salmon P. Chase, who in private letters to his daughters stated that they were as competent to vote as he was when he was their age, and thought women's suffrage would be a worthy experiment in a few states and was willing to support it in his home state of Ohio, had a male-dominated view of marriage and advised his daughter Kate to submit to her husband's misconduct, which no good father would agree to today.

The act was only one step forward in what would continue to be a long march. The fact is black women were recognized as citizens. Congressman Bingham noted on the floor of Congress that citizenship protected women in their freedom of speech, protected them from illegal search and seizure, and gave them the protections of the entire Bill of Rights. Notwithstanding its failure to live up to modern views, the act did elevate black women to the same legal status as white women

5. Thomas R. R. Cobb, *An Inquiry into the Law of Negro Slavery in the United States of America* (1858; repr., New York: Negro Universities Press, 1968); this was the only legal analysis of slavery produced by a southerner. Special thanks to Nancy Chawla (class of 2015) for researching Cobb's views.
6. Ibid., chap. 15, "Of Contracts by slaves, and herein of marriage," 240–46. See also chap. 20, "Of manumission by will or executory contract," 296–305. Of course, contracts could play a role in other matters, such as the purchase and ownership of land.
7. Ibid., "Table of Cases," xxiii–xxxii. In chap. 15, concerning the inability of people held in slavery to make and enforce contracts, Cobb cited cases thirty-three times, treatises or other books thirty-one times, and one statute. Stanley, *From Bondage to Contract*, 9, indicated that "the absence of contract marked the slave." Further, she quoted George M. Stroud, *Sketch of Laws Relating to Slavery* (1827), 10, 31, for the proposition that a universal principle of all slave states was that "a slave cannot make a contract" (18 and n. 39).
8. Cobb, *Inquiry into the Law of Negro Slavery*, 240.
9. State v. Mann, 13 N.C. 203, 266 (1830). A jury of twelve white men found Mann guilty of battery for shooting Lydia in the back when she tried to run away from a punishment, but this was reversed by the North Carolina Supreme Court.
10. It is generally thought that House Judiciary chair James F. Wilson (R-Iowa) drafted the enforcement clause. I have suggested that this was needed because of the Republican theory that without such a clause the Fugitive Slave Act could not be enforced, and consistency might produce the same result here. Richard L. Aynes, "On Misreading John Bingham and the Fourteenth Amendment," 103 *Yale L. J.* 57, 71 (1993) (outlining the prewar argument that there was no power to enforce the Fugitive Slave Act). Many Republicans believed the citizenship clause of the act was merely "declaratory" of existing law. E.g., *Cong. Globe*, 39th Cong., 1st Sess., 1124

(March 1, 1866.), Representative Burton C. Cook (R-Ill.) ("this is the law now"). Others thought the rights outlined in the act, including the right to make or enforce contracts, were the rights conferred by nature of being a citizen (Representative Martin R. Thayer, R-Pa.) and stemmed from the rights of citizens guaranteed under Article 4 and the republican form of government clause (Representative William Lawrence, R-Ohio) or were the rights of human nature (Representative and future Secretary of the Treasury William Windom, R-Minn.). *Cong. Globe*, 39th Cong., 1st Sess., 1159 (March 2, 1866).

11. 16 U.S. Stat. 140.
12. *Cong. Globe*, 39th Cong., 1st Sess., 1833 (April 7, 1866) (citations omitted). Lawrence referred to the right of contract as one of the "inherent and inalienable rights."
13. Ibid., 475–76 (January 29, 1866) (Senator Trumbull speaking of "rights of a freeman," "every man as a free man," and "every free man"). Indeed, even modern scholars take the view that the right to contract was one of the "undeniable civil rights." E.g., George Rutherglen, *Civil Rights in the Shadow of Slavery: The Constitution, Common Law, and the Civil Rights Act of 1866* (New York: Oxford University Press, 2013), 89.
14. *Cong. Globe*, 39th Cong., 1st Sess., 127 (January 30, 1866).
15. One can hardly write about the Civil Rights Act of 1866 without taking into account the status of people held in slavery before and after the adoption of the Thirteenth Amendment and how it affected their rights. The starting point is who were citizens and what prompted the 1866 Civil Rights Act citizenship clause. Linking the status and prohibitions imposed upon people held in slavery helps explain why the framers of the act felt that a contracts provision was necessary. My goal here is to simply point out that respected people in the field of law articulated the view that, if followed, would have made the citizenship clause unnecessary. James Kent, approximately twenty-five years old at the time of the adoption of the U.S. Constitution, was said to have been "stoutly conservative." *Concise Dictionary of American Biography* (New York: Charles Scribner's Sons, 1964), 522. Timothy Walker's book on American law, during its day, is said to have been "the most generally used text-book in the country." Charles Frederick Greve, *Centennial History of Cincinnati and Representative Citizens* (Chicago: Biographical Publishers, 1904), 1:8. Congressman Bingham was one of the top eleven men of "prominent influence" in the House of Representatives. Michael Les Benedict, *Compromise of Principle: Congressional Republicans and Reconstruction, 1863–1869* (New York:

W. W. Norton, 1974), 31. For a more detailed account of the history of citizenship, see Benedict's and Zietlow's chapters in this volume on the 1866 act's citizenship clause.

16. "Letter from Hon. John A. Bingham to the Colored Citizens of Lynchburg," *New York Times*, May 23, 1867, 5, col. 4 ("citizen-slaves" were now "citizen freemen"); "Letter from Hon. John A. Bingham," *Cadiz (Ohio) Republican*, April 22, 1870, 2, col. 3. (African Americans held in slavery as "an enslaved race" were nevertheless "natural born citizens of the United States under disabilities").
17. We know, for example, that the Congress that drafted the Civil Rights Act of 1866 was not court-centric because its citizenship clause directly conflicted with the very well known but despicable *Dred Scott* case.
18. Chancellor James Kent, *Commentaries*, 4th ed. (New York: E. B. Clayton, 1840), 2:257. This portion of Kent was quoted by Congressman Bingham in Congress, *Cong. Globe*, 35th Cong., 2d Sess., 892 (1859).
19. Timothy Walker, *Introduction to Law*, 2d ed. (Cincinnati: Derby, Bradley, and Co., 1844), 131. Biographical data on Walker can be found in Walter Theodore Hitchcock, "Timothy Walker," in *The Yale Biographical Dictionary of American Law*, ed. Roger K. Newman (New Haven: Yale University Press, 2009), 568.
20. It is worth noting that both of these prominent jurists had taken these positions well before the *Dred Scott* decision and yet Chief Justice Taney ignored them in his opinion.
21. Cobb, *Inquiry into the Law of Negro Slavery*, 313. The disability to contract placed upon a person held in slavery operated "every place he may go, so long as he remains a slave" (246).
22. William H. Barnes, *History of the Thirty-Ninth Congress of the United States* (1868; repr., New York: Negro Universities Press, 1869), 95–96.
23. Ibid., 98.
24. Ibid., 100. See also W. E. B. DuBois, *Black Reconstruction in America, 1860–1880* (repr., New York: Touchstone Books, 1995), 271 (including contracts within these rights and citing *Cong. Globe*, 39th Cong., 1st Sess., part 1, 90 and 91)
25. DuBois, *Black Reconstruction in America*, 329.
26. *Cong. Globe*, 39th Cong., 1st Sess., 571 (February 1, 1866).
27. Ibid., 211 (January 12, 1866).
28. Benedict, *Compromise of Principle*, 149.
29. *Cong. Globe*, 39th Cong., 1st Sess., 600 (February 2, 1866). This might be acceptable from a contracts standpoint, if one could rely upon Cobb's

treatise indicating that free African Americans could contract with anyone capable of contracting. But we have reason to be skeptical. We know, for example, that freed people could not enter into the contract of marriage with white people and that they could not enter into contracts to purchase firearms. If those unstated limitations existed, what else might not be covered by Cobb's broad claim? Cobb, *Inquiry into the Law of Negro Slavery*, 313. This probably did not extend to the ability to contract to buy arms because these were generally prohibited (314). This undoubtedly explains why the Freedmen's Act explicitly included the right to bear arms in the rights it protected. See 15 U.S. Stat. 83 (1866) ("to have full and equal benefit of all laws and proceedings for the security of person and estate, including the constitutional right of bearing arms"). Further, given Guthrie's political views, it is unlikely that he intended the result to be as broad as a modern reader would conclude.

30. *Cong. Globe*, 39th Cong., 1st Sess., app. 75 (February 3 or 5, 1866).
31. Scott v. Sandford, 60 U.S. 393, 407 (1857).
32. There was a certain degree of cowardice in this. See generally Richard L. Aynes, "*McDonald v. Chicago*, the Fourteenth Amendment, the Right to Bear Arms and the Rights of Self-Defenses," *Cardozo L. Rev. de*novo* (special print edition of an online journal) (multiple examples of southern aristocrats backing down when confronted by northerners proficient with weapons and willing to use them, 192–94 and 196n142).
33. Benedict, *Compromise of Principle*, 148.
34. Ibid., 164–70.
35. Unidentified report read in the speech of William Lawrence, *Cong. Globe*, 39th Cong., 1st Sess., 1833 (April 7, 1866).
36. Of course, others opposed the bill on wider grounds that would have defeated the entire bill, including the contract provision.
37. *Cong. Globe*, 39th Cong., 1st Sess., 1782 (April 5, 1866).
38. Eric Foner, *Reconstruction* (New York: Harper and Row, 1988), 244.
39. See generally Richard L. Aynes, "The Fourteenth Amendment and the Bill of Rights: Enforcing the Bill of Rights against the States: The History and the Future," 18 *J. Contemp. Legal Issues* 77, 101–5 (2009).
40. William Gillette, *Retreat from Reconstruction, 1869–1879* (Baton Rouge: Louisiana State University Press, 1979); Heather Cox Richardson, *The Death of Reconstruction, Race, Labor, and Politics in the Post–Civil War North, 1865–1901* (Cambridge, Mass.: Harvard University Press, 2001).
41. *Century Edition of the American Digest*, vol. 10 (St. Paul, Minn.: West Publishing, 1899).

42. Ibid., 250–651.
43. Ibid., 2651–831.
44. Ibid., 3–26.
45. E.g., Mark R. Brown, "A Primer on the Law of Attorney's Fees under § 1988," 37 *Urb. Law.* 663 (2005).
46. Rutherglen, *Civil Rights in the Shadow of Slavery*, 138–42.
47. Batson v. Kentucky, 476 U.S. 79 (1986).
48. Jones v. Alfred Mayer Co., 392 U.S. 409, 439 (1968).
49. Rutherglen, *Civil Rights in the Shadow of Slavery*, 147. It should also be noted that in the nineteenth century there were numerous references to the "German race," the "Irish race," and the like, suggesting that what are considered ethnic groups in modern times were thought of as different races.
50. *Cong. Globe*, 39th Cong., 1st Sess., 599 (1866). Rutherglen recites this very quote at the beginning of his chap. 3, "Reconceiving Civil Rights," in *Civil Rights in the Shadow of Slavery*, 40.
51. *Jones*, 392 U.S. 409 (Congress's authority, under the Thirteenth Amendment, to legislate against private racial discrimination and overruling a portion of the *Civil Rights Cases*, 109 U.S. 3 [1883]. *Jones* was a 1982 case, involving the refusal to sell a house because the attempted buyer was African American).
52. Runyon v. McCrary, 427 U.S. 160 (1976) (right to contract in Section 1981 prohibits private nonsectarian school from denying admission based on race).
53. Patterson v. McLean Credit Union, 491 U.S. 164 (1989) (in a harassment case based upon race, limited *Runyon* and Section 1981 to the contract itself and not post-contract formation behavior).
54. Theodore Eisenberg, "*Jones v. Alfred H. Mayer Co.*," in *The Oxford Companion to the Supreme Court of the United States*, ed. Kermit L. Hall (New York: Oxford University Press, 1992), 453.
55. The Court eschews the term "overruled" and refers to this as legislative action that "supersedes" the Court's decision. See CBOCS West, Inc. v. Humphries, 553 U.S. at 452 (2008); 1991 Civil Rights Act, 105 Stat. 1071.
56. *CBOCS West*, 553 U.S. at 445.
57. "Brief of Historians as amici," filed January 3, 2008, generally and at 6. The details of these reprisals and the sources for the information are set forth in the brief. Report of the Commissioner of the Bureau of Refugees, Freedmen, and Abandoned Lands, 1865, H.R. Ex. Doc. No. 11, 39th Cong., 1st Sess. (1865).

58. "Brief of Historians," 6. See also 7, 10, 11, 12, and 13.
59. Ibid., 14.
60. In the interest of disclosure: I participated in that case as a party-amicus and helped, in a small way, to edit the brief of the amici before it was filed. Both the majority and the dissent discussed statutory construction of the 1991 act and the majority discussed some legislative history of that act, but neither discussed the legislative history of the original statute.
61. Sullivan v. Little Hunting Park, Inc., 396 U.S. 229 (1969). This was a case involving property and retaliation, also under the Civil Rights Act of 1866.
62. Lane v. Wilson, 307 U.S. 268, 275 (1939).
63. Senator Trumbull borrowed existing language from the Northwest Ordinance in the drafting of the Thirteenth Amendment. However, unlike the Fourteenth Amendment framers, he did *not* copy the language of Article 1, Section 10 ("No State shall . . ."), which would have evidenced intent to apply a state action doctrine to all of the rights listed. Further, the reference to "acting under color" of state law is used only in the second section of the act, not the first.
64. *Cong. Globe*, 39th Cong., 1st Sess., 500 (January 30, 1866). While some have argued that there is some state action requirement in the act, this is contrary to the language of the statute, and even George Rutherglen admits that "reading the state action doctrine back into the debates of the 1866 Act creates an inescapable risk of anachronism." Rutherglen, *Civil Rights in the Shadow of Slavery*, 61. I would state this more strongly and submit that reading the state action doctrine into the statute is contrary both to its legislative history and to its statutory language. Rutherglen seems to be concerned that the statute's use of the word "custom" could be read to imply a state action requirement (14, 61, 77, 81, 84, 132, 140, 145). However, Foner takes the opposite approach and uses the word "custom" to reach private action. Foner, *Reconstruction*, 249.
65. Theodore Eisenberg, "*Runyon v. McCrary*," in *The Oxford Companion to the Supreme Court of the United States*, ed. Kermit L. Hall (New York: Oxford University Press, 1992), 453.
66. "Time Limits for Filing a Charge," U.S. Equal Employment Opportunity Commission web page (last accessed March 3, 2014.) However, for federal employees or job applicants, one must contact the EEOC within forty-five days. In age discrimination the complaint time is extended to three hundred days only if there is a *state law* prohibiting age discrimination in employment and a state agency or authority enforcing that law. (A

local law does not extend the time.) I am grateful to law librarian Annette Souare and her research assistants for research on this issue.

67. Ibid.
68. See Owen v. Okure, 448 U.S. 235 (1989).
69. E.g., Nada v. Mbah, 119 Ohio St. 3rd 305 (1992) (selecting R.C. 2305.10 as the applicable statute for a 1983 case). The same rationale would produce the same decision in a 1981 claim, unless one could prevail on the argument that the state contract's statute of limitations applies.
70. Enforcement Act of 1879, 16 Stat. 140 (Section 16 and supporting Sections 17 and 18). See also Revised Statutes of 1874, Sections 1977 and 1978.
71. Aynes, "Fourteenth Amendment and the Bill of Rights," 77, 101–5.
72. This era is generally said to have spanned 1905–37 and is named after the U.S. Supreme Court's case in *Lochner v. New York*, 198 U.S. 45 (1905).
73. E.g., Randy E. Barnett, "Foreword: What's So Wicked about Lochner?," 1 *N.Y. L. & Liberty* 325, 333 (2005) (stating the Civil Rights Act identified its contract clause as one of the privilege or immunities protected by the Fourteenth Amendment, "the very right protected by the Court in *Lochner*"); and Kurt T. Lash, "Two Movements of a Constitutional Symphony: Akhil Reed Amar's The Bill of Rights," 33 *U. Rich. L. Rev.* 485, 499–500 (1999) ("It is possible to argue that Lochner itself was based upon Fourteenth Amendment equal protection and due process principles in its strong protection against freedom of contract without government interference. After all, the Civil Rights Act of 1866 expressly protected freedom of contract"). Note, however, the conflict between the two.
74. 14 Stat. 546 (1867) and codified in 42 U.S.C., Section 1994. See also Aviam Soifer, "Federal Protection, Paternalism, and the Virtually Forgotten Prohibition of Voluntary Peonage," 112 *Columbia L. Rev.* 1607, 1617n38 (2012) (quoting the prohibition against "*voluntary* or involuntary service or labor of any persons as peons"; emphasis added).
75. Wilson R. Huhn to Richard L. Aynes, e-mail of June 11, 2014 (on file with author).
76. "Speech of Hon. John A. Bingham, of Ohio, at National Hall," *Cadiz Republican*, November 7, 1860.
77. Ibid.
78. "Father in Israel, the Hon. John A. Bingham Again Takes the Stump in Behalf of the Principles of the Republican Party. An Eloquent Plea for Justice and Equal Rights," *Cincinnati Commercial Gazette*, October 3, 1885, 3, cols. 1–3 (stating that the claim of the Democratic Party to be the friend

of labor was "enough to bring the blush to the cheek of the devil," that it was that party which had "enslaved the labor of the people of one-half of this Union," and that the Democratic Party voted against the amendment freeing these laborers from slavery).

79. *Cadiz Republican*, May 17, 1894, as reprinted in "Twice Told Tales," *Harrison News-Herald*, June 14, 2014, A4, col. 2 ("We have no hesitation in saying that our sympathies are entirely with the men who work in the mines, and we hope, sincerely for their complete success in the contest. Their lot in life is a hard one. Their occupation is full of danger and hardship; their work is indispensable to the business of the world").
80. In re Turner, 24 F. Cas. 337 (C.C. Md. 1867) (No. 14,247).
81. There are two dissents in which the 1866 Civil Rights Act is mentioned. While occurring during the *Lochner* era, neither of these supports the expansive reading of the right to contract articulated in *Lochner* or the claim that contracts are free from government regulations. In *Hodges v. United States*, 203 U.S. 1 (1906), the majority held that the Thirteenth Amendment did not authorize Congress to use criminal statutes to protect contract rights of laborers from racially motivated attacks. Justice Harlan and Justice Day dissented, relying, in part, upon the 1866 Civil Rights Act because "the disability to make valid contracts for one's services was . . . an inseparable incident of the institution of slavery which the Thirteenth Amendment destroyed" and the criminal statutes could be used to enforce the violation of that right by private parties. 203 U.S. 1 at 20, 38. See also Pamela Brandwein, *The Judicial Settlement of Reconstruction* (Cambridge: Cambridge University Press, 2011), 190–92 (discussing *Hodges*). *Brader v. James*, 49 Okla. 734, 154 P. 570 (1916), *aff'd* 246 U.S. 88 (1918) (while the Supreme Court affirmed this decision, no mention was made of the use of the Civil Rights Act in the dissent below). Oklahoma justice Hardy dissented from the majority's holding that a sale of land owned by a Native American was void because the approval of the Secretary of Interior had not been obtained as required by statute. Justice Hardy would have upheld transfer of the land since a later statute of Congress made the same Native Americans U.S. citizens, relying upon the Fifth Amendment to the U.S. Constitution and the "inherit, purchase, lease, sell, hold, and convey" provision of the 1866 Civil Rights Act, but not its contract provision.
82. Jacobus tenBroek, *Equal under Law*, new, enl. ed. (New York: Collier Books, 1965), 239.
83. *Cong. Globe*, 39th Cong., 1st Sess., 1153 (March 2, 1866).

9

THE ORIGINS OF ARGUMENTS OVER AFFIRMATIVE ACTION

Lessons from the Civil Rights Act of 1866

George Rutherglen

Disputes, disagreement, ambiguity, and ambivalence have marked the law of affirmative action since it came to prominence in the civil rights era, nearly fifty years ago. Much the same can be said of the Civil Rights Act of 1866, from its enactment in Reconstruction to its revival, reinterpretation, and recodification over a century later. Charges of reverse discrimination figured in the opposition to the act, nowhere more prominently than in President Andrew Johnson's message vetoing the act after it first passed Congress. Supporters adamantly denied any favoritism to any group under the statute, insisting that it protected the civil rights of all citizens. The contours of this debate at the outset of Reconstruction prefigure debates over affirmative action that have become familiar in modern times, although they were put to quite different uses then than they are now. First, they were over a statute that was, both in its terms and its effects, neutral as between racial groups. The immediate aim of the 1866 act was to secure equality for the newly freed slaves by conferring upon them the same rights as enjoyed by "white citizens." Although framed in racial terms, the purpose of the act was to treat all citizens equally, as did the provisions of the Fourteenth Amendment that were modeled on the act. Second, the Reconstruction arguments over reverse discrimination proved to be most successful in constricting the scope of civil rights legislation, particularly the Freedmen's Bureau Bill, which could become law only after its sponsors narrowed its scope both in time and in aims. Yet, third, these arguments were not tied up, as affirmative action plans are now, with the large role that government currently takes in public education and public employment. Apart from the temporary measures undertaken during the Civil War and Reconstruction, notably through the Freedmen's Bureau, the role of government was limited and the role of the federal government more limited still.

Simultaneously with the revival of the Civil Rights Act of 1866, modern civil rights legislation featured debates over whether it would endorse, permit, or require affirmative action. The Civil Rights Act of 1964[1] gave prominent, if equivocal, voice to doubts about affirmative action, as did the Civil Rights Act of 1991,[2] which made crucial changes to the 1964 act. The 1991 act also reinforced the connection between these developments and the 1866 act by codifying the modern understanding of what the earlier act accomplished: a general prohibition against private discrimination in contracting and real estate transactions, as well as equal access to the courts.[3] Constitutional and statutory decisions confirmed and expanded this understanding of the broad scope of civil rights while at the same time engaging the continuing controversy over affirmative action, charting a course sometimes favorable toward affirmative action and sometimes skeptical, as evidenced by the Supreme Court's two recent decisions in *Fisher v. University of Texas*.[4] Those decisions established stricter standards for affirmative action in higher education while at the same time allowing affirmative action to persist.

These current controversies might be attributed to modern attitudes, and in particular the need to delay enforcement of a strict color-blind conception of prohibitions against discrimination until the continuing effects of racial and ethnic discrimination have been eliminated. But a look at the origins of the civil rights laws in Reconstruction cautions against a modernist perspective, which foreshortens debates to the aftermath of *Brown v. Board of Education*,[5] rather than seeing their origins in Reconstruction. This chapter attempts to rediscover those origins by reexamining the legislative history and immediate reception of the Civil Rights Act of 1866[6] as it bears upon race-conscious remedies for racial discrimination.

We must accept these differences between then and now, but even so we must admit that one disturbing similarity remains: the place of arguments against reverse discrimination among a constellation of objections to any form of remedial civil rights legislation. At the time, these arguments combined with assertions of the unconstitutionality of federal legislation, including intrusion upon states' rights, and the general need to limit the duration of any form of federal assistance. Such claims are still repeated today. If we have learned anything from the Civil Rights Act of 1866 and from its reception in Reconstruction, it is that these arguments cannot be taken at face value. Yet they must be taken into account, if only because they have persisted for so long among so many constituencies. Even supporters of civil rights have acknowledged that extraordinary remedies targeted to benefit a particular group must be of limited duration, as the history of the Freedmen's Bureau amply reveals. Yet opponents of civil rights have been all too ready to conclude that because yesterday's goals have been met, today's no longer need to be pursued.[7] Both as a matter of policy, and as a matter of constitutional doctrine, their objections should be greeted with reservations about their scope and effect—very similar in the end to the reservations that opponents today seek to impose upon race-conscious remedies for discrimination. Just as such remedies must be tailored to the circumstances that make them necessary, so too must legal and constitutional objections to those remedies.

This chapter proceeds in three parts. The first concerns the Civil Rights Act of 1866 and the congressional debates leading to its enactment. The second compares the act with the legislation authorizing the Freedmen's Bureau and the different reactions to each form of legislation. The third part briefly considers the implications of this comparison for modern civil rights law, especially for constitutional arguments over affirmative action. No one-to-one correspondence exists between the legislative debates in 1866 and constitutional arguments today, but the debates then have left their traces now in concerns over special remedies for discrimination and, in particular, over how long they should remain in effect.

THE CIVIL RIGHTS ACT OF 1866

The 1866 act was framed expressly in racial terms, conferring the same right "as is enjoyed by white citizens" upon all citizens "of every race and color, without regard to any previous condition of slavery or involuntary servitude." The act then enumerated a detailed list of protected civil rights: to make contracts, to hold property, to gain access to court, to be protected by the law, and to be subject to equal penalties. Moreover, the act granted citizenship to "all persons born in the United States and not subject to any foreign power, excluding Indians not taxed." All such persons, including the newly freed slaves, were raised up to the same status as white citizens.[8] The act went on to punish as a crime any deprivation of the enumerated rights on the basis of race, color, or previous condition of servitude when done under the authority of law or custom.[9] Just as the basic rights guaranteed by the act were defined in terms of racial equality, the remedy provided by the act was against racial discrimination.

Opponents of the act nevertheless charged that it resulted in reverse discrimination in favor of African Americans by granting them benefits never previously granted to white citizens or to other ethnic groups, notably Native Americans. The basis for this argument seems to lie in the use of the naturalization power mainly over individuals rather than over groups. Supporters of the act countered by relying on historical examples of naturalizing entire tribes and all the residents of former Spanish or Mexican possessions.[10] This objection to mass naturalization was intertwined with several related arguments: that the act exceeded the lawmaking authority power of Congress; that it encroached upon the power of the states over domestic matters; that it constituted an unprecedented expansion of federal law enforcement and the jurisdiction of the federal courts; and that it went too far in protecting too many civil rights. These objections were met by amendments that confined the scope of the act, ironically by adding the explicitly racial clause "as is enjoyed by white citizens." The point of that clause, finally resolved only in the twentieth century,[11] was to raise all citizens to the same status as white citizens.

Strict formalists might object that this clause injects an essential racial element into the legislation and makes it questionable for violating principles of color-blindness. But formalist arguments, if taken to that extreme, would undermine any remedies for racial discrimination because these must, in one way or another, refer to the wrong that they seek to set right. In any event, the changes made to the statute did not silence arguments over its constitutionality, which were put to rest only with the adoption of the Fourteenth Amendment and the reenactment of the statute under that amendment. Until then, the criticism of the act's scope took the paradoxical position that it was both too broad and too narrow.

As originally introduced, the act declared that "there shall be no discrimination in civil rights or immunities among the inhabitants of any State or Territory of the United States on account of race, color, or previous condition of slavery."[12] That language followed a grant of citizenship to "all persons of African descent born in the United States."[13] The first of these provisions was thought to be too broad in its reference to "civil rights or immunities" and the second too narrow in its conferral of citizenship only upon African Americans. The chair of the House Judiciary Committee, Republican James F. Wilson of Iowa, successfully moved to delete the reference generally to "civil rights" because it "might give warrant to a latitudinarian construction not intended."[14] The same amendment added the phrase "as is enjoyed by white citizens" in order to make clear that the act did not confer the same civil rights on women and children as on men.[15] An earlier amendment by the chair of the Senate Judiciary Committee, Republican Lyman Trumbull of Illinois, expanded the grant of citizenship to "all persons born in the United States and not subject to any foreign power."[16] After extended debate over the coverage of Native Americans, this provision was limited by the phrase "excluding Indians not taxed."[17] The last clause was intended as a gloss on those persons "subject to any foreign power," since Indian tribes were regarded as separate sovereign entities, notably in the commerce clause of the U.S. Constitution.[18] Although the phrase "Indians not taxed" had dubious origins next to the three-fifths clause in the original Constitution, it eventually made its way into the Fourteenth Amendment as part of the definition of who was entitled to vote.[19]

These changes, in the end, transformed the explicitly racial provisions of the act, defining who benefited and who was excluded. The changes enabled Senator Trumbull to state that the act "applies to white men as well as black men. It declares that all persons in the United States shall be entitled to the same civil rights."[20] He reiterated this point on several occasions, as did other legislators,[21] responding directly to the criticism of the act as special interest legislation in favor of African Americans. A vocal opponent of the act, Senator Willard Saulsbury a Democrat from Delaware, criticized it in these terms: "I think the time for shedding tears over the poor slave has well nigh passed in this country. The tears which honest white people of this country have been made to shed from the oppressive acts of this Government in its various departments during the last four years call more loudly for my sympathies."[22] Senator Garrett Davis, a Democrat from Kentucky, decried the act as a product of "these times of fanaticism and of unreasonable philanthropy for the negro," just like the legislation establishing the Freedmen's Bureau.[23] While acknowledging that the act provided for equal civil rights, these critics insisted that it resulted in unequal treatment by favoring African Americans over individual aliens and that enough had already been done on their behalf.

These arguments were then combined with the constitutional objection that what the act proposed to do exceeded the limits of congressional power. Critics doubted whether Congress could naturalize African Americans on the same collective basis that had been offered to some Indian tribes and some residents of the territories acquired from Spain and France. The power of Congress to "establish an uniform Rule of Naturalization" did not obviously extend to groups.[24] Nor did it obviously give Congress the power to overrule the holding of *Scott v. Sandford* that African Americans could not become citizens under federal law.[25] Despite the Thirteenth Amendment,[26] this holding technically remained valid and was definitively rejected only by the citizenship provisions of the Fourteenth Amendment. Before that was accomplished, critics argued that the Thirteenth Amendment had already done enough for the former slaves by emancipating them and that Congress could do little more under its power to enforce the amendment "by appropriate legislation."[27] Congress could provide for the physical freedom of the former slaves but not guarantee them equal civil rights. By these means, opponents of the 1866 act transformed objections that it resulted in special treatment of African Americans into arguments that it exceeded constitutional limits on legislative remedies for slavery.

President Johnson carried these arguments to rhetorical and illogical extremes, marshaling objections to the act on any ground regardless of their consistency with another.[28] He began his veto message, as had the opponents of the act in Congress, by acknowledging the breadth of the act but then shifted abruptly to criticizing it as discriminatory. The citizenship provision, he noted, "comprehends the Chinese of the Pacific States, Indians subject to taxation, the people called Gypsies, as well as the entire race designated as blacks, people of color, negroes, and persons of African blood."[29] This broad grant of citizenship nevertheless "proposes a discrimination against large numbers of intelligent, worthy, and patriotic foreigners, and in favor of the negro, to whom, after long years of bondage, the avenues to freedom and intelligence have now been suddenly opened."[30] So, too, the act's enumeration of protected rights sought to "repeal all State laws discriminating between whites and blacks in the subjects covered by this bill" and seemingly extended to laws against miscegenation and on the right to vote and to hold office.[31] The second section of the act, which made it a crime to deny the rights enumerated in the first section, sought "to afford discriminating protection to colored persons in the full enjoyment of all the rights secured to them by the preceding section."[32] And all the enforcement provisions of the act together "establish for the security of the colored race, safeguards which go infinitely beyond any that the General Government has ever provided for the white race. In fact, the distinction of race and color is, by the bill, made to operate in favor of the colored and against the white race."[33] To use modern terminology, Johnson objected that the facially neutral provisions of the act were tainted by the congressional motive mainly to benefit African Americans.

This one-sided motive placed the act beyond the power of Congress to enforce the Thirteenth Amendment. According to Johnson, there was no longer any need for special treatment of African Americans:

> It cannot, however, be justly claimed that, with a view to enforcement of this article of the Constitution, there is at present any necessity for the exercise of all the powers which this bill confers.
>
> Slavery has been abolished, and at present nowhere exists within the jurisdiction of the United States: nor has there been, nor is it likely there will be, any attempt to revive it by the people of the States.[34]

The formal abolition of slavery by the Thirteenth Amendment had already done enough for African Americans, and further measures to protect them were no longer necessary, if they ever were. As free laborers, the former slaves could reach a settlement with their former masters under the laws generally regulating employment: "Each has equal power in settling the terms, and if left to the laws that regulate capital and labor, it is confidently believed that they will satisfactorily work out the problem."[35] Johnson reached this conclusion despite ample evidence of resistance in the southern and border states to recognition of the freed people's civil rights.[36] While the act was too broad in protecting all racial minorities, it was too narrow in doing so primarily for the benefit of African Americans.

The overall lack of coherence in President Johnson's objections to the 1866 act could be attributed to the structure of his veto message: it proceeded as a section-by-section critique that went through the act from beginning to end, with no organizing principle other than the numerical order of the act's provisions. Hence the message contained a lengthy discussion of the act's enforcement provisions, which made up eight of its nine sections. The strident tone of the veto message could also have resulted from Johnson's successful veto of the Freedmen's Bureau Bill, upheld by a narrow margin in the Senate only a month earlier. The message accompanying that veto, examined in more detail in the next part of this chapter, contains the same basic arguments of favoritism, lack of necessity, and unconstitutionality asserted against the civil rights act. The kitchen-sink quality of these objections reinforces the impression that they were hastily drafted and poorly considered, designed to precipitate a confrontation with Congress rather than a compromise over Reconstruction. Instead of seeking common ground with the congressional leadership, Johnson rejected any attempt by Congress to slow or complicate his program of speedy Presidential Reconstruction.

Yet the doubts raised by Johnson's veto message, if not its tenor, were shared by his political opponents. Supporters of civil rights, such as Representative John A. Bingham of Ohio, shared concerns over the constitutionality of the 1866 act and supported the Fourteenth Amendment for that reason. The Republican majorities in the Thirty-Ninth Congress passed both the 1866 act to protect civil rights and the Fourteenth Amendment to place that protection on a more secure constitutional footing. For that reason, Section 1 of the amendment largely tracks the provisions of Section 1 of the act, beginning with citizenship, proceeding to privileges and immunities, and concluding with equal protection and due process.[37] The foundational role that the Fourteenth Amendment now occupies in civil rights law naturally leads to questions about Johnson's motives in vetoing the similar provisions of the 1866 act. How could prohibitions against discrimination, or guarantees of equality, be themselves attacked as discriminatory?

But before the decisive confrontation between congressional Republicans and the president in the election of 1866—leading to the victory of the former despite the latter's strenuous efforts to defeat them—the entire program of Congressional Reconstruction remained in doubt. The Thirteenth Amendment might have made the most radical single change in the structure of the Constitution—confirming the emancipation of four million Americans wrought by the Civil War and replacing the economics of slavery with the regime of free labor—but its consequences had yet to be worked out. The 1866 act began this process of profound social, economic, and political adaptation. The antebellum system of limited federal government did not contemplate a federal takeover of an issue previously reserved entirely to the states. Opposition to the act, and to other steps in Reconstruction to remake the federal system, was backhanded testimony to the radicalism of the steps that needed to be taken. Objections to the 1866 act therefore had a degree of durability belied by the extremism of the rhetoric in which they were framed. The same objections appeared earlier in the debates over the Freedmen's Bureau, and they came up again in more moderate but more effective form in constitutional arguments over the legacy of Reconstruction. The next parts of this chapter address these issues in turn.

THE FREEDMEN'S BUREAU

The Freedmen's Bureau Bill, although considered simultaneously with the Civil Rights Act of 1866, presents a study in contrasts. The bill sought to extend the life of the Freedmen's Bureau, which had been established during the Civil War as part of the War Department, but did not seek to do so permanently. The bureau was created to deal with the refugee crisis created as the advancing Union armies effectively emancipated the slaves within or near their lines.[38] Unlike the Civil Rights Act of 1866, the bill did not create a whole new category of federally protected rights; it only proposed to renew an existing program. Moreover, as its original placement in the War Department suggests, the legislation principally was justified under the war power as part of the effort to secure the consequences of victory in the Civil War. Since the bureau antedated the Thirteenth Amendment, the authority to continue it was only belatedly and incidentally justified under the enforcement provisions of that amendment. The war power also placed a time limit on the duration of the bureau. It could not outlast the authority and the circumstances that gave rise to it or, according to its critics, extend geographically beyond the former Confederate states. The greatest contrast with the 1866 act concerned the essential mission of the bureau, which was to distribute relief and to provide other special benefits to the newly freed slaves and other refugees of the war, which included many white people in the dire conditions in the South as the Civil War came to an end. The bill was accordingly framed in formally neutral terms, to benefit all refugees regardless of race, although "opponents and supporters generally viewed it as largely, if not exclusively, for the assistance of freedmen."[39] The Freedmen's Bureau Bill was therefore vulnerable to the charge that it constituted "class legislation," for the particular benefit of one group rather than for the rights of all, a charge today that would be framed as one of reverse discrimination.

All these differences made for a far more tumultuous reception of the Freedmen's Bureau Bill than of the 1866 act, leading to yet another contrast between the two pieces of legislation. President's Johnson's veto of the bill was upheld, leading to significant concessions that resulted eventually in the passage of the Freedmen's Bureau Act.[40] In fact, supporters of the bill had to qualify and limit its provisions from the very beginning, a pattern set in the legislation originally establishing the bureau. After attempts to place the bureau in the Treasury Department, it was constituted as part of the War Department "to continue during the present war of rebellion and for one year thereafter."[41] The scope of its programs, originally limited to the freed people, was expanded to cover all refugees. Although this step did not entirely succeed in defusing the objection that the bureau benefited only African Americans, it did lend a semblance of formal neutrality to its operations. Even with these limitations, debate over the creation of the bureau lasted through two sessions of Congress, when the growing numbers of slaves liberated by the victorious Union armies made the need for a systematic program of emergency relief undeniable. The necessities of war assured that some acceptable compromise would be enacted.

The Freedmen's Bureau began by providing food, shelter, and medical care to the slaves who had fled to Union lines or who were displaced by the war. They had gained their freedom but often had lost any means of livelihood. The bureau accordingly was authorized to rent confiscated and abandoned southern lands to them in a program that became increasingly contentious as southerners returned to claim their property and were eventually pardoned by President Johnson.[42] When the freed people were denied possession of the land, many migrated to nearby towns or cities, where regular employment was hard to find. The bureau soon adopted a policy of returning them to the land to work for the white people who continued to own the land, almost all of them former slaveholders. This step necessitated the negotiation of contracts of employment, unfamiliar to either party. The former slaveholders wanted to return to a regime of despotic control over their workers and the newly freed slaves, almost all of whom were illiterate and hardly capable of negotiating favorable contracts for themselves. The bureau tried to fill the gap by taking on the role of supervising and regulating the contracts between planters and ex-slaves, with limited success given the magnitude of the task, the hostility of white land owners, and the limited number of bureau agents.[43] A lasting contribution of the bureau involved the establishment of schools for the freed people, often with the assistance of northern charitable organizations.[44] The long-term benefits from education, however, could not address immediate economic relations.

Both possession of the land, where it was possible, and contracts of employment, when they were made, presupposed a functioning legal system that fairly protected the freed people's rights. So, too, did any form of security against personal violence, which remained endemic and often intense throughout the South. The reconstituted southern governments provided a system of civil justice in theory, but it was regularly used against African Americans. Hence the bureau had to step in to provide alternatives, in the form of its own courts or military commissions. These, too, met with only limited success. Nevertheless, they reveal the essential connection between the legislation authorizing the bureau and the Civil Rights Act of 1866. Each depended upon the other: the bureau could be effective only if civil rights were effectively enforced, and those rights could be enforced only if the freed people had access to impartial justice. As it soon became evident, the ambitious goals of each legislative program could not be fulfilled in the disordered and violent conditions of Reconstruction. Incremental reforms based on rigid adherence to the presuppositions of antebellum constitutional structure came at the cost of delayed, and eventually ineffective, enforcement.

The essential compromises that appeared in the legislation creating the Freedmen's Bureau, apart from an explicit limit on duration, formed the basis for the Freedmen's Bureau Bill considered in 1866. The bill provided that the earlier legislation "shall continue in force until otherwise provided by law, and shall extend to refugees and freedmen in all parts of the United States."[45] Only the provision for military protection of civil rights was limited in time and geographic extent, applying only when "the ordinary course of judicial proceedings has been interrupted by the rebellion."[46] Displacement of the ordinary processes of civil litigation by courts in the Freedmen's Bureau and by military commissions quickly emerged as a central and vexing issue. The federal officials on the scene in the South saw that the freed people could not get justice in the state courts, while President Johnson wanted to speed the return to full recognition and normal operation of the reconstituted governments in the South.[47] The bill therefore elicited charges from the beginning that it purported to create a large and permanent federal bureaucracy.[48]

The sponsor of the bill, Senator Trumbull, immediately responded by disclaiming any such intent: "This Freedmen's Bureau is not intended as a permanent institution. It is only designed to aid these helpless, ignorant, and unprotected people until they can provide for and take care of themselves."[49] He made the same point in response to Johnson's veto: "The object of the bill was to continue in existence the Freedmen's Bureau—not as a permanent institution."[50] Although the language of the bill did not quite support Trumbull's disclaimer of its permanent status, the need for him to make this concession revealed the reigning presuppositions of the times: limited government, especially at the federal level; suspicion of relief programs, on the ground that they promoted dependency; and adherence to the principles of free labor in competitive markets. These policies were all reflected in the placement of the bureau in the War Department, making it dependent upon the army for support and vulnerable to demobilization as soldiers left the army, and the South, after the war ended. The bureau, too, lacked significant sources of independent funding: bureau agents were not compensated from federal funds; the lands available to the bureau for relocation of freed people and rent-producing income steadily shrank as Confederate sympathizers were pardoned; and annual appropriations required renewed congressional approval. The ideological, political, and institutional structure in which the bureau was embedded virtually assured that its existence would be temporary. Apparently for that reason, Trumbull could credibly represent that the Freedmen's Bureau Bill did not make the bureau permanent, despite providing that it "shall continue in force until otherwise provided by law."[51]

The provisions to take over the jurisdiction of the state courts in cases involving freed people were subject to more explicit limits: they applied only in areas where the operation of the courts was disrupted by the war and resulted in racial discrimination in the protection of civil rights, and they ended once any "State shall have been fully restored in all its constitutional relations to the United States, and the courts of the State and of the United States within the same are not disturbed or stopped in the peaceable course of justice."[52] Trumbull relied on these provisions to respond to objections that the jurisdiction of bureau and military courts would extend into states that remained loyal to the Union[53] and that it would extend indefinitely into the future, a charge emphasized by Johnson in his veto message.[54] His disclaimers on this issue, and the provisions of the bill, could not be more different from the terms of the Civil Rights Act of 1866. The latter protected almost all the civil rights protected by the former, but it did so permanently, throughout the country, and without qualification, as Trumbull himself emphasized: the Freedmen's Bureau Bill's "provisions are temporary, but there is another bill on your table, somewhat akin to this, which is intended to be permanent, to extend to all parts of the country, and to protect persons of all races in equal civil rights."[55] The 1866 act did not depend upon military courts, but it provided a mechanism for federal jurisdiction where necessary to protect civil rights. Where the one has endured, the other soon expired.

A similar contrast can be drawn between who was protected by each piece of legislation. As its popular name suggests, the principal beneficiaries of the Freedmen's Bureau Bill were the freed people. It did extend to refugees, regardless of race, but the main benefits went almost wholly to African Americans.[56] The protection of civil rights, although listing the same beneficiaries, also reached "any other persons."[57] Trumbull did not, however, emphasize that these provisions applied "to white men as well as black men," as he had in his defense of the 1866 act. All he could point to was the protection of white, as well as black, refugees,[58] and indeed, evidence later submitted to Congress indicated that about a third of food rations distributed by the bureau were to white people.[59] Yet the emphasis in the Freedmen's Bureau Bill on assisting African Americans invited the objection that it was "class legislation for a particular class of the blacks to the exclusion of all whites."[60] These objections merged with concerns that, if extended to white citizens, the legislation represented an assertion of federal power to provide welfare relief to all needy citizens.[61] Johnson combined both arguments in his veto message. The federal government, he asserted, "has never deemed itself authorized to expend the public money for the rent or purchase of homes for the thousands, not to say millions, of the white race, who are honestly toiling from day to day for their subsistence."[62] Although unexceptional now, this federal initiative was extraordinary then in an era when the spending power was much more narrowly interpreted. It could be invoked only on the model of pensions for Civil War veterans, which accounts for many of the references in Congress to the newly freed slaves who had fought on behalf of the Union.

As with the 1866 act, issues of policy became issues of constitutional authority. The arguments over the duration and continued need for the bureau sprang directly from its original source in the war power. Senator Trumbull and other supporters viewed the bill as an extension of a program begun during the war, as did President Johnson in his veto message. Trumbull asserted that "the war powers of the Government do not cease with the dispersion of the rebel armies. They are to be continued and exercised until the civil authority of the Government can be established firmly and upon a sure foundation not again to be disturbed or interfered with."[63] This argument carried within it the seeds of limitations on the scope and duration of any measures adopted because the southern states were still "in the grasp of war." Opponents quickly seized on the fact that the war was over and that there was some evidence, however slim, that the ordinary forms of civil government had returned to states undergoing Presidential Reconstruction. If Congress refused to make the bureau permanent during the war, one opponent asked, how could it do so "when the war is over, when the States are returning to their places in the Union, when the citizens are returning to their allegiance, when peace and quiet, to a very large extent, prevail over that country, when the courts are reestablished . . . ?"[64] These objections were directed particularly to the assertion of jurisdiction by bureau and military courts. Johnson began his veto message on this theme: "If it be asked whether the creation of such a tribunal within a State is warranted as a measure of war, the question immediately presents itself whether we are still engaged in war."[65]

The Thirteenth Amendment made only occasional appearances in the arguments over the bill. Trumbull took it up in his principal speeches only after invoking the war power, so that it appears to be something of an afterthought. Nevertheless, when he introduced the bill, as a companion to the Civil Rights Act, he presented both measures as enforcement legislation under the Thirteenth Amendment.[66] The debate then focused on whether any civil rights legislation was necessary at all if slavery had effectively been abolished by Section 1 of the amendment.[67] The Thirteenth Amendment made its only appearance in Johnson's veto message in the same role—as a sufficient protection that dispensed with the need for further legislation: "The institution of slavery, for the military destruction of which the Freedmen's Bureau was called into existence as an auxiliary, has been already effectually and finally abrogated throughout the whole country by an amendment of the Constitution of the United States."[68] This ironic reliance upon the amendment to defeat the bill led Trumbull to protest that the president had not referred to it at all.[69] The truth was that the amendment figured far more prominently in the debates over the 1866 act, which turned only incidentally upon the war power because of the permanence of the act's provisions.

The reverse was true of the debates over the Freedmen's Bureau Bill and only served to emphasize its temporary nature. Senator Thomas Hendricks, Democrat of Indiana, a staunch opponent of the bill, considered its basis in the Thirteenth Amendment only "very briefly,"[70] and Trumbull gave this ground for the amendment similarly brief consideration, although he did so out of the contrary conviction that the bill was clearly constitutional. He assimilated the bill to the 1866 act, as he had when he announced the introduction of both pieces of legislation, and he professed "no doubt that under this provision of the Constitution we may destroy all these discriminations in civil rights against the black man."[71] Since both pieces of legislation contained nearly the same list of civil rights, both could be justified in this respect by reliance upon the same source of congressional power. But the means chosen for protection differed greatly between the two: the Freedmen's Bureau Bill relied upon military administration and enforcement, while the 1866 act relied mainly upon civil enforcement in the federal courts. One was a temporary consequence of the war, and the other was an enduring institution of civil society.

The temporary duration of the Freedmen's Bureau followed from its limited mission and its origins in the exercise of the war power. It might be continued under the Thirteenth Amendment, but not indefinitely. The response to Johnson's veto made this clear. After the Senate failed to override the veto, by two votes less than the required two-thirds majority,[72] the bill was reintroduced in the House with an explicit time limit of two years. Its principal sponsor there, Representative Thomas Eliot, a Republican from Massachusetts, emphasized both that the revised bill "continues the Bureau for two years, and removes one objection,"[73] and that the authority to pass it rested squarely on the Thirteenth Amendment.[74] This express time limit on the bureau's existence and added limits on the sale or rental of land to the freedmen did not stop the opponents of the original bill from repeating their objections to it.[75] Nor did these changes stop President Johnson from vetoing the legislation again, and for the same reasons that he offered in support of his first veto.[76] He added only that the passage of the 1866 act, over his veto, furnished another reason not to renew and extend the bureau's life. These changes were enough, however, to override the second veto of the bill.[77]

The resulting Freedmen's Bureau Act put the bureau firmly on the course to be phased out, as it was in subsequent legislation enacted in 1868.[78] That legislation initially extended its life for another year but was quickly supplemented by legislation that limited its life to six months.[79] Both acts were caught up in the growing constitutional confrontation with President Johnson. Both elicited vetoes, and the second act, in a provision that was probably unconstitutional, sought to restrict the president's power to appoint a successor to General Oliver Howard, the commissioner of the bureau.[80] The second act also revealed the political dynamics surrounding the bureau, which constantly placed its supporters on the defensive. The act was titled "An Act relating to the Freedmen's Bureau and providing for its Discontinuance" and made explicit the assumption in the first act that the bureau would be continued for no more than a year, and for less than a year in any state "fully restored in its constitutional relations with the government of the United States."[81] Within three weeks, the one-year extension of the bureau was cut in half. Opponents of the legislation objected to less definite time limits, and Representative Eliot agreed to alter the legislation accordingly.[82] Debate over both acts was brief, focused on the cost of the bureau[83] and the absence of any continuing need for it as African Americans gained the right to vote.[84] The same Congress passed the Fifteenth Amendment, signaling a shift from protecting the freed people through administrative programs to reliance upon political safeguards.

It also opened the bureau to renewed charges that it furnished a system of political patronage and control of the black vote.[85] The debate over termination of the bureau did not focus on what it had accomplished and what still needed to be done—all of which supported its continuation—but on its inconsistency with the spirit of the times, which favored self-reliance according to the ordinary processes of the law. The opponents of the bureau might be dismissed as longtime Confederate sympathizers, but the supporters had to recognize the limits of what they could accomplish. The bureau discontinued its operations in the South on January 1, 1869, and its affairs were entirely wound up by June 30, 1872.[86]

This sequence of legislation taught a harsh lesson, as did the mixed reception of the bureau in the field. Affirmative efforts to assist the freed people could last only as long as the perceived need for emergency measures. After that, they succumbed to the array of pressures to preserve the status quo, which Johnson and the other opponents of the bureau might have expressed in extreme form but which had broad appeal that the supporters of the bureau had to take into account. The suspicion attached to class legislation, the expense of any program adequate to the freed people's needs, and the desire to adhere to the traditionally limited role of the federal government kept any legislation permanently establishing the bureau well outside the bounds of political possibility. The 1866 act, with its neutral protection of civil rights for everyone, enforceable by traditional judicial remedies, stood a far better chance of survival.

Even so, the 1866 act had to meet objections that it, too, exceeded the power of Congress. Those objections were overcome by adoption of the Fourteenth Amendment and the reenactment of the act under its provisions, conferring upon the act a degree of constitutional confirmation that further differentiated it from the Freedmen's Bureau Act. As the former became a source of fundamental law, the latter began to lapse according to its own time limits. Like other aspects of Congressional Reconstruction, the Freedmen's Bureau expired before it could be subject to a successful constitutional challenge.

The extent of congressional power remained a matter of intense debate throughout Reconstruction, and many of the arguments against the Freedmen's Bureau reappeared as arguments against neutrally framed civil rights legislation, foremost among them the Civil Rights Act of 1875,[87] whose main provisions were struck down in the *Civil Rights Cases*.[88] These arguments did not vanish with the disappearance of the bureau but persisted long after it was dismantled.

CONSTITUTIONAL IMPLICATIONS

Both supporters and critics of affirmative action have turned to the statutes passed by Congress in 1866 to argue over the meaning of the Fourteenth Amendment, which Congress drafted, debated, and passed at nearly the same time. Their arguments from the legislative record take on a formalist cast, perhaps inevitably so, because the record yields only the terms of the enacted statutes and the statements made in the congressional debates: Did the statutes take account of race, and if so, in what way? Did the members of Congress regard these measures as race-conscious or race-neutral? Both sides in the debate, however, have additional motives in deploying such arguments. Liberals, although generally unsympathetic to originalism or textualism, seek to persuade conservative judges and scholars who are sympathetic to these methods of interpretation and to draw on them to support the constitutionality of affirmative action. Liberals therefore emphasize the reference to the newly freed slaves in the Freedmen's Bureau Act, as well as similar references to African Americans in legislation on soldiers' pay and on relief and schools in the District of Columbia.[89] Conservatives, who defend a color-blind interpretation of the Constitution, must contend with the fact that the Fourteenth Amendment contains no express prohibition against discrimination, let alone one that bars any consideration of race. They can find a substitute, however, by looking to the Civil Rights Act of 1866 and its requirement that all citizens be treated equally regardless of race. They can also get around the protection of freedmen in the Freedmen's Bureau Act because the statute additionally covered white refugees. Some go even further and assert that "the category of 'freedman' was not a racial category."[90] White people conceivably could have been slaves, and in any event, remedies for freed people were remedies for slavery, not benefits conferred solely on the basis of race.

In fact, neither side in this debate goes as far as it could. The liberals argue that the race-conscious measures in the Freedmen's Bureau Act are consistent with principles adopted at the same time in the Fourteenth Amendment. They could add that the same principles were adopted in the act itself, in its provisions protecting civil rights in almost exactly the same terms as the Civil Rights Act of 1866. The provisions in both acts have the same structure as Section 1 of the Fourteenth Amendment and can be used, as the Supreme Court has recently recognized, to interpret that amendment.[91] Whether or not Congress felt itself bound by the constitutional requirements that it sought to impose upon the states, it adopted virtually the same principles in the civil rights provisions of the Freedmen's Bureau Act. Those provisions granted civil rights in absolute terms, as freestanding rights, not just rights good against the former Confederate states.[92] By putting those provisions for the relief of freedmen in the same act, Congress evidently believed that they were entirely consistent with race-neutral principles of equal civil rights. Indeed, the members of Congress who supported it were almost entirely the same as the members who supported the 1866 act and the Fourteenth Amendment.[93] Conservatives, on the other hand, minimize the references to race in the Freedmen's Bureau Act to make them consistent with a color-blind interpretation of the Constitution. They could add that the act had a limited life span, which added to its political acceptability. The act's focus on African Americans, even if it also benefited white refugees, came at the cost of making the program temporary. Both sides miss the temporal dimension of the legislation authorizing the bureau and then dismantling it. Neither side wants to admit the possibility that race-conscious measures might be constitutional in one era and then unconstitutional in another—not because constitutional principles change but because circumstances might justify different measures at different times.[94] Arguments over affirmative action tend to be framed in all-or-nothing terms that do not easily admit pragmatic adjustment to the needs of the times.

In 1866, the Thirty-Ninth Congress reached a different conclusion. It readily concluded that the Freedmen's Bureau accorded in principle with the goal of equal civil rights but that its unpopularity as a product of special legislation prevented it from becoming a durable means to that goal. Many historians attribute the unpopularity of the bureau to the efforts of President Johnson to subvert its activities, combined with propaganda about "carpetbaggers" in the South and fatigue with Reconstruction efforts in the North.[95] On this view, supporters of the bureau eventually had to cave in to the erroneous but widespread caricature of the bureau's work. There is much to this view, but it neglects the limited lifespan contemplated for the bureau from the very beginning. It was the supporters of the bureau, not its critics, who readily conceded its temporary nature. No doubt they did so under some political pressure, but this pressure has never been absent from debates over race-conscious remedies for racial discrimination. It cannot be dismissed as a passing feature of the politics of Reconstruction. Nor is it easily dismissed as a matter of politics rather than constitutional law. In theory, it might be relegated to questions of policy, to be taken up by Congress and other politically responsive officials, leaving the courts only to decide whether these officials have the power to adopt race-conscious measures. Yet the Thirty-Ninth Congress regarded the legislation that it enacted as elucidating constitutional principles, including those in the Fourteenth Amendment, which it approved. Realism about the need for extraordinary remedies has been tempered—and often overcome—by the need for political assurances that such remedies are only temporary. The Freedmen's Bureau fell under the influence of such political necessities.

The existence of these necessities calls into question the need for judicial review to revisit such arguments as a matter of constitutional doctrine. Although the pedigree for this form of judicial review stretches back to decisions in Reconstruction—and forward to recent decisions of the Roberts Court—the lessons of the past sound a cautionary note for the future. In the *Civil Rights Cases,* the Supreme Court struck down the public accommodations provisions of the Civil Rights Act of 1875, even though they were framed in entirely neutral terms that would later be substantially reenacted in the Civil Rights Act of 1964.[96] As Justice Joseph Bradley wrote in his opinion for the Court,

> When a man has emerged from slavery, and by the aid of beneficent legislation has shaken off the inseparable concomitants of that state, there must be some stage in the progress of his elevation when he takes the rank of a mere citizen, and ceases to be the special favorite of the laws, and when his rights as a citizen, or a man, are to be protected in the ordinary modes by which other men's rights are protected.[97]

As a statement of the ultimate goal of civil rights law, this passage is unexceptional. When fully effective remedies have erased all the adverse effects of slavery, the law can revert to its normal operation and victims of slavery can seek recourse through the normal operation of the judicial system. Yet the justices in the *Civil Rights Cases* in 1883, like President Johnson in his veto messages in 1866, were altogether too ready to believe that this goal had been met. Much the same criticism can be advanced of the decisions of the Roberts Court casting doubt on affirmative action and, even more pointedly, invalidating crucial provisions of the Voting Rights Act of 1965.[98] As a matter of policy, the need for extraordinary remedies always remains open for debate. As a matter of legal doctrine, the need for the courts to go over the same ground that the political process has already covered remains to be established. The evidence from Reconstruction reveals that Congress is fully capable of addressing the duration of extraordinary remedies for racial discrimination.

CONCLUSION

The arguments dating from the creation of civil rights at the outset of Reconstruction cannot perfectly correspond to the arguments advanced today over affirmative action. Legislation enacted in 1866 cannot resolve controversies current in 2018. What the arguments from Reconstruction do reveal is the fundamental similarity in the problems confronted then and now—in prohibiting discrimination and in devising remedies for it, in framing such measures in neutral and universal terms where possible, and in limiting their scope and duration where it is not. Where supporters have seen an urgent problem demanding extraordinary remedies, opponents have found such steps to be both unnecessary and unconstitutional. The debate between the two sides has proved to be less illuminating in the contours of the arguments they advance than in the concessions they have had to make. No matter how strong the case for reform, its supporters have had to acknowledge the limits of public support, while its opponents have had to accept expanded conceptions of equal treatment. The positions and concessions of each side have been fully aired in the legislative process, and particularly over the scope and duration of race-conscious remedies. Congress took those issues seriously in Reconstruction and limited the duration of the Freedmen's Bureau for precisely such reasons, while it made the neutral prohibitions in the Civil Rights Act of 1866 universal and permanent. This example from the birth of civil rights, a century and a half ago, hardly determines the outcome of debates today, but it offers a salutary lesson in how the political process first addressed issues of racial equality that have remained with us ever since.

Notes

I would like to thank Barry Cushman, Darrell Miller, and Ted White for comments on previous drafts of this chapter.

1. Pub. L. No. 88-352, 78 Stat. 241 (1964).
2. Pub. L. No. 102-166, 105 Stat. 1071 (1991).
3. 42 U.S.C., Sec. 1981 (2012).
4. 133 S. Ct. 2411 (2013); 136 S. Ct. 2198 (2016).
5. 347 U.S. 483 (1954).
6. 14 Stat. 27. The act is reproduced in the appendix and its provisions are quoted several times in this chapter.
7. For a comprehensive survey of such arguments, see Darren Lenard Hutchinson, "Racial Exhaustion," 86 *Wash. U. L. Rev.* 917 (2009).
8. 14 Stat. 27, Sec. 1 (codified as amended at 42 U.S.C., Secs. 1981–1982 [2012]).

9. Ibid., Sec. 2.
10. George Rutherglen, *Civil Rights in the Shadow of Slavery: The Constitution, Common Law, and the Civil Rights Act of 1866* (New York: Oxford University Press, 2013), 65.
11. McDonald v. Santa Fe Trail Transp. Co., 427 U.S. 273, 285–96 (1976).
12. *Cong. Globe*, 39th Cong., 1st Sess., 474 (January 29, 1866) (statement of Senator Trumbull).
13. Ibid.
14. Ibid., 1366 (March 13, 1866). A reference to "civil rights" was also deleted from a proposed draft of the Fourteenth Amendment. William E. Nelson, *The Fourteenth Amendment: From Political Principle to Judicial Doctrine* (Cambridge, Mass.: Harvard University Press, 1988), 54–57.
15. See *Cong. Globe*, 39th Cong., 1st Sess., 474; ibid., 1115 (March 1, 1866); ibid., 157.
16. Ibid., 498 (January 30, 1866).
17. Ibid., 527 (January 31, 1866).
18. U.S. Const., Art. 1, Sec. 8. The clause treats commerce "with the Indian Tribes" like commerce "with foreign Nations, and among the several States."
19. Ibid., Sec. 2; ibid., Fourteenth Amend., Sec. 2.
20. *Cong. Globe*, 39th Cong., 1st Sess., 599 (February 2, 1866).
21. Rutherglen, *Civil Rights*, 51, 191n40.
22. *Cong. Globe*, 39th Cong., 1st Sess., 477 (January 29, 1866).
23. Ibid., 577 (February 1, 1866).
24. U.S. Const., Art. 1, Sec. 8.
25. Scott v. Sandford, 60 U.S. 393, 423 (1857). Lincoln's attorney general Edward Bates nevertheless offered an opinion that, on the issue of citizenship of African Americans, *Dred Scott* did not constitute binding law. Citizenship, *Official Opinions of the Attorneys General of the United States*, 10:382, 383, 409–13 (1862).
26. U.S. Const., Thirteenth Amend., Sec. 1 ("Neither slavery nor involuntary servitude, except as a punishment for crime whereof the party shall have been duly convicted, shall exist within the United States, or any place subject to their jurisdiction").
27. See *Cong. Globe*, 38th Cong., 1st Sess., 1465 (April 8, 1864) (statement of Senator Henderson in debate over the Thirteenth Amendment); U.S. Const., Thirteenth Amend., Sec. 2.
28. Drafts of the veto message reveal that President Johnson rejected advice, most likely from Secretary of State Seward, to moderate his criticism of

Congress. LaWanda Cox, *Freedom, Racism, and Reconstruction: Collected Writing of LaWanda Cox*, ed. Donald G. Nieman (Athens: University of Georgia Press, 1997), 70–93. For a detailed account of how the veto of the act confirmed the complete break between the president and Congress, see Eric L. McKitrick, *Andrew Johnson and Reconstruction* (New York: Oxford University Press, 1960), 298–325.

29. *Cong. Globe*, 39th Cong., 1st Sess., 1679 (March 27, 1866).
30. Ibid.
31. Ibid., 1680.
32. Ibid.
33. Ibid., 1681.
34. Ibid.
35. Ibid.
36. Ibid., 1759 (April 4, 1866) (statement of Senator Trumbull).
37. For an elaboration of this comparison, see Rutherglen, *Civil Rights*, 71–80; see also John Harrison, "Reconstructing the Privileges or Immunities Clause," 101 *Yale L. J.* 1385, 1402–25 (1992).
38. Donald G. Nieman, *To Set the Law in Motion: The Freedmen's Bureau and the Legal Rights of Blacks, 1865–1868* (Millwood, N.J.: KTO Press, 1979), 36–37.
39. Eric Schnapper, "Affirmative Action and the Legislative History of the Fourteenth Amendment," 71 *Va. L. Rev.* 753, 763 (1985).
40. See Act of July 16, 1866, Sec. 1, 14 Stat. 173; *Cong. Globe*, 39th Cong., 1st Sess., 943 (February 20, 1866).
41. See Act of March 3, 1865, Sec. 1, 13 Stat. 507; Schnapper, "Affirmative Action," 760.
42. Nieman, *To Set the Law in Motion*, 47–53.
43. Ibid., 53–66, 156–90.
44. Eric Foner, *Reconstruction: America's Unfinished Revolution, 1863–1877* (New York: Harper and Row, 1988), 144–48.
45. Sec. 1, reprinted in E. McPherson, *The Political History of the United States of America during the Period of Reconstruction* (Washington, D.C.: Philp and Solomons, 1871), 73.
46. Secs. 7–8, reprinted in ibid., 73–74.
47. Nieman, *To Set the Law in Motion*, 104–55.
48. *Cong. Globe*, 39th Cong., 1st Sess., 315 (January 19, 1866) (statement of Senator Hendricks).
49. Ibid., 319 (statement of Senator Trumbull).
50. Ibid., 936 (February 20, 1866).

51. See note 45.
52. See note 46.
53. *Cong. Globe*, 39th Cong., 1st Sess., 320 (January 19, 1866); ibid., 318 (remarks of Senator Hendricks).
54. Ibid., 938 (February 20, 1866); ibid., 916 (February 19, 1866) (veto message).
55. Ibid., 322 (January 19, 1866) (remarks of Senator Trumbull).
56. Schnapper, "Affirmative Action," 763, 772.
57. Secs. 7–8, reprinted in McPherson, *Political History*, 73–74. Sec. 7 used the phrase "any other persons," while sec. 8 used "other person."
58. *Cong. Globe*, 39th Cong., 1st Sess., 940 (February 20, 1866).
59. Ibid., 40th Cong., 2d Sess., 3056 (June 11, 1868) (statement of Representative Eliot).
60. Ibid., 39th Cong., 1st Sess., 544 (January 31, 1866) (statement of Representative Taylor); ibid., 630 (February 3, 1866) (statement of Representative Marshall); see also Schnapper, "Affirmative Action," 765–66; and Herman Belz, *Abraham Lincoln, Constitutionalism and Equal Rights during the Civil War Era* (New York: Fordham University Press, 1997), 143, 151, 160–61.
61. *Cong. Globe*, 39th Cong., 1st Sess., 317 (January 19, 1866) (statement of Senator Hendricks); John M. Bickers, "The Power to Do What Manifestly Must Be Done: Congress, the Freedmen's Bureau, and Constitutional Imagination," 12 *Rogers Williams U. L. Rev.* 70, 102 (2006).
62. *Cong. Globe*, 39th Cong., 1st Sess., 916 (February 19, 1866).
63. Ibid., 320 (January 19, 1866). He also invoked passing the privileges and immunities clause and the republican form of government clause to justify the prosecution of the Civil War. Ibid., 319. For the basis of the Freedmen's Bureau in the war power and its relation to military occupation, see Michel Les Benedict, *Preserving the Constitution: Essays on Politics and the Constitution in the Reconstruction Era* (New York: Fordham University Press, 2006), 10–14; and Gregory P. Downs, *After Appomattox: Military Occupation and the Ends of War* (Cambridge, Mass.: Harvard University Press, 2015), 45–47. For modern endorsement of the proposition that "the war power does not necessarily end with the cessation of hostilities," see *Woods v. Cloy W. Miller Co.*, 333 U.S. 138, 141 (1948).
64. *Cong. Globe*, 39th Cong., 1st Sess., 315 (January 19, 1866) (statement of Senator Hendricks).
65. Ibid., 916 (February 19, 1866).
66. Ibid., 43 (December 13, 1865); ibid., 322 (January 19, 1866); see ibid., 630 (February 3, 1866) (statement of Representative Hubbard). For a later, equally brief reference to the Thirteenth Amendment in debate over

legislation terminating the bureau, see *Cong. Globe*, 40th Cong., 2d Sess., 4007 (July 13, 1868) (statement of Representative Paine).

67. *Cong. Globe*, 39th Cong., 1st Sess., 42–43 (December 13, 1865) (statement of Senator Saulsbury); ibid. 318 (January 19, 1866) (statement of Senator Hendricks).
68. Ibid., 916 (February 19, 1866).
69. Ibid., 941 (February 20, 1866).
70. Ibid., 318 (January 19, 1866) (statement of Sen. Hendricks); see ibid., 934 (February 20, 1866) (statement of Senator Davis).
71. Ibid., 322 (January 19, 1866).
72. Ibid., 943 (February 20, 1866).
73. Ibid., 2772 (May 23, 1866).
74. Ibid., 2773.
75. Ibid. (statement of Representative Le Blond); ibid., 3839–41 (July 16, 1866) (statement of Senator Hendricks); ibid., 3840–41 (statement of Senator Saulsbury).
76. Ibid., 3838.
77. Ibid., 3842, 3850; Act of July 16, 1866, Sec. 1, 14 Stat. 173.
78. Act of July 6, 1868, Sec. 1, 15 Stat. 83.
79. Act of July 25, 1868, Sec. 2, 17 Stat. 193.
80. Ibid., Sec. 1.
81. Ibid., Sec. 2.
82. 40th Cong., 2d Sess., 4005–07 (July 13, 1868).
83. Ibid., 1813–15 (March 11, 1868) (statement of Representative Eliot); ibid., 1994–95 (March 19, 1868) (statements of Representatives Wood and Arnell); ibid., 4004–05 (July 13, 1868) (statements of Representatives Brooks and Eliot).
84. Ibid., 1815 (March 11, 1868) (statement of Representative Trimble); ibid., 3053–54 (June 11, 1868) (statement of Senator Hendricks).
85. Ibid., 3054, 3055–56, 3058 (June 11, 1868) (statement of Senator Hendricks); ibid., 4004 (July 13, 1868) (statement of Representative Brooks).
86. Act of June 10, 1872, 17 Stat. 347, 366.
87. Act of March 1, 1875, 18 Stat. 335.
88. 109 U.S. 3 (1883).
89. Schnapper, "Affirmative Action." For a recent restatement of these views and citations to others who have made similar arguments, see Amicus Brief of Constitutional Scholars, 5–17, in *Fisher v. University of Texas*, 133 S. Ct. 2411 (2013).
90. "Town Hall: McConnell and Rosen Debate Affirmative Action," Constitution Daily website: "But as you must realize, the category of 'freedman'

was not a racial category; it referred to people who until recently were held in chattel slavery. A close look at the laws passed by the Reconstruction Congress indicates only one, almost trivial, example of genuinely race-based legislation—designed to make sure that black soldiers serving the Union in the War received their full entitlement to pay and pension." Available at http://blog.constitutioncenter.org/2013/06/town-hall-mcconnell-and-rosen-on-affirmative-action/; Michael Rappaport, "Originalism and the Colorblind Constitution," available at https://papers.ssrn.com/sol3/papers.cfm?abstract_id=2244610

91. McDonald v. City of Chicago, 561 U.S. 742, 774–75 (2010).
92. The provision applied "in every State or district where the ordinary course of judicial proceedings has been interrupted by the rebellion," until ordinary judicial remedies were restored and the state's relations with the federal government reestablished. Act of July 16, 1866, Sec. 14, 14 Stat. 173, 176–77. The rights, however, were granted to everyone in those areas and were good against both the state and the federal government. For instance, the act explicitly protects "the constitutional right to bear arms," which at the time applied only against the federal government.
93. The votes on all these measures were nearly the same. For the Freedmen's Bureau Act, 33 to 12 in the Senate, and 104 to 33, with 45 not voting, in the House. *Cong. Globe*, 39th Cong., 1st Sess., 3842, 3850 (July 16, 1866); for the Civil Rights Act of 1866, 33 to 15 in the Senate, and 122 to 41, with 21 not voting, in the House. Ibid., 1809, 1861 (April 6, 1866). The votes on the Fourteenth Amendment were 33 to 11 in the Senate, and 120 to 32, with 32 not voting, in the House. Ibid., 3042 (June 8, 1866); ibid., 3149 (June 13, 1866).
94. See Barry Cushman, *Rethinking the New Deal Court: The Structure of a Constitutional Revolution* (New York: Oxford University Press, 1998), 90–91 (attributing a similar application of constitutional principle to changed circumstances by Chief Justice Hughes in the New Deal).
95. See William Gillette, *Retreat from Reconstruction 1869–79* (Baton Rouge: Louisiana State University Press, 1979), x–xii (summarizing the causes typically assigned for the failure of Reconstruction).
96. Compare ch. 114, Sec. 1, 18 Stat. 335, 336 (1875) with Pub. L. No. 88-352, tit. II, 78 Stat. 241, 243 (1964) (codified as amended at 42 U.S.C., Secs. 2000a to 2000a-6).
97. Civil Rights Cases, 109 U.S. 3, 25 (1883).
98. Shelby County v. Holder, 133 S. Ct. 2612 (2013).

10

THE JANUS OF CIVIL RIGHTS LAW

Darrell A. H. Miller

The Civil Rights Act of 1866 is the Janus of American civil rights law. In one way, the act looks backward, to the wreckage of slavery and the Civil War and to the power of the Thirteenth Amendment, ratified a few weeks before. In another way, the act looks forward, to Reconstruction, to the power of the Fourteenth Amendment, and, further still, to the Civil Rights Movement of the 1960s and the Second Reconstruction, a century yet to come. Justice Sandra Day O'Connor recognized the act's peculiar quality when she referred to it as "both a Thirteenth and a Fourteenth Amendment statute."[1]

To say that the Civil Rights Act is a product of both the Thirteenth Amendment, which abolished slavery, and the Fourteenth Amendment, which guarantees equality, raises issues that go far beyond the mere timing of its enactment. It is to raise fundamental questions about the very meaning of Reconstruction. Is the act concerned primarily with the rights of African Americans, or is it concerned with the rights of all people, whatever their identity? Does the act target coercion, no matter the source, or only coercion by the government? What does the act's history tell us about the respective roles of Congress and the Supreme Court in defining and enforcing civil rights? And finally, what can the act tell us about our current attitudes toward the legacy of slavery and its aftermath? Because the act stands as a gateway between the Thirteenth and Fourteenth Amendments, its history, interpretation, enforcement, and influence can help us better understand American civil rights commitments, the meaning of equality, and what exactly it means to say a person is free.

THE PAST

Passage

On January 5, 1866, Lyman Trumbull, the Democrat-turned-Republican senator from Illinois, introduced the first civil rights bill in American history.[2] Trumbull proposed the bill, marked S. 61, on the heels of the Thirteenth Amendment, ratified just weeks before. Debate over the "emancipation amendment" had consumed the prior Congress, and political opinion ranged from the exultant to the bewildered. Supporters considered the emancipation amendment a "permanent disposition of the whole question of slavery,"[3] a "consummation"[4] of the founding generation's republican vision. Ratification, for them, finally inscribed the Declaration of Independence into the Constitution.[5] For the most zealous, the amendment did everything: it broke the black man's bonds and simultaneously bestowed upon him the bounty of rights, protections, and opportunities available to every other citizen of the United States.[6]

Opponents denounced the emancipation amendment as an uncompensated taking of private property and the first step toward centralized government.[7] To them, federal abolition of slavery repudiated, rather than perfected, the Founders' design.[8] Some even suggested that an emancipation amendment was unconstitutional. For these skeptics, slavery, property rights, and federalism formed an alloy impervious to change, invulnerable even to the constitutional amendment process itself.[9] Others conceded the amendment was constitutional, but they insisted that emancipation meant only freedom from coerced labor—nothing more.[10]

Given the wide disagreement, Congress produced a Thirteenth Amendment that was both terse and elliptical. It has just two sections: a declaration (poached from the Northwest Ordinance), "Neither slavery nor involuntary servitude, except as a punishment for crime whereof the party shall have been duly convicted, shall exist within the United States, or any place subject to their jurisdiction,"[11] and an assertion, "Congress shall have power to enforce this article by appropriate legislation."[12] This was the thin scaffold from which national reconstruction would begin.

Trumbull introduced S. 61 aware of the gulf between the Thirteenth Amendment's aspiration and its implementation. The amendment's "abstract truths and principles" meant nothing "unless the persons who are to be affected . . . have some means of availing themselves of their benefits."[13] To "give effect" to the Thirteenth Amendment, to secure "practical freedom" for its beneficiaries, Congress needed a legal apparatus for emancipation.[14] But Congress had never passed a civil rights act before, and there was little agreement on how to guarantee civil rights, or even on how to define them. Certainly the civil rights of the newly emancipated must reach further than "the bare privilege of not being chained,"[15] but how much further? What distinguished a civil right from a political right? What distinguished a civil right from a social right? Were civil rights positive rights? If so, what kind? Were they the duties citizens owed to each other, or the duties that the government owed to its citizens? If the latter, which government: state or federal? Were civil rights prohibitions or obligations? All the questions of federal and state power, private and public coercion, citizenship and freedom that Congress deferred in wrangling over the Thirteenth Amendment returned in debates over its enforcement.[16]

Congress was doing something new, but it was compelled to act. The emancipation amendment was not the talisman some abolitionists had hoped. Recalcitrant southerners flaunted their sense that, although the war was lost, they would win the peace. "'Things will work back again into their old grooves,'" chirped an Alabama planter.[17] To assist the process, southern legislatures enacted Black Codes that proclaimed the equal status of African Americans in one paragraph and inflicted crippling social and economic disabilities in another.[18] The codes barred African Americans from certain trades, obliged them to be employed under threat of criminal prosecution, subjected them to special taxation, and restricted their ability to travel, assemble, possess firearms, and associate with white persons.[19] In ways blatant and subtle, "combinations" of officials, quasi-officials, and private citizens worked to thwart emancipation.[20] White individuals would not sell emancipated persons the necessaries of life,[21] refused to hire them without permission from former masters,[22] and arrested them almost at will.[23] The former slaves were placed in impossible straits. Private parties prevented them from obtaining employment or property, courts convicted them for failure to have either, and then sheriffs forced them into hard labor as punishment.[24] The goal was to keep freed people "'as near to the condition of slavery as possible.'"[25] The secretary of state declared slavery dead on December 18, 1865, but to millions, it must have felt very much alive. Something had to be done, and the Civil Rights Act was Congress's first attempt.

Federal protection of civil rights was novel, but the bill itself was a bricolage. The act contained ten sections: a declaration of citizenship in Section 1 rounded out by a "machinery for enforcement," pieced together from various extant sources, in the remaining sections.[26] Section 1 federalized U.S. citizenship and used the apolitical place of birth as the metric.[27] It then went on to guarantee to those citizens "the same right . . . to make and enforce contracts, to sue, be parties, and give evidence, to inherit, purchase, lease, sell, hold, and convey real and personal property, and to full and equal benefit of all laws and proceedings for the security of person and property, as is enjoyed by white citizens." Congress lifted much of this list from Justice Bushrod Washington's 1823 circuit decision in *Corfield v. Coryell*, which had construed the citizenship rights implicit in the privileges and immunities clause of Article 4 of the Constitution.[28] Congress enumerated these rights in the act partially to repudiate the Black Codes and partially to reassure the act's more timorous supporters.[29] For the remaining sections, Congress borrowed from familiar sources in foreign relations law and, ironically, from the Fugitive Slave Act of 1850—an antebellum measure designed to enforce the Constitution's fugitive slave clause.[30] The act supplied federal forums for adjudication, specified punishment for those who "under color of any law" deprive a person "of any right secured or protected by this act," and criminalized the obstruction of federal law enforcement.[31]

Given the circumstances and its borrowed language, Republicans considered the bill fairly moderate and felt confident President Andrew Johnson would sign it.[32] Instead, he rejected the Civil Rights Bill as an unwarranted extension of federal power and as an unwise intervention into the free market.[33] And, foreshadowing modern zero-sum attitudes to race-conscious legislation,[34] he disparaged "safeguards which go infinitely beyond any that the [federal government] has ever provided for the white race."[35] Republicans were incensed. Congress overrode the president's veto,[36] determined that the Thirteenth Amendment would not be reduced to a "paper guarantee."[37]

Jubilation, rancor, and bloodshed followed the act's passage. In Fort Greene, Brooklyn, a hundred-gun salute thundered in celebration.[38] The *Lowell Daily Citizen and News* proclaimed, "Great News—Passage of the Civil Rights Bill over the Veto."[39] A reporter for the *Boston Advertiser* applauded "the representatives of the people" who made "good the guarantees of emancipation."[40] Others predicted an apocalypse. Scare quotes collared any mention of the act. The *Harrisburg Patriot and Union* suggested that the "Negro 'Civil Rights Bill'" perverted the Founding Fathers' design and would lay waste to state constitutions.[41] The *Macon Daily Telegraph* mocked the "iniquitous"[42] measure as a "Civil Wrongs Bill" and predicted its quick judicial demise.[43]

The battles did not remain confined to newsprint. In April 1866, a riot erupted in Norfolk, Virginia, when black citizens celebrating passage of the act clashed with hostile police officers and white citizens.[44] Two other cities, Memphis and New Orleans, experienced their own deadly racial and political turmoil before the summer was over.[45] The year 1866 also witnessed another birth, besides that of the first civil rights act, the birth of a new "social club" dedicated to "the inalienable right of self-preservation"—it called itself the Ku Klux Klan.[46]

The violence of 1866, the rise of the Klan, uncertainty over the act's constitutional foundation, and the abject failure of Presidential Reconstruction spurred Congress and the country to further action. From 1868 to 1875, the nation added to the Constitution the Fourteenth Amendment (1868) and the Fifteenth Amendment (1870), and Congress passed the 1870 Enforcement Act (including a reenactment of the Civil Rights Act of 1866), the 1871 Ku Klux Klan Act, and the Civil Rights Act of 1875, the first federal public accommodation law.

The Fourteenth Amendment entrenched many of the Civil Rights Act's protections in the Constitution, but it also expanded and abstracted them.[47] The act's guarantee of federal birthright citizenship remains in the Fourteenth Amendment, but the amendment extends a guarantee of residential *state* citizenship as well.[48] The act's itemized entitlements and protections, pinched from *Corfield v. Coryell,* are gone. In their stead, the amendment prohibits a state from abrogating the "privileges *or* immunities"[49] of U.S. citizens, depriving any person of "life, liberty, or property, without due process of law," or denying any person "equal protection of the laws."[50] But in one crucial respect, the Fourteenth Amendment appears narrower; it expressly speaks of the behavior of *states,* whereas the Civil Rights Act of 1866 is not so limited.[51] Consequently, when Congress reenacted the 1866 act in 1870, as part of the post–Fourteenth Amendment Enforcement Act, it clouded the earlier, clearer, Thirteenth Amendment source of civil rights norms.

This minor change had profound consequences in subsequent litigation. First, it raised questions about who was supposed to benefit from the 1866 act's protections. The 1866 act grew out of Congress's power to prohibit and prevent "slavery"—an institution with an indubitable racial character in the United States. The 1870 act relied on Congress's power to protect "privileges or immunities," "due process," and "equal protection"—norms that do not necessarily require deep knowledge of a racialized custom. Second, it sowed doubt as to the target of the 1866 act's prohibitions. Slavery, forbidden by the Thirteenth Amendment, was an institution maintained by private coercion as much as by public sanction. As a result, it is plausible to construe the amendment's enforcement power to reach both public and private actors. By contrast, the Fourteenth Amendment restrains only the state, raising questions as to whether Congress intended the act's recodification in 1870 to limit the act's prohibitions only to government agents.[52]

As history shows, courts soon began to pull civil rights in this direction: away from African Americans as the beneficiaries of protection and away from private parties as the targets of prohibition—moves that helped to usher in the long period of Jim Crow.

Retreat

Retreat from Reconstruction is a familiar tale. The newly formed Department of Justice and other federal officials initially pursued civil rights cases with vigor, but within a generation, enforcement had languished.[53] Southern states evaded scrutiny by enacting laws that offered equality in form but denied it in fact. Congress, once generous with its civil rights support, turned miserly in the face of southern resistance. High court decisions like the *Slaughterhouse Cases, United States v. Cruikshank,* the *Civil Rights Cases,* and *Plessy v. Ferguson* whittled civil rights protections for African Americans until they covered only the narrowest types of legal disabilities and the most literal forms of coerced labor. The *Civil Rights Cases,* for example, restricted Congress's authority to enforce the Thirteenth Amendment against private actors and narrowed the Fourteenth Amendment prohibitions to state agents. *Plessy* went further and held that even *state*-mandated racial discrimination did not violate the Fourteenth Amendment's equal protection clause, so long as the state guaranteed "separate but equal" facilities. So, while the Court's obiter dicta continued to place black civil rights at the heart of Reconstruction, the Court's holdings betrayed an ever-more sclerotic notion of what civil rights were or could be.

Scholars and historians dispute the reasons for Reconstruction's decline. For writers like Robert Kaczorowski, the cause was almost entirely political. In his classic *Politics of Judicial Interpretation,* Kaczorowski sees the first few bold and broad constructions of the Civil Rights Act of 1866 crumble under the pressure of persistent racial and political terrorism, federal inconstancy, and flagging public interest.[54] The problem was not constitutional authority or legislative intent but political will.[55] Other writers, like Herman Belz, are less certain that Congress intended broad constructions of either the Thirteenth Amendment or the Civil Rights Acts. For these writers, there was no retreat; Reconstruction politics and litigation reflected a genuine belief in the limited role of federal law in state affairs, even after the Civil War. To them, Reconstruction supplied only "minimum national standards" for local law enforcement, not a broad license for federal intervention.[56] The federal state arrangements from 1789 remained largely intact. According to Belz, progressive critics of

Reconstruction unfairly measure nineteenth-century civil rights law with a modern yardstick.[57] And these are but two of the numerous writers who have explored this literature. For whatever reason, whether because of political failure or legal insufficiency, or both, by the turn of the century, the Civil Rights Act of 1866 was moribund.

Return

The 1968 case of *Jones v. Alfred H. Mayer Co.* conventionally marks a short-lived revival of the 1866 act in the national imagination.[58] In *Jones*, Joseph Lee Jones, an African American federal employee, and his white wife attempted to buy a house in a St. Louis, Missouri, suburb. Agents of the Alfred H. Mayer Company told the Joneses it was their policy not to sell houses to black people, and Jones, with the support of the St. Louis fair housing community, sued. Initially, the litigation followed familiar Fourteenth Amendment traces: the new subdivision was large, more like a municipality than a private enterprise; the defendants were land developers, not individual homeowners. This was the familiar language of state action. Ever since the *Civil Rights Cases*, only governments could be liable for Fourteenth Amendment violations. Mayer's development had to look like a government, or be so deeply entangled with a government that its activities amounted to that of a state, in order for it to violate any rights guaranteed by the Constitution or its enforcement legislation. Later, and by degrees, the 1866 act gained prominence, and with it, its Thirteenth Amendment roots. According to Jones's lawyers, Congress had evidence of rampant collusion by white southerners in 1866 to keep freed people in bondage, and Congress passed the act under its authority to enforce the Thirteenth Amendment; surely Congress had not intended to impose a state action requirement drawn from a yet-unratified Fourteenth Amendment? Besides, Jones argued, what good is an equal right to property if no one will sell you any?[59]

The Supreme Court accepted the argument. Justice Potter Stewart, writing for the majority, held that the Civil Rights Act of 1866 forbids a private property owner from refusing to sell to a willing buyer due to race and that Congress has power under the Thirteenth Amendment to pass such a law.[60] As the majority wrote, Congress wanted to eliminate racial discrimination against African Americans, whether the barriers were erected by the Black Codes or "by private individuals and unofficial groups . . . unrelated to any hostile state legislation."[61] It was up to Congress to identify "badges," "incidents," and "relic[s]" of slavery rationally and to design appropriate legislation.[62] Private refusal to sell homes because of race tends to "herd[]" African Americans into ghettos, and that segregation is a relic of slavery that Congress may prevent.[63] The Court ended with a strong statement of economic empowerment: "The freedom that Congress is empowered to secure under the Thirteenth Amendment includes the freedom to buy whatever a white man can buy, the right to live wherever a white man can live."[64] If Congress cannot so define freedom, the majority concluded, "then the Thirteenth Amendment made a promise the Nation cannot keep."[65]

Detractors panned *Jones* as an unprincipled, unprecedented Warren Court invention, its legal theories cooked up in the chambers of Justice Stewart.[66] But interest in the Thirteenth Amendment and the Civil Rights Act of 1866 goes back at least a generation before *Jones*. As Risa Goluboff has documented, totalitarian propaganda machines were eager to exploit America's racial hypocrisies, leading the Roosevelt administration to recognize black civil rights as a critical wartime issue. The newly formed Civil Rights Division in the Department of Justice enlisted its lawyers to protect racial minorities, and especially African Americans, from egregious racial abuse.[67] The new division had to work under hostile conditions. Claims that the Constitution guaranteed liberty of contract and unregulated markets ebbed after the New Deal, but separate-but-equal was still black-letter law.[68] Faced with these challenges, the Civil Rights Division reached back to the Thirteenth Amendment and its laws for new theories of civil rights—theories less burdened by laissez-faire constitutionalism, theories that could outflank the state-action, separate-but-equal barriers of the *Civil Rights Cases* and *Plessy*.[69] Even though the division would not systematically tackle disenfranchisement, lynching, police brutality, and similar outrages for another decade, Justice Department lawyers did mount a successful campaign against peonage, suffered in many cases by African Americans, with theories drawn from Reconstruction statutes.[70]

Mid-twentieth-century civil rights leaders also tapped into the potential of the Thirteenth Amendment and 1866 act, although with less deliberation and coordination than they did with the Fourteenth Amendment. George Vaughn, a maverick St. Louis lawyer, initially attempted to litigate the famous case of *Shelley v. Kraemer* as an 1866 act case.[71] In *Shelley*, the Kraemers sought to keep a black family, the Shelleys, from moving into a home in St. Louis. The Kraemers alleged that a racially restrictive covenant prevented the Shelleys from living in the neighborhood. Initially, Vaughn argued that the covenant violated the Shelleys' statutory right to contract for property the same as white citizens. But the national NAACP, fearful of the pitfalls of this approach, soon took over and steered the litigation onto a more conventional course.[72] The NAACP persuaded the Court that state judicial enforcement of a privately negotiated racially restrictive covenant violates the Fourteenth Amendment's equal protection clause. Although Vaughn's 1866 argument failed in *Shelley*, he was soon vindicated. In *Hurd v. Hodge*, a companion case to *Shelley*, Chief Justice Frederick Vinson held that *federal* judicial enforcement of racially restrictive covenants in the District of Columbia is unlawful, not because of the equal protection clause of the Fourteenth Amendment (which had yet to be applied to the federal government) but because of the 1866 act.[73]

The early civil rights pioneer Dr. Pauli Murray wrote a thesis in law school that traced public accommodation and antidiscrimination norms to the Thirteenth Amendment.[74] Her sense that the amendment provided authority for federal public accommodations law prefigured arguments in support of the Civil Rights Act of 1964, many years later.[75] During hearings on the 1964 act, Justice Department officials appealed to the Reconstruction amendments and legislation as precedential, if not for strictly legal reasons, at least for moral ones. Although Burke Marshall of the Department of Justice's Civil Rights Division ventured that "the [Thirteenth] amendment positively gives the Congress power to move in this area [of civil rights],"[76] Congress justified its power to prohibit discrimination in hotels, restaurants, and other public accommodations largely on its authority to regulate interstate commerce. Even so, in the 1964 Supreme Court case *Heart of Atlanta Motel v. United States*, Justice Hugo Black concurred that congressional power to protect African Americans from discrimination in commerce is clear "in view of the Thirteenth, Fourteenth and Fifteenth Amendments."[77]

By 1968, the justices were also finding it increasingly difficult to finesse the state-action barrier to private discrimination in civil rights litigation. In opinions like *Shelley*, the *White Primary Cases*, and, to a lesser extent, the *Sit-In Cases*, the justices resorted to ever-more ingenious reasoning to conclude that ostensibly private discrimination was really government discrimination prohibited by constitutional norms. The Court was plainly eager for an alternative, and the time was ripe.[78] The *Jones* litigation team supplied a theory that plausibly linked concerns of widespread, coordinated private action in 1866 with those same concerns a century later. *Jones* subtly shifted emphasis from *express* discrimination by groups in the form of state authority (a Fourteenth Amendment problem) to the *risk* of discrimination by groups in the form of private housing markets (a Thirteenth Amendment problem), but it did so within the context of the same statute, the Civil Rights Act of 1866. Although *Jones* appeared a wild, unruly decision to detractors, civil rights leaders had prepared the ground for this shift years before. The fruit of this effort, however, could flourish only so long as the Court was willing to accept congressional judgments about how best to enforce the Reconstruction amendments. For some time in the late 1960s and early 1970s, the Court was willing to defer to Congress's opinion, both as to the scope of the problem of discrimination and to the propriety of its remedies. That deference would gradually turn to skepticism as the Warren and Burger Courts transitioned to the Rehnquist and Roberts Courts.

As important as *Jones* is as a matter of the 1866 act, it did not yield a whole new generation of civil rights acts or Thirteenth Amendment litigation. Although lawyers slowly refined its precedential impact in the latter twentieth century, the legacy of *Jones* is more muted, and perhaps more telling. In 1976, in *Runyon v. McCrary*,[79] the Court extended the logic of *Jones* to racial discrimination in all contracting, not just for real property. *Runyon* dealt with alleged racial discrimination at a private school. The plaintiffs argued that by failing to accept their black children, the school had denied them an opportunity to contract the same as whites. *Runyon* upheld the act, even though the defendants plausibly claimed that the act, so construed, violated their First Amendment rights of association and their constitutional rights to privacy and parenthood.[80] Some *Runyon* justices even hinted that *Jones* was a mistake and should be overturned.[81] But Congress intervened and settled the matter in the 1991 Civil Rights Act. That bill specified that the 1866 act prevented discrimination in contracting by both private and public actors.[82] In other words, Congress reinforced the notion that the 1866 act is "both a Thirteenth and a Fourteenth Amendment statute."[83] Congress amended Trumbull's bill in a way that raises many questions, but largely they are of an academic variety. Today, the 1866 act mostly duplicates other types of protections, from other constitutional sources, and has faded from the civil rights agenda.

TENSIONS AND TRANSITIONS

The Civil Rights Act of 1866 and its protections today appear an adjunct to other statutes, if not an afterthought. Congress enforces modern civil rights priorities primarily through its power to tax and spend, to regulate interstate commerce, and to enforce the Fourteenth Amendment. As a tool of civil rights policy, the Civil Rights Act of 1866 is at best supplementary.[84]

Recent decisions are mostly incidental, technical refinements.[85] So why should we investigate the Civil Rights Act of 1866 as anything more than a historical curiosity?

For two familiar reasons: First, to understand the Civil Rights Act of 1866, to appreciate its transitional position in American civil rights history, is to come to understand how we have arrived at this place in the twenty-first century. Without apprehending this past, our current civil rights doctrine and discourse is episodic and incomprehensible. (What does protecting the channels of commerce have to do with race discrimination at a diner?) The Civil Rights Act of 1866 occurred at a historical juncture where America debated fundamental issues of political economy and morality: slave versus citizen, war versus peace, form versus function, and principle versus politics. Those debates still take place. Second, to understand the act's role in getting us to where we are may give us a sense of where we are going. The act refracts the Reconstruction amendments and the contested values implicit in those amendments. Understanding how the act addresses matters of freedom, race, citizenship, equality, and coercion may offer clues about how law may speak to the issues in the future.[86]

Slave and Citizen

The Civil Rights Act of 1866 forced the nation to ask what distinguishes a slave from a citizen. Slavery has generated an enormous literature, on subjects as varied as the economics of slave labor to the sociology of slave communities. But one issue that remains pertinent to the legacy of the act is whether Congress thought it would be race-conscious or race-blind.

An early draft of the Civil Rights Act specifically conferred citizenship upon persons of "African descent." Congress abandoned this phrasing for a race-neutral alternative.[87] However, civil rights continued to be conceptualized in race-conscious ways: the statute as enacted says the rights protected shall be the same as those for "white citizens." As George Rutherglen has remarked, the act used "the rights of whites among themselves [as] the natural measure of equality for everyone."[88] The contemporaneous Freedmen's Bureau Bill, occasionally read in pari materia with the 1866 act, and other similar bills are easily characterized as race-conscious legislation.[89]

The suggestion of residual race-consciousness in the 1866 act provides insight into the race-consciousness of the Thirteenth Amendment, and perhaps of the Fourteenth Amendment as well. Without race-consciousness, the ideas of "slavery" and "involuntary servitude" in the Thirteenth Amendment collapse into ahistorical synonyms.[90] And without a race-conscious theory of the Thirteenth Amendment, the power to enforce against the "badges," "incidents," and "relics" of slavery become peculiarly color-blind. Justice Thurgood Marshall, in the 1976 case *McDonald v. Santa Fe Trail Transportation Co.*, appeared to endorse this color-blind reading of the 1866 Civil Rights Act and, implicitly, Congress's power to enforce the Thirteenth Amendment. *McDonald* held that the 1866 act protects white persons as well as African Americans from employment discrimination, and the language about "white citizens" in the act speaks only to the racial nature of the forbidden motive.[91] Marshall understood the act to prohibit racial discrimination, not racial discrimination against any particular group.

Santa Fe may be the correct outcome, but it could be over-read to scrub the racial coding that informs both slavery and its abolition through the Thirteenth Amendment. Slavery in the United States wasn't just a labor practice. It was an institution. In particular it was a *racialized* institution with black people subordinate and white people dominant. By 1865, the institution's core racial characteristic was firm: in America, only black people could be slaves; and all slaves were black people.[92] As an American institution, slavery encompassed a set of racially denominated behaviors, norms, and practices that penetrated almost every aspect of our society—either directly or indirectly.[93]

The shift in civil rights focus from the Thirteenth Amendment, and the rights of Africans as free people, to the Fourteenth Amendment, and the rights of citizens in general, unquestionably made the Reconstruction project more durable, but at the cost of a certain racial sensitivity and context.[94] It supports arguments that race-consciousness in the pursuit of racial equality is in tension with itself, a temporary evil rather than a structural imperative, and perhaps illegitimate.[95]

Less than one generation after emancipation, members of the High Court were already impatient with the pace of transition from liberated slave to undifferentiated citizen. As Justice Joseph Bradley wrote in the *Civil Rights Cases*, "There must be some stage in the progress of his elevation when [the freed person] . . . ceases to be the special favorite of the laws."[96] But the sentiment is familiar in our own time, especially in debates over affirmative action and other forms of race-conscious remediation. In *Grutter v. Bollinger*, Justice O'Connor suggested that maybe in twenty-five years, race-conscious affirmative action will no longer be necessary to advance the compelling government interest of diversity.[97] During oral argument over Congress's ability to enforce the Fifteenth Amendment, Justice Antonin

Scalia disparaged sections of the Voting Rights Act as a "racial entitlement" scheme.[98] The shift in civil rights away from slavery toward citizenship also tends to feed into a certain vision of the Civil War's meaning, one in which the war had nothing to do with race, or even slavery, but was a fight over the Union, states' rights, and federalism.

Recapturing some measure of the race-consciousness of the Civil Rights Act of 1866 may slow those who want to drain Reconstruction of its racial history. It also may help color our understanding of other types of legislation, whether generated from Thirteenth Amendment enforcement power or some other power. Just as Justice Black suggested that Congress may use the commerce clause to protect black people from discrimination "in view of the Thirteenth, Fourteenth and Fifteenth Amendments," so other race-conscious measures, voting rights, or voluntary affirmative action by municipalities may be legitimate in light of the race-conscious construction of these amendments. It does not suggest that race-conscious measures are required. It does not suggest that race-conscious measures are even effective. But it does suggest that appropriately tailored, race-conscious measures would be constitutional.

War and Peace

The 1866 act attempts to transform civil rights protections from a wartime expedient into a permanent feature of American society.[99] But lost in the transition from war to peace is an appreciation of Reconstruction's meaning. The desire for normalcy after the Civil War and the desperate effort to harmonize 1866 with 1776 leads some today to minimize the impact of Reconstruction as a moment of profound structural and social change.

Representative Ignatius Donnelly was convinced that the Civil War had broken with the past and that Congress was engaging in nothing short of a re-founding. "Shall nothing be born of this mighty convulsion," he asked, "mightier by far than the old Revolution, mightier than all the revolutions of the world? . . . Sir, this is a new birth of the nation."[100] Carl Schurz initially expressed similar thoughts, noting, "It is not only the political machinery of the States and their constitutional relations to the General Government, but the whole organism of Southern society that must be reconstructed, or rather constructed anew."[101]

The Reconstruction Congress was constrained by a desire for normalcy and a need to restore established institutions. To do so, it ironically ignored certain traditions that long had been used to support the legitimacy of slavery itself. The ancient punishment for losing a war of rebellion was execution or servitude.[102] Confederate president Jefferson Davis suffered neither. Despite grumblings by some Unionists, and despite precedent stretching far into antiquity, Congress did not permanently dissolve the Confederate States and rule them as conquered territory.[103] As Harold Hyman and William Wiecek have written, the "[c]ongressmen who framed the Thirteenth Amendment in 1865 and who enforced it in 1866 perceived themselves to be in a constitutional world characterized by both continuities and changes."[104] A measure of this desire for continuity and change is evident from the Reconstruction enactments themselves: the Thirteenth Amendment borrowed from the older Northwest Ordinance, the Civil Rights Act of 1866 borrowed from the Thirteenth Amendment, and the Fourteenth Amendment borrowed from the Civil Rights Act of 1866.

Doubtless, the transition from war to peace kept many of the institutions that existed before 1865. It infused these institutions with the equality and liberty norms of the Declaration of Independence, but it did not eradicate them. The historical record is strong on that score. To suggest that everything was different in American federalism, politics, and society because of the Civil War is a gross distortion of the historical record. But, as a matter of legal construction, too intense a focus on continuity is equally distorting. It leads to "selective ancestor worship,"[105] where Founding Fathers like James Madison and Thomas Jefferson are venerated and Reconstruction fathers like Lyman Trumbull, John Bingham, and Charles Sumner are recognized infrequently, and only when they ape Madison and Jefferson.[106] It also permits spectacles like *Shelby County v. Holder*, the Voting Rights Act case, where the values of eighteenth-century federalism trump the values of nineteenth-century voter protection, even in the face of constitutional language that meant to reorder these priorities.[107]

The issue is a matter of emphasis and attention. Recapturing the revolutionary aspects of the Civil Rights Act and the Reconstruction amendments counters other popular narratives in which Reconstruction is an anomaly, a slightly embarrassing hiccup in an otherwise unbroken historical arc that begins with an idealized set of arrangements set down in Philadelphia in 1787 and ends with the victory of small government populism in the first decade of the twenty-first century. It also links those Reconstruction efforts to the subsequent course of civil rights in the twentieth century, a course that permits equality and nondiscrimination to become just as constitutive of the American experiment as federalism and private property.

Form and Function

With the 1866 act, the Reconstruction Congress addressed a functional problem with formalist tools. The functional problem was obvious: a massive black population, under- or uneducated, some with skills, some without, beset on every side by individuals who were, at best, tepid in their support for the new citizens and at worst actively hostile to their presence. But the tools Congress deployed were largely formalistic and procedural. Congress committed to a peacetime system of litigation to enforce civil rights, not to an open-ended military occupation.[108] As a result, African Americans were left to deal with recondite legal processes, surly law enforcement, and formal evasion with few resources.[109]

Formalism manifested itself in three ways: emphasis on de jure discrimination over de facto discrimination, focus on public action over private action, and attention to action versus inaction. De facto versus de jure discrimination was pursued through enforcement of race-neutral laws in racially discriminatory ways. Laws prohibiting vagrancy or regulating firearms were written in race-neutral terms but were notoriously meant to be enforced against only African Americans.[110] Private collectives acted in concert to frustrate black rights in ways that mirrored public collectives.[111] Finally, Congress in the Civil Rights Act of 1866 kept in place a state law enforcement apparatus, relying on federal enforcement when the state apparatus failed. But that raised questions of what constituted a failure sufficient to implicate federal protection. As federal enforcement began to flag, courts and Congress seemed less inclined to peer beyond the formal equality of legislation to see how states actually enforced these rights.[112]

In some sense, Congress members cannot be blamed; they did not know any other way. Theirs was a world in which words like "private," "public," "property," "contract," "local," "national," "civil," "political," and "social" were assumed to have well-defined meaning and internal coherence. Even when they did not have such well-defined meaning, local custom and common-law adjudication filled in the gaps. But the Civil War and Reconstruction weakened this method of reasoning and the institutions responsible for delivering content to these categories. The legal realists wanted to understand and evaluate law by the function it performed rather than rely on formal labels like "contract" or "tort." One can identify the beginning of this more functional approach in debates over the 1866 act. Generations before Louis Jaffee wrote "Law Making by Private Groups"[113] and Robert Hale wrote "Coercion and Distribution in a Supposedly Non-coercive

State"[114]—two canonical texts of legal realism—members of Congress complained of "customs" and "combinations" and asked, "If a man can be sold as a vagrant because he does not labor, without any inquiry as to whether he can or cannot procure labor, is he a freeman?"[115]

Freed people and their allies needed protection, property, education, and political power; mostly they received process.[116] This shouldn't diminish the real effect that the act worked on the American constitutional structure. Without question Reconstruction left emancipated persons, and African Americans in general, better off. But to understand the Civil Rights Act of 1866 and the mix of Thirteenth and Fourteenth Amendment power from which it operates, one must understand the functional nature of discrimination and inequality then and now. Discrimination and inequality persist not only through positive pronouncements and malign intent but also through custom, inattention, and invisible structural constraint.[117] Acknowledging this reality does not itself dictate a remedy. Still, recognizing that Congress's first attempt to address civil rights showed at least some sensitivity to the functional aspects of the problem is to rebuke those who say that policy makers are powerless to act against these more intractable legacies of our slave-owning past. Even if Congress's remedy was incomplete in 1866, the history of the act speaks to a constitutional exercise of legislative power to address actual, not just formal, manifestations of discrimination today.

Principle and Politics

From its inception, the Civil Rights Act of 1866 exhibited a tension between principle and politics. It was passed with ambitions to be "the greatest and the grandest act"[118] of Congress, an attempt to "define in legislative terms the essence of freedom."[119] But, to become an act, it had to pass Congress and to navigate the multiplicity of interests that inhabit that body under the best of times, not to mention under the stress of a civil war. The compromises began early: the elimination of the race-specific language from the initial draft of the bill, the protestations that interracial marriage could still be punished. It continued in the slow and fitful retreat from civil rights enforcement on a federal level. It progressed in the later shift to a more race-neutral, state-action construction of the Fourteenth and Fifteenth Amendments, a shift that "reflected limitations that white America wished to set on the search for justice-as-equality."[120] And, of course, it appears in the Compromise of 1877, which effectively ended civil rights as a national priority for at least a generation.

Even after the civil rights revival of the 1960s, neither the Civil Rights Act of 1866 nor the Thirteenth Amendment generated as much interest or law as the Fourteenth Amendment or its enforcement legislation. One reason may be that the Thirteenth Amendment and the early Reconstruction enactments offer less opportunity for what the late Derrick Bell called "interest-convergence."[121] According to Bell, racial majorities resist protecting racial minorities unless something is in it for them. Once white people stopped being the target of reactionary behavior on the part of southern terrorists, the interests of white voters moved on to other matters, and there was no longer any impetus for continued protection of black interests. As William Carter has noted, the more the 1866 act is grounded in Congress's power to enforce the Thirteenth Amendment against the "badges," "incidents," and "relics" of slavery, and the more that power is historically tied to the protection of persons with African ancestry, the more difficult it is to identify convergent interests.[122]

Even when the Thirteenth Amendment and the Civil Rights Act of 1866 enjoyed renewed interest by power brokers, it seemed instrumental. The Civil Rights Division protected African Americans with old law because of an administration goaded by totalitarian propaganda and political necessity as much as, or perhaps more than, by any deep sense of moral obligation. Similar arguments apply to the attack on Jim Crow and the ascent of civil rights in the middle of the twentieth century. Domestic civil rights priorities were shaped by concerns over foreign policy: the United States needed to win more hearts and minds in the developing world than the Eastern Bloc.[123]

What does this say about the 1866 act and its legacy? One lesson is raw realpolitik. Civil rights protections that grow out of the Reconstruction amendments will continue to succeed only when they advance the interests of other groups that have broader political appeal. So, for instance, the Matthew Shepard and James Byrd, Jr., Hate Crimes Prevention Act of 2009, the federal hate-crime legislation, cites the Reconstruction amendments for authority but extends its protections against hate-motivated violence to victims of not only racial violence but also violence motivated by religion, national origin, gender, sexual orientation, gender identity, or disability.[124] A second lesson is the unsurprising conclusion that minorities—and African Americans in particular—must vigilantly maintain institutions that allow them to form coalitions and exercise political influence, especially in an environment where the traditional racial binary between black and white is steadily eroding. If, as Bell once quipped, American politics are "'the only game in town,'"[125] this outcome may be the best that can be hoped for. Interpretation of civil rights guarantees, congressional authority to legislate under any of the Reconstruction amendments, and any number of other forms of constructive political engagement will never be attentive to minority interests if minorities are frustrated in their ability to exercise a voice in the process. Social change is powered by a dynamic between principle and politics, as Judge J. Harvie Wilkinson has observed.[126] But politics is most effective for minorities when principle and persuasion is coupled with power.

THE FUTURE

Civil rights in America, beginning with the Civil Rights Act of 1866, often is framed as a story of redemption. Not southern-style redemption: the purging of southern Republican governments and the triumph of white supremacy, although that is in our story too. Instead, it is a story of biblical redemption: the fallen Constitution of the Framers is redeemed by the virtue of Reconstruction lawmakers and the blood of civil rights heroes.[127] This is a good story, suffused with Judeo-Christian tropes, and there is much truth to it. But, as Kermit Roosevelt has noted, another trope operates in this narrative as well, one that *does* involve southern redemption. It is a story less teleological, more Eastern; a story of cycles, revolutions of death and rebirth, death and rebirth. As Roosevelt puts it, Reconstruction begets southern redemption, begets a Second Reconstruction, begets a second southern redemption, and so on.[128]

We are reaching another point of transition when it comes to the Civil Rights Act of 1866 and its legacy. Whether we are in a moment of death or of rebirth in civil rights is difficult to tell. The Supreme Court has chipped ever more steadily at congressional power to enforce equality norms, whether that power comes from the Fourteenth or Fifteenth Amendments[129] or from the commerce clause,[130] although in other ways—for sexual minorities, for example—the notion of freedom and citizenship first discussed in the 1866 act has broadened.[131] In both cases, however, there is less room for congressional action and less potential for civil rights to mean anything other than what the justices say they mean.

Evidence for this transition is apparent from litigation over the Matthew Shepard and James Byrd, Jr., Hate Crimes Prevention Act. President Barak Obama signed the Hate Crimes Prevention Act into law in October 2009. The act makes it a federal crime for a person to willfully cause or attempt bodily harm, "whether or not acting under color of law," where the violence was due to race or color or "because of the actual or perceived religion, national origin, gender, sexual orientation, gender identity, or disability" of the victim.[132] The Hate Crimes Prevention Act is a descendant of the Civil Rights Act of 1866. Its legislative DNA first appears in that act's criminal penalties for those who deprive a citizen of federal rights.[133] The family resemblance is apparent in the 1870 Enforcement Act and the 1871 Ku Klux Klan Act, which protect individuals from violence when they exercise their rights under the Constitution.[134] Congress passed the Hate Crimes Prevention Act by asserting its power to regulate interstate commerce; but, perhaps aware of the constitutional weakness of that assertion standing alone, Congress also relied on its Thirteenth Amendment enforcement power.[135]

United States v. Cannon,[136] a Fifth Circuit case, is the among the first decisions to address the Reconstruction enforcement authority for the Hate Crimes Prevention Act, and its opinion is emblematic of the transitional stage we are in when it comes to the legacy of 1866. The same judge writes both for the majority and for the concurrence. In *Cannon*, the defendants challenged the Hate Crimes Prevention Act as exceeding congressional power to enforce the Thirteenth Amendment, the same type of constitutional authority that has upheld the Civil Rights Act of 1866 since *Jones*. Speaking for the majority, Judge Jennifer Walker Elrod held that "racially motivated violence was essential to the enslavement of African-Americans and was widely employed after the Civil War in an attempt to return African-Americans to a position of de facto enslavement."[137] The Hate Crimes Prevention Act, therefore, was a rational exercise of Congress's Thirteenth Amendment enforcement power.[138]

Speaking for the special concurrence, Judge Elrod cast doubt upon her own opinion. "[The Supreme Court's] articulation of congressional power under § 2 of the Thirteenth Amendment . . . is in tension with the Supreme Court's discussion of congressional power under the Fourteenth Amendment."[139] Noting that the Supreme Court has "cautioned against . . . expansions of federal law into areas, like police power, that are the historical prerogative of the states," Judge Elrod wondered whether Congress may still regulate "acts between private actors, within the heart of the states' traditional police powers, without any findings that states currently and consistently fail to adequately address the problem."[140] So it is that the Hate Crimes Prevention Act, the legislative scion of the very first Civil Rights Act, begets an opinion speaking with two voices. One voice speaks of Reconstruction and its amendments as a broad grant of congressional authority to protect freedom and equality from all threats in perpetuity; the other voice speaks of Reconstruction and its amendments as a set of narrow remedial provisions, limited in scope and limited in time. The future direction of civil rights law, beginning with the 1866 act, is uncertain. We stand at the threshold.

Janus was the Roman god of doorways, of war and peace, of endings and beginnings. Where we are, on which side of this passage, or at what point in its revolution, it is difficult to tell. Perhaps we should take comfort in one last story of Janus, told by Ovid. Long ago, a great war erupted between two peoples and Janus loosed a flood of fire, and the land was strewn with the bodies of fathers and sons. But after the bloodshed, the two peoples agreed to form one nation, and to rule wisely, with universal justice, as one. Whether we will achieve that state is not the question; whether we will continue to work toward it is.

Notes

1. Jett v. Dallas Indep. Sch. Dist., 491 U.S. 701, 722 (1989).
2. *Cong. Globe*, 39th Cong., 1st Sess., 129 (January 5, 1866) (statement of Senator Trumbull). For more on Lyman Trumbull, see generally Horace White, *The Life of Lyman Trumbull* (Boston: Houghton Mifflin, 1913).
3. "Peace and Slavery," *New York Times*, February 4, 1865, 4.
4. "The Consummation!," ibid., December 19, 1865, 1.
5. Michael Vorenberg, *Final Freedom: The Civil War, the Abolition of Slavery, and the Thirteenth Amendment* (New York: Cambridge University Press, 2001), 108.
6. See ibid., 86 ("Many [lawmakers] . . . believed that the mere absence of slavery was enough to guarantee equal opportunity and equal rights").
7. See George Rutherglen, *Civil Rights in the Shadow of Slavery: The Constitution, Common Law, and the Civil Rights Act of 1866* (New York: Oxford University Press, 2013), 35; see also Vorenberg, *Final Freedom*, 109–11.
8. *Cong. Globe*, 38th Cong., 1st Sess., 1458 (April 7, 1864) (statement of Senator Hendricks).
9. See Rutherglen, *Civil Rights in the Shadow of Slavery*, 35; see also Vorenberg, *Final Freedom*, 109–11. See also U.S. Const., Art. 5 (providing for a process to amend the Constitution).
10. See *Cong. Globe*, 39th Cong., 1st Sess., 476 (January 29, 1866) (statement of Senator Saulsbury).
11. U.S. Const., Thirteenth Amend., Sec. 1.
12. Ibid., Sec. 2.

13. *Cong. Globe*, 39th Cong., 1st Sess., 474 (January 29, 1866) (statement of Senator Trumbull).
14. Ibid.
15. Herman Belz, *A New Birth of Freedom: The Republican Party and Freedmen's Rights, 1861–1866* (New York: Fordham University Press, 2000), 160 (quoting Representative James A. Garfield) (internal quotation marks omitted).
16. Vorenberg, *Final Freedom*, 67.
17. John Townsend Trowbridge, *The South: A Tour of Its Battle-Fields and Ruined Cities, a Journey through the Desolated States, and Talks with the People* (Hartford, Conn.: L. Stebbins, 1866), 427.
18. See Rutherglen, *Civil Rights in the Shadow of Slavery*, 47.
19. See Donna L. Dickerson, *The Reconstruction Era: Primary Documents on Events from 1865 to 1877* (Westport, Conn.: Greenwood Press, 2003), 44–46.
20. See Darrell A. H. Miller, "The Thirteenth Amendment and the Regulation of Custom," 112 *Colum. L. Rev.* 1811, 1832–34 (2012) (citing contemporary use of this term in Congress).
21. *Cong. Globe*, 39th Cong., 1st Sess., 589 (February 1, 1866) (statement of Representative Donnelly).
22. Leon F. Litwack, *Been in the Storm So Long: The Aftermath of Slavery* (New York: Random House, 1979), 415–16.
23. Carl Schurz, sent to investigate the immediate postwar period, commented on a "spirit" in the South where freedmen were kept under "permanent martial law" and where "every white man [is invested] with the power and authority of a police officer as against every black man." Carl Schurz, *Report on the Condition of the South* (1865), reprinted in *Speeches, Correspondence and Political Papers of Carl Schurz*, vol. 1, ed. Frederic Bancroft (New York: Knickerbocker Press, 1913), 325–26.
24. See, e.g., Douglas A. Blackmon, *Slavery by Another Name: The Re-enslavement of Black Americans from the Civil War to World War II* (New York: Doubleday, 2008), 53–54; and Rutherglen, *Civil Rights in the Shadow of Slavery*, 113.
25. Stephen Budiansky, *The Bloody Shirt: Terror after Appomattox* (New York: Viking, 2008), 24 (quoting a letter from Edmund Rhett dated October 14, 1865).
26. Rutherglen, *Civil Rights in the Shadow of Slavery*, 59.
27. Civil Rights Act of 1866, ch. 31, 14 Stat. 27, Sec. 1. The act is reproduced in full in the appendix to this volume and is quoted from throughout the chapter.

28. See Rutherglen, *Civil Rights in the Shadow of Slavery*, 25–28, 52–53.
29. See ibid., 52–57; and Vorenberg, *Final Freedom*, 234–36.
30. See Rutherglen, *Civil Rights in the Shadow of Slavery*, 59; see also U.S. Const., Art. 4, Sec. 2, Cl. 3.
31. Civil Rights Act of 1866, ch. 31, Secs. 2–6, 14 Stat. 27–30.
32. See Eric Foner, *Reconstruction: America's Unfinished Revolution, 1863–1877* (1988; repr., New York: HarperCollins, 2005), 243, 245, 247.
33. President Andrew Johnson, "Veto of the Civil Rights Act" (March 27, 1866), reprinted in *Presidential Documents: The Speeches, Proclamations, and Policies That Have Shaped the Nation from Washington to Clinton*, ed. J. F. Watts and Fred L. Israel (New York: Routledge 2000), 146–50.
34. Compare Shelby County v. Holder, 133 S. Ct. 2612 (2013) (striking down portions of the Voting Rights Act). See also Randall Kennedy, "Race Relations Law in the Canon of Legal Academia," 68 *Fordham L. Rev.* 1985, 1995 (2000).
35. Johnson, "Veto," 150.
36. Vorenberg, *Final Freedom*, 234.
37. See *Cong. Globe*, 39th Cong., 1st Sess., 1151 (March 2, 1866) (statement of Representative Thayer).
38. "Brooklyn News," *New York Times*, April 11, 1866, 2.
39. "Great News—Passage of the Civil Rights Bill over the Veto," *Lowell Daily Citizen and News*, April 7, 1866, 2.
40. Ibid. (quoting "Dixon" of the *Boston Advertiser*).
41. "The Negro 'Civil Rights Bill,'" *Harrisburg Patriot and Union*, April 9, 1866, 2.
42. "The Civil Rights Act," *Macon Daily Telegraph*, April 14, 1866, 2.
43. "The Civil Wrongs Bill," ibid.
44. See George C. Rable, *But There Was No Peace: The Role of Violence in the Politics of Reconstruction* (Athens: University of Georgia Press, 2007), 31–32.
45. Ibid., 33–58.
46. Foner, *Reconstruction*, 342; *The Ku Klux Klan, Organization and Principles* (1868), in *Documents of American History*, 7th ed., vol. 1, ed. Henry Steele Commager (New York: Appleton-Century-Crofts, 1963), 500.
47. See Rutherglen, *Civil Rights in the Shadow of Slavery*, 71.
48. See U.S. Const., Fourteenth Amend., Sec. 1.
49. Emphasis added.
50. U.S. Const., Fourteenth Amend., Sec. 1.
51. Rutherglen, *Civil Rights in the Shadow of Slavery*, 71–72.

52. See, e.g., Runyon v. McCrary, 427 U.S. 160, 201–2 (1976) (J. White, dissenting).
53. See Robert J. Kaczorowski, *The Politics of Judicial Interpretation: The Federal Courts, Department of Justice and Civil Rights, 1866–1876* (1985; repr., New York: Fordham University Press 2005), 1–26, 79, 101–15.
54. See generally ibid.
55. See ibid., 49–78.
56. See Herman Belz, *Emancipation and Equal Rights: Politics and Constitutionalism in the Civil War Era* (New York: W.W. Norton, 1978), 139, 146–47.
57. See ibid.
58. See Judith Olans Brown, Daniel J. Givelber, and Stephen N. Subrin, "Treating Blacks as If They Were White: Problems of Definition and Proof in Section 1982 Cases," 124 *U. Pa. L. Rev.* 1, 2 n4 (1975); Douglas L. Colbert, "Liberating the Thirteenth Amendment," 30 *Harv. C.R.-C.L. L. Rev.* 1, 29 (1995).
59. See Brief of Petitioners at 14, Jones v. Alfred H. Mayer Co., 392 U.S. 409 (1968) (No. 645), reprinted in *Landmark Briefs and Arguments of the Supreme Court of the United States: Constitutional Law*, ed. Philip B. Kurland and Gerhard Casper, vol. 67 (Arlington, Va.: University Publications of America, Inc., 1975), 70.
60. For more on this history, see Darrell A. H. Miller, "White Cartels, the Civil Rights Act of 1866, and the History of *Jones v. Alfred H. Mayer Co.*," 77 *Fordham L. Rev.* 999 (2008).
61. *Jones*, 392 U.S. at 427.
62. Ibid. at 439, 440, 443.
63. Ibid. at 442–43.
64. Ibid. at 443.
65. Ibid.
66. See, e.g., Charles Fairman, *History of the Supreme Court of the United States: Reconstruction and Reunion 1864–88, Part One*, ed. Paul A. Freund, vol. 6 (New York: Macmillan 1971), 1258; and Sam J. Ervin Jr., "*Jones v. Alfred H. Mayer Co.*: Judicial Activism Run Riot," 22 *Vand. L. Rev.* 485 (1969).
67. See Risa Goluboff, *The Lost Promise of Civil Rights* (Cambridge, Mass.: Harvard University Press, 2007), 112; and Risa Goluboff, "The Thirteenth Amendment and the Lost Origins of Civil Rights," 50 *Duke L. J.* 1609, 1623–26 (2001).
68. See Goluboff, "Lost Origins," 1631–32.
69. Goluboff, *Lost Promise*, 130–31; Goluboff, "Lost Origins," 1628–34, 1640–44.

70. See Goluboff, "Lost Origins," 1642–44, 1647–68.
71. See Richard R. W. Brooks and Carol M. Rose, *Saving the Neighborhood: Racially Restrictive Covenants, Law, and Social Norms* (Cambridge, Mass.: Harvard University Press, 2013), 146–49; and Shelley v. Kraemer, 33 U.S. 1 (1948).
72. Brooks and Rose, *Saving the Neighborhood*, 149.
73. Hurd v. Hodge, 334 U.S. 24 (1948).
74. See Kenneth W. Mack, *Representing the Race: The Creation of the Civil Rights Lawyer* (Cambridge, Mass.: Harvard University Press, 2012), 230–32.
75. See Linda C. McClain, "Involuntary Servitude, Public Accommodations Laws, and the Legacy of *Heart of Atlanta Motel, Inc. v. United States*," 71 *Md. L. Rev.* 83, 124–28 (2011).
76. Ibid., 126, quoting *A Bill to Eliminate Discrimination in Public Accommodations Affecting Interstate Commerce: Hearings on S. 1732 before the Senate Comm. on Commerce*, 88th Cong., 1st Sess., 28, 244 (1963) (statement of Burke Marshall, Assistant Attorney General, Civil Rights Division, Department of Justice).
77. Heart of Atlanta Motel, Inc. v. United States, 379 U.S. 241, 276 (1964) (J. Black, concurring); see also McClain, "Involuntary Servitude," 110–11.
78. See Miller, "White Cartels," 1009–21, for a similar discussion.
79. See *Runyon*, 427 U.S. 160 (construing the Civil Rights Act of 1866 as codified at 42 U.S.C., Sec. 1981).
80. See ibid., 175–80.
81. For a discussion, see Bernard Schwartz, "Rehnquist, Runyon, and Jones—the Chief Justice, Civil Rights, and Stare Decisis," 31 *Tulsa L. Rev.* 251 (1995).
82. See Civil Rights Act of 1991, Pub. L. No. 102-166, § 101(2), 105 Stat. 1071, 1071–72, codified at 42 U.S.C., Sec. 1981(b)-(c) (2012).
83. *Jett*, 491 U.S. at 722.
84. See Rutherglen, *Civil Rights in the Shadow of Slavery*, 12.
85. See CBOCS West, Inc. v. Humphries, 553 U.S. 442 (2008) (discussing whether Sec. 1981 forbids retaliation); and Campbell v. Forest Preserve Dist. of Cook County, Ill., 752 F.3d 665, 671 (7th Cir. 2014) (holding that 42 U.S.C., Sec. 1981 does not give a private right action against government actors and Sec. 1983 is the exclusive remedy).
86. I claim no originality for this notion. Looking to history for guidance about who we are and where we are going is the basis of almost all works of history, including the history of this act. See, e.g., Rutherglen, *Civil Rights*

in the Shadow of Slavery, 17 ("A sustained examination of [the history of the 1866 act] casts a new light on . . . where we have been . . . and . . . where we might yet go").

87. See Ryan C. Williams, "Originalism and the Other Desegregation Decision," 99 *Va. L. Rev.* 493, 529–30 (2013).
88. Rutherglen, *Civil Rights in the Shadow of Slavery*, 4.
89. For further discussion, see Eric Schnapper, "Affirmative Action and the Legislative History of the Fourteenth Amendment," 71 *Va. L. Rev.* 753 (1985); and Jed Rubenfeld, "Affirmative Action," 107 *Yale L. J.* 427 (1997). For a differing view, see Michael B. Rappaport, "Originalism and the Colorblind Constitution," 89 *Notre Dame L. Rev.* 71 (2013).
90. In this sense I agree with James Pope that "the Thirteenth Amendment does not appear to be uniquely unambiguous or unsuited for interpretation," but I disagree with his suggestion that the word "slavery" is necessarily narrower in meaning than the words "involuntary servitude." See James Gray Pope, "What's Different about the Thirteenth Amendment, and Why Does It Matter?," 71 *Md. L. Rev.* 189, 197–98 (2011).
91. McDonald v. Santa Fe Trail Transportation Co., 427 U.S. 273 (1976).
92. See Miller, "Thirteenth Amendment and the Regulation of Custom," 1829–31.
93. Ibid., 1837–42.
94. As Harold M. Hyman and William M. Wiecek wrote, "No one in 1866, or in 1870, anticipated that lawyers and judges would reverse the stream of history and begin to interpret the 1866 Civil Rights act in light of the Fourteenth and Fifteenth Amendments rather than the Thirteenth Amendment." Harold M. Hyman and William M. Wiecek, *Equal Justice under Law: Constitutional Development, 1835–1875* (New York: Harper and Row, 1982), 465.
95. See George Rutherglen's chapter in this volume.
96. Civil Rights Cases, 109 U.S. 3, 25 (1883).
97. Grutter v. Bollinger, 539 U.S. 306, 343 (2003).
98. See Justin Levitt, "Section 5 as Simulacrum," 123 *Yale L. J. Online* 151, 166 (2013), quoting transcript of oral argument at 47, *Shelby County*, 133 S. Ct. 2612 (No. 12–96).
99. See Belz, *Emancipation and Equal Rights*, 114–15; Foner, *Reconstruction*, 242–43; and Kaczorowski, *Politics of Judicial Interpretation*, 2–5.
100. *Cong. Globe*, 39th Cong., 1st Sess., 586 (February 1, 1866) (statement of Representative Donnelly).

101. See Schurz, *Report on the Condition of the South*, 355.
102. See Orlando Patterson, *Slavery and Social Death: A Comparative Study* (Cambridge, Mass.: Harvard University Press, 1982), 111–12, 128.
103. See Foner, *Reconstruction*, 243; and William Mason Grosvenor, "The Law of Conquest: The True Basis of Reconstruction," 24 *New Englander* 111–31 (January 1865).
104. Hyman and Wiecek, *Equal Justice under Law*, 392. See also Foner, *Reconstruction*, 245 (noting that the 1866 act "combined elements of continuity and change").
105. See Akhil Reed Amar, *The Bill of Rights: Creation and Reconstruction* (New Haven, Conn.: Yale University Press, 1998), 293.
106. See Peruta v. County of San Diego, 742 F.3d 1144, 1152 (9th Cir. 2014) (citing the Framers and Charles Sumner as all supporting an individual right to keep and bear arms), *vacated* 781 F.3d 1106 (9th Cir. 2015).
107. For a full discussion of this issue, see Joseph Fishkin, "The Dignity of the South," 123 *Yale L. J. Online* 175 (2013).
108. Rutherglen, *Civil Rights in the Shadow of Slavery*, 57 ("For better or for worse, litigation became the only enduring means of protecting civil rights").
109. See Kaczorowski, *Politics of Judicial Interpretation*, 39–40; and Rutherglen, *Civil Rights in the Shadow of Slavery*, 124–25.
110. See Foner, *Reconstruction*, 201; see also Robert J. Cottrol and Raymond T. Diamond, "Never Intended to Be Applied to the White Population: Firearms Regulation and Racial Disparity—the Redeemed South's Legacy to a National Jurisprudence?," 70 *Chi.-Kent L. Rev.* 1307 (1995).
111. See notes 21–23 above and accompanying text.
112. See Kaczorowski, *Politics of Judicial Interpretation*, 25, 33, 88–89.
113. Louis L. Jaffee, "Law Making by Private Groups," 51 *Harv. L. Rev.* 201 (1937).
114. Robert L. Hale, "Coercion and Distribution in a Supposedly Non-coercive State," 38 *Pol. Sci. Q.* 470 (1923).
115. *Cong. Globe*, 39th Cong., 1st Sess., 1124 (March 1, 1866) (statement of Representative Cook).
116. See Laura F. Edwards, *A Legal History of the Civil War and Reconstruction: A Nation of Rights* (New York: Cambridge University Press, 2015), 123–25.
117. See Darrell A. H. Miller, "Racial Cartels and the Thirteenth Amendment Enforcement Power," 100 *Ky. L. J.* 23 (2012) (discussing aspects of structural racism).

118. *Cong. Globe*, 39th Cong., 1st Sess., 603 (January 29, 1866) (Senator Wilson).
119. Foner, *Reconstruction*, 244.
120. Hyman and Wiecek, *Equal Justice under Law*, 466.
121. See Derrick A. Bell Jr., "*Brown v. Board of Education* and the Interest-Convergence Dilemma," 93 *Harv. L. Rev.* 518, 523 (1980).
122. See generally William M. Carter Jr., "The Thirteenth Amendment, Interest Convergence, and the Badges and Incidents of Slavery," 71 *Md. L. Rev.* 21 (2011). Carter adds that this perception is mistaken.
123. See Bell, "*Brown v. Board of Education* and the Interest-Convergence Dilemma," 524–25 (observing that the *Brown v. Board of Education* decision provided "credibility" in a "struggle" for the "hearts and minds of emerging third world peoples"); see also Derrick A. Bell Jr., "Racial Equality: Progressives' Passion for the Unattainable," 94 *Va. L. Rev.* 495, 511–12 (2008) (reviewing Goluboff, *Lost Promise*).
124. See Matthew Shepard and James Byrd, Jr., Hate Crimes Prevention Act of 2009, Pub. L. No. 111–84, Div. E, 123 Stat. 2838–2842 (codified in relevant part at 18 U.S.C., Sec. 249 [2012]).
125. See Bell, "Racial Equality," 520 (quoting legendary gambler Canada Bill).
126. J. Harvie Wilkinson III, "The Dual Lives of Rights: The Rhetoric and Practice of Rights in America," 98 *Cal. L. Rev.* 277 (2010).
127. See Jack M. Balkin, *Constitutional Redemption: Political Faith in an Unjust World* (Cambridge, Mass.: Harvard University Press, 2011).
128. See Kermit Roosevelt III, "Reconstruction and Resistance," 91 *Tex. L. Rev.* 121, 144 (2012).
129. See, e.g., *Shelby County*, 133 S. Ct. 2612; Bd. of Tr. of the Univ. of Ala. v. Garrett, 531 U.S. 356 (2001); and Kimel v. Fla. Bd. of Regents, 528 U.S. 62 (2000).
130. See United States v. Morrison, 529 U.S. 598 (2000) (striking down portions of the Violence against Women Act as exceeding Congress's power to regulate interstate commerce).
131. Obergefell v. Hodges, 135 S. Ct. 2071 (2015); United States v. Windsor, 133 S. Ct. 2675 (2013). The Court's recent decision upholding affirmative action at the University of Texas is a counter to this trend as well. See Fisher v. University of Texas, 136 S. Ct. 2198 (2016).
132. See 18 U.S.C., Sec. 249(a) (2012).
133. See Civil Rights Act of 1866, ch. 31, Sec. 2, 14 Stat. 27.

134. See Kami Chavis Simmons, "Subverting Symbolism: The Matthew Shepard and James Byrd, Jr., Hate Crimes Prevention Act and Cooperative Federalism," 49 *Am. Crim. L. Rev.* 1863, 1876 (2012).
135. Pub. L. 111-84, Sec. 4702, 123 Stat 2190, 2836.
136. United States v. Cannon, 750 F.3d 492 (5th Cir. 2014).
137. Ibid., 502.
138. Ibid., 505.
139. Ibid., 511 (J. Elrod, specially concurring).
140. Ibid., 512, 514.

APPENDIX

CONTRIBUTORS

INDEX

APPENDIX: THE CIVIL RIGHTS ACT OF 1866

April 9, 1866

An Act to protect all Persons in the United States in their Civil Rights, and furnish the Means of their Vindication.

Be it enacted by the Senate and House of Representatives of the United States of America in Congress assembled, That all persons born in the United States and not subject to any foreign power, excluding Indians not taxed, are hereby declared to be citizens of the United States; and such citizens, of every race and color, without regard to any previous condition of slavery or involuntary servitude, except as a punishment for crime whereof the party shall have been duly convicted, shall have the same right, in every State and Territory in the United States, to make and enforce contracts, to sue, be parties, and give evidence, to inherit, purchase, lease, sell, hold, and convey real and personal property, and to full and equal benefit of all laws and proceedings for the security of person and property, as is enjoyed by white citizens, and shall be subject to like punishment, pains, and penalties, and to none other, any law, statute, ordinance, regulation, or custom, to the contrary notwithstanding.

Sec. 2. *And be it further enacted,* That any person who, under color of any law, statute, ordinance, regulation, or custom, shall subject, or cause to be subjected, any inhabitant of any State or Territory to the deprivation of any right secured or protected by this act, or to different punishment, pains, or penalties on account of such person having at any time been held in a condition of slavery or involuntary servitude, except as a punishment for crime whereof the party shall have been duly convicted, or by reason of his color or race, than is prescribed for the punishment of white persons, shall be deemed guilty of a misdemeanor, and, on conviction, shall be punished by fine not exceeding one thousand dollars, or imprisonment not exceeding one year, or both, in the discretion of the court.

Sec. 3. *And be it further enacted,* That the district courts of the United States, within their respective districts, shall have, exclusively of the courts of the several States, cognizance of all crimes and offences committed against the provisions of this act, and also, concurrently with the circuit courts of the United States, of all causes, civil and criminal, affecting persons who are denied or cannot enforce in the courts or judicial tribunals of the State or locality where they may be any of the rights secured to them by the first section of this act; and if any suit or prosecution, civil or criminal, has been or shall be commenced in any State court, against any such person, for any cause whatsoever, or against any officer, civil or military, or other person, for any arrest or imprisonment, trespasses, or wrongs done or committed by virtue or under color of authority derived from this act or the act establishing a Bureau for the relief of Freedmen and Refugees, and all acts amendatory thereof, or for refusing to do any act upon the ground that it would be inconsistent with this act, such defendant shall have the right to remove such cause for trial to the proper district or circuit court in the manner prescribed by the "Act relating to habeas corpus and regulating judicial proceedings in certain cases," approved March three, eighteen hundred and sixty-three, and all acts amendatory thereof. The jurisdiction in civil and criminal matters hereby conferred on the district and circuit courts of the United States shall be exercised and enforced in conformity with the laws of the United States, so far as such laws are suitable to carry the same into effect; but in all cases where such laws are not adapted to the object, or are deficient in the provisions necessary to furnish suitable remedies and punish offences against law, the common law, as modified and changed by the constitution and statutes of the State wherein the court having jurisdiction of the cause, civil or criminal, is held, so far as the same is not inconsistent with the Constitution and laws of the United States, shall be extended to and govern said courts in the trial and disposition of such cause, and, if of a criminal nature, in the infliction of punishment on the party found guilty.

Sec. 4. *And be it further enacted,* That the district attorneys, marshals, and deputy marshals of the United States, the commissioners appointed by the circuit and territorial courts of the United States, with powers of arresting, imprisoning, or bailing offenders against the laws of the United States, the officers and agents of the Freedmen's Bureau, and every other officer who may be specially empowered by the President of the United States, shall be, and they are hereby, specially authorized and required, at the expense of the United States, to institute proceedings against all and every person who shall violate the provisions of this act, and cause him or them to be arrested and imprisoned, or bailed, as the case may be, for trial before such court of the United States or territorial court as by this act has cognizance of the offence. And with a view to affording reasonable protection to all persons in their constitutional rights of equality before the law, without distinction of race or color, or previous condition of slavery or involuntary servitude, except as a punishment for crime, whereof the party shall have been duly convicted, and to the prompt discharge of the duties of this act, it shall be the duty of the circuit courts of the United States and the superior courts of the Territories of the United States, from time to time, to increase the number of commissioners, so as to afford a speedy and convenient means for the arrest and examination of persons charged with a violation of this act; and such commissioners are hereby authorized and required to exercise and discharge all the powers and duties conferred on them by this act, and the same duties with regard to offences created by this act, as they are authorized by law to exercise with regard to other offences against the laws of the United States.

Sec. 5. *And be it further enacted,* That it shall be the duty of all marshals and deputy marshals to obey and execute all warrants and precepts issued under the provisions of this act, when to them directed; and should any marshal or deputy marshal refuse to receive such warrant or other process when tendered, or to use all proper means diligently to execute the same, he shall, on conviction thereof, be fined in the sum of one thousand dollars, to the use of the person upon whom the accused is alleged to have committed the offense. And the better to enable the said commissioners to execute their duties faithfully and efficiently, in conformity with the Constitution of the United States and the requirements of this act, they are hereby authorized and empowered, within their counties respectively, to appoint, in writing, under their hands, any one or more suitable persons, from time to time, to execute all such warrants and other process as may be issued by them in the lawful performance of their respective duties; and the persons so appointed to execute any warrant or process as aforesaid shall have authority to summon and call to their aid the bystanders or posse comitatus of the proper county, or such portion of the land or naval forces of the United States, or of the militia, as may be necessary to the performance of the duty with which they are charged, and to insure a faithful observance of the clause of the Constitution which prohibits slavery, in conformity with the provisions of this act; and said warrants shall run and be executed by said officers anywhere in the State or Territory within which they are issued.

Sec. 6. *And be it further enacted,* That any person who shall knowingly and wilfully obstruct, hinder, or prevent any officer, or other person charged with the execution of any warrant or process issued under the provisions of this act, or any person or persons lawfully assisting him or them, from arresting any person for whose apprehension such warrant or process may have been issued, or shall rescue or attempt to rescue such person from the custody of the officer, other person or persons, or those lawfully assisting as aforesaid, when so arrested pursuant to the authority herein given and declared, or shall aid, abet, or assist any person so arrested as aforesaid, directly or indirectly, to escape from the custody of the officer or other person legally authorized as aforesaid, or shall harbor or conceal any person for whose arrest a warrant or process shall have been issued as aforesaid, so as to prevent his discovery and arrest after notice or knowledge of the fact that a warrant has been issued for the apprehension of such person, shall, for either of said offences, be subject to a fine not exceeding one thousand dollars, and imprisonment not exceeding six months, by indictment and conviction before the district court of the United States for the district in which said offense may have been committed, or before the proper court of criminal jurisdiction, if committed within any one of the organized Territories of the United States.

Sec. 7. *And be it further enacted,* That the district attorneys, the marshals, their deputies, and the clerks of the said district and territorial courts shall be paid for their services the like fees as may be allowed to them for similar services in other cases; and in all cases where the proceedings are before a commissioner, he shall be entitled to a fee of ten dollars in full for his services in each case, inclusive of all services incident to such arrest and examination. The person or persons authorized to execute the process to be issued by such commissioners for the arrest of offenders against the provisions of this act shall be entitled to a fee of five dollars for each person he or they may arrest and take before any such commissioner as aforesaid, with such other fees as may be deemed reasonable by such commissioner for such other additional services as may be necessarily performed by him or them, such as attending at the examination, keeping the prisoner in custody, and providing him with food and lodging during his detention, and until the final determination of such commissioner, and in general for performing such other duties as may be required in the premises; such fees to be made up in conformity with the fees usually charged by the officers of the courts of justice within the proper district or county, as near as may be practicable, and paid out of the Treasury of the United States on the certificate of the judge of the district within which the arrest is made, and to be recoverable from the defendant as part of the judgment in case of conviction.

Sec. 8. *And be it further enacted,* That whenever the President of the United States shall have reason to believe that offences have been or are likely to be committed against the provisions of this act within any judicial district, it shall be lawful for him, in his discretion, to direct the judge, marshal, and district attorney of such district to attend at such place within the district, and for such time as he may designate, for the purpose of the more speedy arrest and trial of persons charged with a violation of this act; and it shall be the duty of every judge or other officer, when any such requisition shall be received by him, to attend at the place and for the time therein designated.

Sec. 9. *And be it further enacted,* That it shall be lawful for the President of the United States, or such person as he may empower for that purpose, to employ such part of the land or naval forces of the United States, or of the militia, as shall be necessary to prevent the violation and enforce the due execution of this act.

Sec. 10. *And be it further enacted,* That upon all questions of law arising in any cause under the provisions of this act a final appeal may be taken to the Supreme Court of the United States.

SCHUYLER COLFAX,
Speaker of the House of Representatives.
LAFAYETTE S. FOSTER,
President of the Senate, *pro tempore.*

In the Senate of the United States, April 6, 1866.
The President of the United States having returned to the Senate, in which it originated, the bill entitled "An act to protect all persons in the United States in their civil rights, and furnish the means of their vindication," with his objections thereto, the Senate proceeded, in pursuance of the Constitution, to reconsider the same; and,

Resolved, That the said bill do pass, two-thirds of the Senate agreeing to pass the same.

Attest:

J. W. Forney,
Secretary of the Senate.

In the House of Representatives U.S. April 9th, 1866.
The House of Representatives having proceeded, in pursuance of the Constitution, to reconsider the bill entitled "An act to protect all persons in the United States in their civil rights, and furnish the means of their

vindication," returned to the Senate by the President of the United States, with his objections, and sent by the Senate to the House of Representatives, with the message of the President returning the bill:

Resolved, That the bill do pass, two-thirds of the House of Representatives agreeing to pass the same.

Attest:

EDWARD MCPHERSON, Clerk,
by CLINTON LLOYD, Chief Clerk.

CONTRIBUTORS

Aaron Astor, an associate professor of history at Maryville College in Tennessee, is the author of two books, *Rebels on the Border: Civil War, Emancipation, and the Reconstruction of Kentucky and Missouri, 1860–1872*, and *The Civil War along Tennessee's Cumberland Plateau*. He has also written eleven articles for the award-winning *New York Times* Disunion series.

Richard L. Aynes, dean emeritus and a professor of law emeritus at the University of Akron School of Law, also held the John F. Seiberling Chair of Constitutional Law. He is a nationally recognized scholar on the Fourteenth Amendment and its principal author, John A. Bingham, and his work has been cited in many scholarly works and by courts, including the U.S. Supreme Court.

Michael Les Benedict is a professor emeritus of history at the Ohio State University, where he is also a visiting scholar at the Moritz College of Law. He is the author of numerous books, including *A Compromise of Principle: Congressional Republicans and Reconstruction, 1863–1869* and *Preserving the Constitution: Essays on Politics and the Constitution in the Civil War Era*.

Millington W. Bergeson-Lockwood specializes in the history of race, politics, and the law in nineteenth-century U.S. history. He has taught at George Mason University and the University of Maryland. In 2012 and 2013 he was the postdoctoral fellow in the Center for Africanamerican Urban Studies and the Economy (CAUSE) at Carnegie Mellon University. He lives currently in Lilongwe, Malawi.

Darrell A. H. Miller is the Melvin G. Shimm Professor of Law at Duke University, where he teaches and writes in the areas of civil rights, legal history, and constitutional law.

George Rutherglen, the John Barbee Minor Distinguished Professor of Law at the University of Virginia School of Law, clerked for Supreme Court justices William O. Douglas and John Paul Stevens. The author of *Civil Rights in the Shadow of Slavery: The Constitution, Common Law, and the Civil Rights Act of 1866*, he has written widely on civil rights, employment discrimination, and civil litigation.

Christian G. Samito holds a law degree and a doctorate in history, practices law, and teaches legal history at Boston University School of Law. He wrote *Lincoln and the Thirteenth Amendment* and *Becoming American under Fire: Irish Americans, African Americans, and the Politics of Citizenship during the Civil War Era* and edited a legal history documentary reader and two collections of Union officers' letters.

Jeff Strickland is an associate professor of history at Montclair State University and a historian of race and ethnicity in the United States. His first book is *Unequal Freedoms: Ethnicity, Race, and White Supremacy in Civil War Era Charleston.* He is currently writing a second book on the Charleston workhouse escape of 1849.

Michael Vorenberg is an associate professor at Brown University. His first book, *Final Freedom: The Civil War, the Abolition of Slavery, and the Thirteenth Amendment,* was a finalist for the Lincoln Prize. He is also the author of *The Emancipation Proclamation: A Brief History with Documents.*

R. Owen Williams, president of the Associated Colleges of the South, has been awarded five fellowships, including the Raoul Berger Fellowship at Harvard Law School and the Samuel I. Golieb Fellowship at the New York University School of Law.

Rebecca E. Zietlow is the Charles W. Fornoff Professor of Law and Values at the University of Toledo College of Law. Her scholarly interest is in the study of the Reconstruction era, including the meaning and history of the Thirteenth and Fourteenth Amendments. Zietlow is also an expert on constitutional theory, examining constitutional interpretation outside of the courts. Her book *Enforcing Equality: Congress, the Constitution and the Protection of Individual Rights* studies the history of congressional protection of rights and the implications of that history for constitutional theory.

INDEX